ALSO BY ANTHONY ARTHUR

Radical Innocent: Upton Sinclair

GENERAL
JO SHELBY'S
MARCH

GENERAL
JO SHELBY'S
MARCH

Anthony Arthur

RANDOM HOUSE

NEW YORK

Published in the United States by Random House,
an imprint of The Random House Publishing Group, a division of
Random House, Inc., New York.

RANDOM HOUSE and colophon are registered
trademarks of Random House, Inc.

LIBRARY OF CONGRESS CATALOGING-IN-PUBLICATION DATA
Arthur, Anthony.
General Jo Shelby's march / Anthony Arthur.
p.   cm.
ISBN 978-1-4000-6830-2
eBook ISBN 978-0-679-60395-5
1. Shelby's expedition to Mexico, 1865.   2. Shelby, Joseph Orville,
1830–1897.   3. Mexico—History—European intervention, 1861–1865.
4. Americans—Mexico—History—nineteenth century.   I. Title.
F1233.A795 2010   972'.07—dc22   2009041661

Printed in the United States of America on acid-free paper

www.atrandom.com

2 4 6 8 9 7 5 3 1

FIRST EDITION

Book design by Caroline Cunningham

For Duncan,
who likes adventure stories,
and, as always and forever,
for Carolyn

Tho' much is taken, much abides; and tho'

We are not now that strength which in old days

Mov'd earth and heaven, that which we are, we are:

One equal temper of heroic hearts,

Made weak by time and fate, but strong in will

To strive, to seek, to find, and not to yield.

"Ulysses" BY ALFRED TENNYSON, 1842

CONTENTS

PART THREE
FROM RESENTMENT TO RECONCILIATION, 1867–97

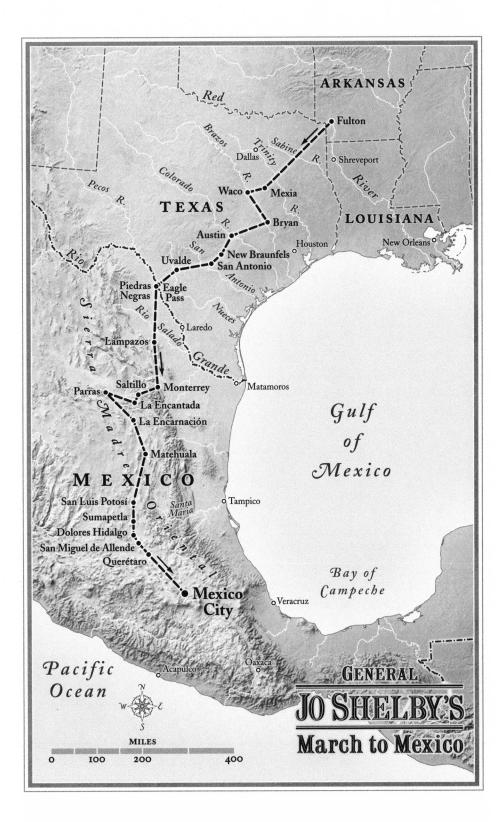

ARKANSAS

Red

Brazos

Trinity

Sabine

Fulton

Dallas

Shreveport

R.

Pecos R.

Colorado

Waco

Mexia

LOUISIANA

TEXAS

R.

Bryan

Rio

Austin

San

Uvalde

New Braunfels

Houston

New Orleans

San Antonio

Piedras
Negras

Eagle
Pass

Antonio

Rio

Nueces

Laredo

Salado

Lampazos

Grande

Matamoros

Sierra

Saltillo

Monterrey

Parras

La Encantada

Gulf
of
Mexico

Madre

La Encarnación

Matehuala

MEXICO

San Luis Potosí

Sumapetla

Santa
María

Tampico

Oriental

Dolores Hidalgo

San Miguel de Allende

Querétaro

Bay of
Campeche

Mexico
City

Veracruz

Pacific
Ocean

Acapulco

Oaxaca

GENERAL

N
W · E
S

JO SHELBY'S

March to Mexico

MILES

0   100   200   400

The Burial of the Flag: Eagle Pass, Texas, July 1, 1865

F ive men stood knee-deep in the muddy shallows of the Rio Grande, each clutching an edge of a tattered Confederate flag that billowed lightly in the soft early morning breeze. On the other side of the wide river, still rushing from the late spring rains, were the low adobe huts of Piedras Negras and two thousand troops loyal to their beleaguered and exiled president, Benito Juárez. Beyond lay the turbulent nation of Mexico—vast, hostile, alien—uneasily ruled by the French army supporting the Hapsburg interloper known as the emperor Maximilian.

Above the men, on a bluff overlooking the river, lay the dusty border town of Eagle Pass, Texas. This desolate crossroads had been the last outpost of the shattered Confederacy. Behind it loomed the newly triumphant United States, now nearly as foreign as Mexico—and, to their minds, no less hostile—to these men who had tried for so many long years to dismember it.

Gaunt, bearded, clad in threadbare gray tunics, the five soldiers looked years older than their age—yet only one was over forty. Their names were Slayback, Elliott, Williams, Gordon, and Blackwell, and they were colonels in General Jo Shelby's "Iron Brigade" of Missouri Volunteers. That is, they had been. Now the war was lost and the brigade disbanded. Most of its thousand-plus survivors had gone back to their farms and villages, and to their families. Fewer than two hundred of the Missourians remained, along with a motley crew of adventurers, fortune hunters, and deserters from half a dozen armies who had stuck to Shelby like cockleburs on his march through Texas.

Shelby's colonels and his men knew why they stayed with him, and it was more than mere self-interest. He was the Jeb Stuart of the Trans-Mississippi West, as the newspapers had it—the daring cavalry commander renowned for his slashing forays behind Union lines in Missouri and Arkansas, and tarred by some as a bushwhacker who harbored the infamous William Quantrill and the James brothers. Shelby's brigade had followed him on his famous raid into Missouri in 1863—six weeks of attack and parry, of plundering Union storage depots and capturing Union soldiers, of sleeping in saddles. And they had been with him in 1864 when he rescued the Confederate forces under the lumbering general Sterling Price from certain destruction at the critical Battle of Westport, near Kansas City. Jo Shelby had risked their lives many times for the Confederacy, which was no more. Now they would place an all-or-nothing bet on his latest gamble, this grand final adventure, the march into Mexico.

Some of those watching the flag ceremony from the bluff above the river were not Shelby's soldiers but prominent men, years and—in some cases—decades older than the young general. They had been senators, congressmen, and governors, and there was a clutch of high-ranking officers, including Major General John Magruder, hero of the Battle of Galveston. Like Shelby, whose home and businesses in western Missouri had long since been reduced to smoldering ruins, these men had nothing to go back to. When Shelby had vowed to seek a new life in Mexico, they willingly acknowledged him as their leader.

Shelby sat silently on a sorrel mare near his officers in the river, leaning forward slightly, resting his crippled right arm on the pommel of his saddle. In his left hand he held his slouch hat with its famous curling black ostrich plume. His face was deeply tanned under a thatch of black hair, his expression remote and stern under a heavy russet beard. Not a large man, bow-legged from years in the saddle, lean but broad-shouldered, he conveyed motion and force even in re-pose. And violence: "He fought like a man who invented fighting," wrote an admiring biographer, "and the men of the Missouri Cavalry Brigade looked on him as the perfect commanding officer: colorful and dashing," reckless with his own life but careful with those of his men.

Abruptly Shelby spoke, halting the officers as they prepared to fold and sink the flag. They waited as he dismounted and waded slowly toward them. He withdrew the black plume from his hat brim and laid it gently within the folds of the flag before it vanished beneath the muddy water. This battle, his typically picturesque gesture said—this four-year battle that the North called the Civil War and the South the War of the Rebellion—was over.

Another struggle beyond the Rio Grande awaited. For Shelby and his men, as Tennyson said of Homer's Ulysses, it was "not too late to seek a newer world." None of them could know whether that world would be better or worse than the one they were rejecting.

PART ONE

THE CALL TO ARMS

1830–65

ONE

From Privileged Youth to
Border Ruffian

I n the early 1850s, a dozen years before he crossed into Mexico, nothing could have compelled Jo Shelby to leave the world of privilege and wealth into which he had been born. Well before his birth, the Shelby name was a famous one in Virginia, Tennessee, and Kentucky, denoting a numerous, widespread, and very successful clan. A common ancestor from Wales, Evan Shelby, had arrived in Pennsylvania in 1735 with his wife and four sons. Evan set the tone for the strain of violence and eccentric independence that would emerge in some of his progeny: Presiding at a wedding in Maryland, he blessed the couple by saying "Jump Dog, Leap Bitch, and I'll be damned if all the Men on Earth can unmarry you." He also threatened to "job a fork into the Gutts" of the groom when he showed signs of backing out.

Evan's energetic sons soon moved west and south, becoming wealthy entrepreneurs and men of property along the Appalachian frontier. His second son, David, sowed crops and begat children, eleven in all; the ninth of these was Orville, Jo's father, born in 1803.

Orville's short life was shadowed by illness, but he had a golden touch when it came to business and marriage. His first wife was an heiress who died young and left him wealthy. His second, in 1829, was Anna Maria Boswell, daughter of a prominent physician in Lexington, Kentucky. Their son Joseph Orville—called J.O. or Jo for his initials from the day of his birth on December 12, 1830—would barely remember his father, who died, just thirty-two, in 1835. Orville left behind enough for his family to live on, including a trust fund for his son that would be his on his twenty-first birthday, in 1851—a healthy sum of $80,000, the equivalent of more than $2 million today.

In 1843, when Jo was twelve, his mother married Benjamin Gratz, who was already related to Jo by marriage: Benjamin's recently deceased wife was Anna Shelby's aunt. Gratz was then forty-nine, with three sons in their late teens and a fourth, Cary, who was just a year and a half older than Jo.

Benjamin Gratz was the scion of a family of eighteenth-century German Jewish immigrants who became merchants and men of distinction in prerevolutionary Philadelphia. Educated as a lawyer at the University of Pennsylvania, he had met Maria Gist, Anna's aunt, while on a business trip to Lexington in Kentucky, one of several states where his family owned land. Among the Gratz holdings in Kentucky was the farmland where Mammoth Cave was discovered in the late eighteenth century.

In the opening decades of the nineteenth century, Lexington developed from a rough frontier village into one of the country's more sophisticated inland cities; it liked to call itself the "Athens of the West." Gratz become a wealthy hemp merchant and a leading citizen. One indication of Lexington's sophistication may be suggested by its apparent willingness not only to tolerate but to welcome a Jew—even an essentially secular, nonobservant Jew like Gratz—into its aristocratic hierarchy. It could not have hurt that Gratz's sister Rebecca was said to be Sir Walter Scott's model for the beautiful heroine of that name in the hugely popular historical novel *Ivanhoe:* Scott's novels had long provided models of chivalric behavior for those in the South who considered themselves aristocrats, as the wealthy planters and commercial barons of Kentucky did.

For seven years, young Jo Shelby lived a charmed life of privilege and ease in Benjamin Gratz's brick Georgian mansion. He was an impressionable boy, with an intellectually acute and involved new father who saw Jo's education in all things—or tried to. Too restless to be a good student, Jo was tutored at home by a succession of frustrated young men, students at Transylvania University, just down the street. His mother offered only occasional supervision; she would bear three children by her new husband within the first five years of their marriage, and whatever free time she had was devoted to her passions for cultivating roses, reading Shakespeare, and supporting the city's orphans' home.

Riding was Jo's passion, and it was readily indulged. In a part of the country devoted to fine horses and daredevil feats of equestrian agility, he excelled. Slender and lithe, Jo sat his horse like a young centaur—no fence was too high, no ditch too wide for the sorrel roans he preferred because they rarely stumbled.

Jo's exemplar as a horseman was his neighbor John Hunt Morgan, five years his senior, and destined, like Shelby, to become one of the Confederacy's greatest cavalry officers. Another older youth who impressed Shelby with his brilliant mind and argumentative nature was his stepcousin B. Gratz Brown, who would later become governor of Missouri and Horace Greeley's running mate in the 1872 presidential election.

But the most striking of his youthful influences was the darkly handsome Frank Blair, who would later become one of William T. Sherman's generals in Georgia and a key adviser to Abraham Lincoln. Combative from the day of his birth in 1821, Blair was kicked out of Yale for carousing and left Princeton after shooting a man in a barroom brawl. Sent by his father to calm down at Transylvania, in 1842 and 1843, Blair lived for a time in the Gratz house and was Jo's tutor—one of the more successful ones because they shared the same rebellious temperament.

Benjamin Gratz was well known for his hospitality and often opened his home to the great men of his own and earlier generations. One of these, the Marquis de Lafayette, provided a link with George Washington himself. In 1826, Lafayette, by that time a hale sixty-eight years of age, was feted at a ball in Lexington while on his sentimental tour of the nation during the fiftieth anniversary of its

Revolution. While there, he dined with the Gratz family and dandled the infant Howard Gratz—the stepbrother, five years his senior, with whom Jo Shelby would become closest—on his knee.

Another frequent Gratz guest over many years was Frank Blair's father, Francis Preston Blair, Sr., the newspaper publisher and intimate friend of President Andrew Jackson. (Blair's former house in Washington, D.C., remains today the official state guesthouse for the president of the United States.) Other renowned visitors were Missouri senators Thomas Hart Benton and Henry Clay, who devoted their careers to heading off the great war between North and South that they saw coming. (Clay lost the presidential election in 1844 to James K. Polk, who promptly embroiled the United States in a war with Mexico whose echoes would touch Shelby profoundly in 1865. In 1873, Clay's grandson would marry Jo Shelby's half sister Anna.)

Benjamin Gratz, like most of his guests, was strongly pro-Union, and he would remain loyal to it when war did break out. He was also like Henry Clay and other patriots in that he owned slaves. Jo himself was attended by a black servant close to his own age named Billy Hunter; his mother bought him at the Lexington slave mart as an eleventh-birthday present for her son. (Billy later said that he had cost Mrs. Shelby $2,000—the equivalent of $50,000 today.) Both boys assumed the rightness of the world into which they had been born, and they became close friends in a way that would baffle later generations of Americans. Billy would stay by his master's side throughout much of the war and would weep at Shelby's grave more than thirty years after he had won his freedom.

Young Jo was not only indifferent to formal study but inclined toward horseplay and practical jokes. One day, according to family legend, he and some friends crept into a room at the Transylvania University medical school where a cadaver had been prepared for dissection in an adjoining classroom. The boys lifted the cadaver from the coffin, and one of them—perhaps Jo—took his place while the others replaced the lid. The pranksters hid in the shadows as young black slaves came in to carry away the coffin. As they began to lift it, the slaves were terrified to hear a sepulchral moan from within the coffin, and then a hoarse voice pleading, "Lift me gently, lift me gently!"

When Jo was sixteen, Benjamin Gratz decided to send him east for a year to have some of his rough edges sanded off at a finishing school in eastern Pennsylvania. His stepbrother Cary would accompany him for at least part of the stay, and both boys would be able to visit frequently with their aunt Rebecca, who lived with one of her other brothers in Philadelphia.

Born in 1781, Rebecca Gratz was still a beautiful woman in her old age. Like her namesake in *Ivanhoe,* she had never married. It was rumored that she had spurned a secret Gentile lover—Henry Clay and Washington Irving were among those suggested—but in fact she had chosen to devote herself to caring for her extended family, and she was greatly revered as "the foremost American Jewish woman of the nineteenth century" for her intelligence and her philanthropic works. In 1844 she had spent the summer with her brother's family in Lexington. Much taken with both Jo and Cary, she assured their father that they would be welcome in her house.

Often sickly, with a tendency toward whooping cough, Cary was quieter than the obstreperous Jo. Rebecca said Cary was a "sweet" boy, "the beauty and the cadet of the family, still in my mind's eye the loveliest of children." She was also touched by Cary's solicitude for Jo, who had his virtues but was never "sweet": For defying the headmaster at the school he and Cary briefly attended in Philadelphia, Jo was locked in his room and put on bread and water rations for three days, until Cary intervened.

By the time he returned home in 1847, Jo had won his aunt's heart completely. Impish and irrepressible, he "seems to have the spirit of mirth inborn in him," Rebecca told Ann. "He is as merry as a bird, or rather as a boy let loose from School, which he illustrated in a way to justify the adage." She would miss his lively presence, Rebecca said, but knew that Jo's parents would certainly "rejoice" in his new application to "his studies."

Jo Shelby's inclinations would always be more practical than academic. As an adolescent and a young man in the late 1840s, he was groomed as a merchant prince, not as a scholar. He did his best to absorb his stepfather's essential injunction—"those who get along best in the world are those who conduct themselves with amiability, urbane in their manners, and perfectly honorable in all their transactions"—

and began work in Benjamin Gratz's hemp factory when he was seventeen.

Commercial hemp is virtually unknown today in the United States; for years it was legally proscribed because of a spurious association with its cousin, marijuana. But in the first half of the nineteenth century it was a major cash crop in Kentucky. Farmed and then processed into bags and cordage for baling cotton, among other uses, hemp was the foundation of an industry that was both profitable and labor intensive in the extreme.

Benjamin Gratz's "ropewalk," where Shelby began his business career, was typical of the factories that dotted southern Appalachia in general and Kentucky in particular. Two stories high, the main building was a narrow structure nearly two hundred feet long and twenty-five feet wide; workers at spindles and looms lined the sides of both floors. Black slaves tied hemp strands around their waists and hooked them onto spinning wheels, then walked back and forth to form extended strands that were twisted into ropes of varying thickness.

It was Shelby's job to see that the men kept up a regular pace. There is no record of him whipping slaves—as Harriet Beecher Stowe's villain Simon Legree does in *Uncle Tom's Cabin*—but the work for the men on the floor was at best monotonous, often hot and always dirty, and deadening to mind and spirit alike. To pay free men the kind of wages they demanded for such labor would have made the products of the hemp industry ruinously expensive. Simple business economics thus made slavery necessary for the survival of these enterprises, and of their owners' way of life. Convinced as they were that blacks were inferior to whites, most slave owners, including even Benjamin Gratz, ignored the moral quandary in which their successful businesses inevitably landed them.

In 1851, Shelby came of age and into his munificent inheritance. His decision to move some three hundred miles west to the village of Waverly, Missouri, must have caused his mother some pain—earlier, when he had briefly considered moving to St. Louis, his aunt Rebecca wrote sympathetically to Anna Gratz that she would certainly miss the presence of so "amiable affectionate & clever" a son. But Shelby was eager to strike out on his own. Stirred by the lure of the frontier, he was more than ready to heed the advice of an Indiana editor in

1851, made famous later, in a shorter version, by Horace Greeley: "Go West, young man, and grow with the country."

It had been Howard Gratz, Shelby's cautious and sobersided step-brother, who initially suggested that he and Jo begin their own hemp business in western Missouri, where land was fertile and cheap. They decided upon Waverly, one of dozens of American villages whose name was inspired by Sir Walter Scott's novel *Waverley* and its sequels, early nineteenth-century bestsellers about the Scottish rebellion in 1745 and its consequences. A William Shelby—a distant cousin—had lived with his family on a farm near Waverly for many years and would ease the path of the new arrivals into the community.

Attractively perched on a wooded bluff above the Missouri River, three-quarters of a mile wide at that point, Waverly had been a distribution point for shipping lumber, furs, and farm products for thirty years. It had a flour mill, an iron foundry, a blacksmith shop, a few stores, and a scattering of wood-frame dwellings for its several hundred inhabitants. A far cry from sophisticated Lexington, the placid village of Waverly in those days must have been much like that of Mark Twain's hometown of Hannibal as he recalled it in *Life on the Mississippi*—an isolated mote of the universe where old men sat languidly whittling on the porch of the mercantile until the effort "broke them down," and yellow dogs slept in the dusty streets until the arriving steamboat's whistle shrieked and the town jumped to life.

Waverly was exciting enough, though, for Jo Shelby during the three years that it took him and Howard to build their new business—years that coincided with a boom in the national economy. By 1855, Shelby and Gratz were prospering as the proud owners of the Waverly Steam Rope Company, which depended on the hard labor of twenty slaves. They also owned a warehouse and a seven-hundred-acre farm, raising not just hemp but wheat and corn, as well as five thousand hogs, a thousand head of cattle, and hundreds of fine horses.

The market for hemp alone was so strong—in 1853 they sold more than four hundred tons at $120 a ton—that the brothers expanded their horizons. They built a giant sawmill a few miles away, made plans to move into real estate with a new town to be called Berlin, and bought their own steamboats in order to avoid being gouged by the piratical private owners who transported their goods to St. Louis. Shelby even thought about founding a college. But for Shelby, the most visible and satisfying symbol of his success was the bachelor palace he built in 1853, a columned white frame house halfway up the bluff—grandly known as Mount Rucker—above his shoreside ropewalk.

Shelby enjoyed his bachelor years in Waverly. Plantation parties and riverboat excursions gave him needed breaks from the press of business, and he became known in the county as a man of style as well as substance. Snub-nosed and larky as a boy, he grew into dignified manhood and sported a thick, flowing beard to enhance his maturity. Always something of a dandy, he wore broadcloth coats and fawn-colored trousers that accentuated his broad chest and narrow hips. A fearless horseman, a graceful dancer, and a witty conversationalist, he was admired equally by the young men and women of his circle. "He was the finest looking man I ever saw, black hair and handsome features," an acquaintance recalled. "He looked like somebody. He looked like someone who had something to him, like he was a fine strong man, which no doubt he was."

Though famously impatient and hot-tempered, Shelby was not notably aggressive in those early years of his manhood. Unlike most of the men he would befriend and later lead in battle, he fought no duels at a time when personal feuds and exaggerated concepts of honor made dueling commonplace. Nor was he, in contrast to his boyhood idol John Hunt Morgan, fascinated by military history and anxious to prove himself as a warrior. He took the South's side in the never-ending quarrels of the day over slavery and secession, but less fiercely than his friend and former tutor Frank Blair supported the North— Blair was already famous as a Free-Soil Democrat in St. Louis. Rather, Shelby simply assumed the rightness of his society, whose economic pillars were balanced on the backs of slaves.

But in the mid-1850s, as the pressure from Northern abolitionists to destroy slavery started to peak, Shelby began to understand the argument he had heard so many times in the Gratz household from Henry Clay, Thomas Hart Benton, and his stepfather. Geography is destiny, they had said. Where you are born and where you live shapes your fate more than you can ever imagine.

Shelby's destiny was determined in 1854. It was in that fateful year that Congress passed the Kansas-Nebraska Act, granting those two territories the right to statehood, with the proviso that voters in the territories could decide for themselves whether they would allow slavery. Nebraska would certainly reject slave-state status. If Kansas, too, rejected slavery, the precarious balance of Henry Clay's 1820 Missouri Compromise would tilt strongly toward the North.

The Missouri Compromise had proscribed slavery in the so-called unorganized territory of the Great Plains—including Kansas—but had allowed it in Missouri and in the Arkansas Territory. Its basic premise was that Missouri would be admitted to the Union in 1821 as a slave state, but that its southern border, when extended westward, would form the northernmost boundary for possible additional slave states.

Missouri's status as a slave state had always been a problem for the North because of its intrusive geography. It stretches more than three hundred miles from its southern border with Arkansas to its northern border with Iowa. Abraham Lincoln's rock-solid Northern state of Illinois shared most of Missouri's long eastern border, down the Mississippi River to Cairo—just above Missouri's very short border with the slave state of Kentucky, which was famous as an escape route for slaves fleeing to freedom in the North.

Missouri's geography made it the linchpin of the then-western United States. That, and its size: It was nearly as large in area as Pennsylvania, Maryland, and New Jersey combined, with a white population of more than half a million, third behind Virginia and Kentucky of the slave states. Its slave population, however, was much less than that of its sister states in the South; this meant that there was a substantial part of the citizenry, especially in the northeastern counties, with no vested interest in defending slavery. Those who defended it were mostly in the western part of the state, and they sought to go on the offensive by expanding their influence in Kansas.

The eastern third of Kansas was a mirror of Missouri—richly fertile land watered by a network of rivers and streams, and heavily wooded along the Missouri and Kaw rivers. There were abundant coal deposits, fuel for the iron horse and the railroads that were already coming onto the scene. Missouri farmers who owned slaves had long viewed the area as a logical area for expansion of their interests, but now Northern abolitionists were bankrolling settlers who they hoped would vote Kansas into the Union as a free-soil state. If that happened, some of Missouri's leaders argued, their state would be three-quarters encircled by zealous enemies determined to destroy the lifeblood of Missouri's economy and culture: slavery.

Many in the North, especially in New England, did their best to make the fears of Missouri take tangible shape. The poet John Green-leaf Whittier called for pioneers to make Kansas "the homestead of the free." Stowe's *Uncle Tom's Cabin* appeared in 1852, even as Jo Shelby was embarking on his business in Waverly, and raised such a storm of moral outrage that Abraham Lincoln would later jest that its author was responsible for the Civil War. Stowe's brother, the Congregationalist minister Henry Ward Beecher, worked with the New England Emigrant Aid Company in Boston to sponsor settlers willing to fight for Kansas as a free-soil state. Beecher was an advocate of muscular Christianity at its most militant, eager to support such requests as this from a typical new Kansan: "Cannot your secret society send us 200 Sharps rifles as a loan," as well as "a couple of field-pieces? If they will do that, I think they will be well *used*."

Such weapons shipments were confiscated if discovered by authorities, especially those found along the long Missouri River passage from St. Louis to Westport (today part of Kansas City, Missouri). Many were hidden in boxes labeled "Bibles," leading to the boast that the west was being won, and slavery challenged, with "Beecher bibles."

The steamboats bearing some of these hidden guns, and the slavery-hating settlers who came with them, passed within hailing distance of Jo Shelby's office window and his factory floor. They seldom stopped at the Waverly dock, as it was only a few hours farther to their final destination at Westport, and the captains knew they would be greeted less than warmly. But one morning in late May 1855, a young couple disembarked hurriedly from a steamboat; the man carried the body of their four-year-old son, who had died of cholera. Their names were Jason and Ellen Brown, they said. They were on their way to join Jason's brothers near Lawrence, Kansas, about forty miles west of Kansas City; Lawrence was one of the new free-state towns that had already become famous as an abolitionist stronghold. Their request to bury the dead child in the Waverly cemetery was granted, and the couple continued on their way to Kansas on foot— the steamboat captain, fearful of an outbreak of cholera because of the child, had left without them.

Several months later, in early October, a tall, strongly built man in his fifties rode into Waverly from the east, leading a heavily loaded wagon driven by two other men. His name was John Brown, and he had come to exhume his grandson's body rather than leave it buried in the tainted soil of a slave state. He did not want to tarry, eager as he was to move on to his final destination of Lawrence. Brown brusquely turned aside questions about where he and the other men were from and what they intended to do in Kansas. He bristled when a rough-looking Waverly man persisted in nosing around the tightly covered wagon; perhaps the local suspected that the wagon was loaded with ammunition, rifles, revolvers, and heavy cutlasses, as indeed it was. The roughneck threatened Brown, saying that he should forget about Kansas: "You won't live to get there." Eyes blazing with righteous anger, John Brown glowered at the Waverly man. That might be so, he said. Everybody had to die at some time. But he warned, "We are prepared *not to die alone.*"

Other fierce and powerful old men in Missouri, as prone to violence as John Brown, were roused to fury by the abolitionists' promise to vote Kansas into the Union as a free-soil state. They formed a quasi-military organization called the Blue Lodge, modeled after the Masons, with similar oaths of allegiance to secrecy and complicated hierarchies. Two Blue Lodge leaders who strongly influenced Shelby, and who flattered him by lavishing attention upon him, were Claiborne Jackson and David Atchison. Each was formidable in his own way, despite aspects of their characters that bordered on the comic.

Jackson was born in Kentucky in 1806 and grew up in Missouri. He served in the state legislature for twelve years, earning power as well as enemies who charged that he was secretly a Jew and that he lusted in an unseemly way after women—he was said to have married in succession two short-lived daughters of a wealthy couple, a doctor and his wife. When he returned to marry the third daughter, her father consented once again but muttered, "I reckon you'll be back next for the old woman." The rumors may have been meant to disparage Jackson's impressive mind and political acumen: He was a classical scholar versed in Latin, Greek, and Hebrew who would become governor of Missouri in 1861 and a leading figure in the state's attempts to secede from the Union.

David Atchison, once a U.S. senator, was born a year after Jackson in a section of Lexington, Kentucky, called "Frogtown." He moved to western Missouri as a young man and thrived as a politician. He was enormous—"a florid, sociable man-mountain, fond of horses, hunting, fishing, and liquor," in the words of historian Jay Monaghan—and sufficiently shrewd as a politician to win his U.S. Senate seat at the age of thirty-six. He had made one huge political miscalculation, however: It was Atchison who urged Senator Stephen Douglas to expedite the passage of the Kansas-Nebraska Act, including the provision for local determination that now threatened western Missouri's way of life, which had slavery at its core. The once-moderate Atchison had since become a notorious fire-eater, urging pro-slavery forces to settle in Kansas and "kill every God-damned abolitionist" who crossed them.

Shelby became involved with the Blue Lodge from around the time of the first key vote on Kansas statehood, on March 30, 1855, in Lawrence. He raised a group of about fifty men and joined several hundred others under Claiborne Jackson to camp outside of town the day before the election. Thus far the Missourians seemed to be little more than rambunctious participants in a shivaree—that time-honored frontier tradition of rough hazing. They were "in a boisterous holiday mood," Shelby's biographer Daniel O'Flaherty writes, with "their horses, their flags, their tents, their fiddles, their whiskey jugs, and their bowie knives sticking out of their boot tops into their jeans."

The evening before the Lawrence vote, an election judge accompanied by a local resident named Sam Wood rode out to inform Shelby and the other men of the rules governing the election. The judge was alarmed by one tough's boast that he planned to vote half a dozen times—the most he could do without reloading his revolver—and then once again with his knife. Wood laughed off the threat. Shelby, charmed with Wood's courage, warned off the loudmouth and accepted Wood's invitation to dinner in Lawrence. The two men argued cordially into the evening about politics; it was the beginning of a friendship that would survive the Civil War. Wood was grateful for Shelby's intercession and admired his sense of honor for promising that he had no intention of voting himself if he had to swear that he was a Kansas resident, because his home was eighty miles east, in Missouri.

Shelby was not always so polite. According to the editor of the Lawrence *Tribune* some years later, he took offense at the sight of an abolitionist named Cyrus Bond, who was "assaulted" by a mob of Blue Lodgers, "shot at and driven over the river bank, making a jump of about thirty feet almost perpendicular. It was said that Shelby fired the shots at Bond, but this we do not know, though we saw the shots fired and saw Bond, a very fat man, running like a quarter horse and wheezing like an old locomotive."

Shelby's neighbors in Waverly and the region approved of his cross-border excursions and raids during the next several years. He was praised by *The American Citizen*, a newspaper in nearby Lexington, for "the courage, coolness and dignity of his deportment under the trying circumstances in which we were all placed, and for his kind, careful and impartial conduct and esteem." He was also given "a fine Sharp's rifle" and lauded for his work in establishing permanent settlements in Kansas. The *Citizen* spread Shelby's fame and, incidentally, made him a target for irate Kansas Jayhawkers.

On a cold, clear morning a week before Christmas, 1855, Shelby woke to learn the cost of his celebrity. His new sawmill in Dover, just a few miles to the west, had gone up in flames the previous night. The building was uninsured; the loss came to $9,000, or about $200,000 in today's money. Arson was the cause, and there was little doubt as to who was responsible. Shelby vowed revenge on the Jayhawkers. His stepbrother's reaction was entirely different. Howard Gratz had objected to Shelby's involvement with the Blue Lodge from the start. In a portent of what would become one of the recurrent tragic themes of the Civil War—brother against brother—he packed up and returned to Kentucky to become editor of *The Kentucky Gazette* and an opponent of the expansion of slavery westward.

Howard Gratz had always been the manager of the brothers' complicated business affairs, relying on the personable and gregarious Shelby to be the company's public face. When he left, the unwelcome burden of rescuing the firm from the disaster precipitated by the fire took most of Shelby's time. This is likely the reason that Shelby was not present at one of the critical events of the border war the following spring. On May 21, 1856, Lawrence was sacked for the first time, after repeated threats by David Atchison. The "general" appears to have been in his cups, at least according to the *Boston Evening Telegraph*, admittedly not a neutral observer; Atchison, the newspaper claimed, was known in Missouri as "Staggering Davy." Exhorting his men to action before they entered the town, he called himself "a Kickapoo Ranger, by God!" who was carrying the banner of "Southern rights." "If one man or woman dare stand before you, blow them to hell with a chunk of cold lead!"

Though the population was terrorized and property damage was extensive, no lives were lost, and Atchison's no doubt exaggerated buffoonery gave the affair a comic turn. He personally aimed a cannon at the town's grand three-story hotel and missed it completely, from a distance of only a few yards. The ball sailed over the building and thumped harmlessly amid a group of women who had sought safety on a hill behind the hotel.

A tragic consequence of this farcical affair followed just two days later, on May 23, 1856, near the hamlet of Osawatomie, Kansas. Late that night, John Brown and four of his sons called five men out of their cabins and shot and hacked them to death with cutlasses—perhaps the same weapons that had been packed in Brown's wagon as he passed through Waverly the year before. Three of the dead were a farmer and his two teenage sons by the name of Doyle. Shelby had by this time developed an uncanny knack for appraising the character and abilities of both his allies and his enemies. He knew all of Brown's victims, he said later, and the Doyles were innocent victims of an outrage. But as for the other two—one was a famously abusive pro-slavery legislator, and the other was notorious for terrorizing free-state farmers—he said coldly that they "got only what they deserved."

John Brown's failed raid at Harpers Ferry and his execution followed three years after these murders, turning him into a legend. In a poem called "Brown of Ossawatomie" [*sic*] John Greenleaf Whittier linked the two events, praising Brown as a martyr seeking a noble goal but decrying his means:

> *Perish with him the folly that seeks through evil good!*
> *Long live the generous purpose unstained with human blood!*
> *Not the raid of midnight terror, but the thought which underlies;*
> *Not the borderer's pride of daring, but the Christian's sacrifice.*

The unrest would continue for another two years after Osawatomie, but federal authorities gradually gained control, and Kansas entered the Union as a free state in 1861. The famous border wars were, in reality, a series of intimidating raids, counterraids, and saberrattling skirmishes. There was more to them than just sound and fury, as some in the South have argued. But the notion of "war," the labels "bleeding Kansas" and "bloody Kansas," and the designation of the Blue Lodge raiders as "border ruffians" were largely rhetorical constructs of the Northern press—a masterful effort to shape opinion by Horace Greeley's *New York Tribune* and the eloquent architects of American culture in New England, including Whittier, Ralph Waldo Emerson, and Henry David Thoreau. In three years there were never more than a few thousand men involved, on both sides of the border, and somewhere between sixty and two hundred of them died. The border wars were hardly trivial, but their greater significance lay in setting the tone and mood for what was yet to come.

For Jo Shelby, the border wars' main consequence was the demonstration of his own vulnerability, as a man of property, to the sweeping passions of the time. That, and the revelation that he had a gift for inspiring men to follow him and for devising hit-and-run tactics particularly appropriate for men who had grown up on horseback.

By the summer of 1858, the situation seemed calm enough for Shelby to give up his envied status as a bachelor. After years of squiring beautiful belles from area plantations, he chose as his bride the girl next door—the petite and lively daughter of his distant cousin William Shelby, who had recently moved his family into town. Betty Shelby, barely five feet tall and just turned seventeen, was a popular girl ten years younger than Jo. Their wedding on July 22, 1858, concluded with a stately promenade from the lawn of William Shelby's home on the bank of the Missouri River to Jo Shelby's waiting steamboat, the *A. B. Chambers*. A contemporary account describes "the path leading to the river" as "carpeted in red velvet. At the bend of the river a brilliantly lighted boat awaited the arrival of the wedding party and close friends," all of whom would join the bride and groom "for an excursion to St. Louis." Biographer Daniel O'Flaherty gracefully imagines the moment of departure, "in the cool of the evening, with lights ablaze in the salon, music floating out over the river to serenade the sleepy birds in the cottonwoods on the bank, and the laughter of the young people gayer than any music."

Among the wedding guests was Shelby's young friend and admirer John Newman Edwards, the reporter and editor of the local *Weekly Missouri Expositor*, published in nearby Lexington. Born in Virginia in 1838, Edwards had an ancestor who sounds like a soul mate of Shelby's boisterous great-grandfather, old Evan Shelby. Edwards's forebear was a terror named Colonel Conquest Wyatt, who used his knife at the age of ninety to pin back an assailant's ear. Edwards himself looked anything but martial. Slightly built, shy and bookish, he had Edgar Allan Poe's high forehead and languorous eyes—as well as something of Poe's erratic genius. Growing up poor and friendless, largely self-taught, Edwards was a born writer lusting for an epic subject when he moved to Missouri in 1855.

He found his subject in the holy Southern cause of states' rights, which he defended in the columns of the *Expositor*. His chosen standard-bearer for that cause would be the handsome young aristocrat Jo Shelby. Edwards's glowing accounts of Shelby's adventures in Kansas led to a lasting friendship: "Jo Shelby was wealthy, John Edwards was poor," as an Edwards admirer later wrote, "but they liked the same things: drinking, fishing, hunting, talking, planning for a time of troubles that lay not far ahead."

From the day of Shelby's wedding to their arrival in Mexico City seven years later, Edwards would seldom be far from Shelby's side. He was to Shelby as James Boswell was to Samuel Johnson, or as Sir Arthur Conan Doyle's Dr. Watson would be to Sherlock Holmes—so much a part of him that they seem almost to be one being. When

Edwards finally married, years after the war, it would be at Shelby's house. He addressed Shelby as "My Dear General" in his letters right up to his death.

Edwards wrote an account for the *Expositor* of the wedding and the party's subsequent boat trip to St. Louis. Sadly, it vanished in the early days of the Civil War when Kansas raiders threw the files of the *Expositor* into the Missouri River. But given Edwards's writerly skills, it must have glittered. Everyone from Shelby's affluent world of influence and prestige was there, including his parents: Anna Gratz, who had visited the year before in order to meet Betty, had come this time with Benjamin, and both were happy to see their exuberant son finally settling down.

Gratz Brown, Shelby's stepcousin and boyhood friend, was also on board, as was Frank Blair. Like Shelby, they had enjoyed flourishing careers and growing influence, yet on trajectories that carried them far from his own path. Brown was in his sixth and final year as a member of the Missouri House of Representatives. He walked with a pronounced limp, the result of a duel he had fought in 1856 over his antislavery pronouncements and his role as a leader in Missouri's Free-Soil movement.

Frank Blair had also gone into politics, as an ally and supporter of Gratz Brown. After serving in the Mexican War in 1846, he won influence in St. Louis through his support of its large German immigrant population; the eager democrats who had fled Germany during the revolutionary turmoil of 1848 shared Blair's strong opposition to slavery. Elected with strong immigrant support to the U.S. House of Representatives in 1852, Blair had recently been won over to the new Republican Party. He would lose his seat in 1858 but get it back in 1860, as a Republican supporter of Abraham Lincoln, and go on to a wartime career marked by extraordinary success as well as controversy.

Also present were the very men most responsible for Shelby's recent involvement with the Blue Lodge raids into Kansas: the blustery and bibulous David Atchison and the scholarly, much-married Claiborne Jackson. A great part of the energies of Frank Blair and Gratz Brown in recent months had been directed specifically against Atchison and Jackson's interference in Kansas—a "secessionist cabal," they called it—so it has to be assumed that the celebratory atmosphere on board

Shelby's boat as it wound its way to St. Louis was strained. These were, after all, violent men with very short fuses.

But they were also fellow Southerners—more to the point, Missourians—and they were gentlemen, taking part in one of the glorious rituals of the Old South. Suppose for a moment that the ghost of the romantic and melancholy John Edwards has returned to finish his lost account of the wedding trip, with the advantage of postwar hindsight.

Picture us, Edwards might say, debating our fevered causes like men who still wished we could be friends, sipping fine bourbon and smoking Havana cigars while our gorgeous, gaily lighted steamboat glides along the majestic Missouri River on a soft midsummer evening. Would that this magical night last forever.

TWO

On the March with the Iron Brigade

O
n April 12, 1861, the Civil War began at Fort Sumter, South Carolina. A few weeks later, Frank Blair sent a telegram to Jo Shelby, urging him to come to St. Louis without delay for a "talk" about the war.

Blair's star, already ascending at the time of Shelby's wedding, had streaked ever higher during the intervening three years. Most recently, he was concerned that the puny military protection provided by Washington would let Claiborne Jackson, now governor of Missouri, claim the state for the South. To forestall this possibly mortal blow to the Union cause, he had formed a political alliance with Captain Nathaniel Lyon.

A ferocious little redhead with a temper even hotter than Blair's, Lyon was a highly competent West Point graduate who had helped end the border fracas between Kansas and Missouri. Lyon was now charged with defending St. Louis, in particular its huge weapons arsenal. Blair and the "Home Guard" units he had earlier established, in which he now held the rank of colonel, were essential elements of Lyon's defenses.

Several hundred men strong, mostly composed of German immigrants, the Home Guard was scorned as made up of "lop-eared

Dutchmen" by the native-born Missourians, who considered themselves frontiersmen—or at least their worthy descendants. But many of the Germans had seen active service in Europe, fighting against repressive regimes, and they would prove to be good soldiers in what they regarded as the Union's righteous cause. In the tumultuous period leading up to the war, they gave Blair the power to become, for a time, in the words of Daniel O'Flaherty, the "dictator of the Union party in Missouri and the personification of the Union cause in the state."

Blair's strength was enhanced by his family connections in Washington. His older brother, Montgomery, was Abraham Lincoln's postmaster general—a vital position because communication between Washington and its battlefield commands would rely on an efficient postal service and its innovative technological arm, the telegraph. The role of Frank and Montgomery's father in Washington was also significant. Still vigorous at seventy-one, Francis Preston Blair, Sr., was reprising his role as Andrew Jackson's trusted adviser with the new president, who frequently stayed at the Blairs' sprawling estate in Silver Spring, Maryland.

It is fair to say that the Blair family—Preston and "Monty" in Washington, and Frank in Missouri—exerted an influence in national affairs comparable to that of the Adamses before them and the Kennedys and Bushes afterward. Frank did not hesitate to use his share of that influence, and a nod from him could make or break a man: John Charles Frémont, "the pathfinder" whose competence as a western explorer did not extend to the military command in the west that Lincoln would soon give him, later found himself out of a job after tangling with Blair. *The New York Herald* accurately described Blair's significance: "Whenever Frank Blair is seen in public his left coat pocket is stuffed full with applications and his right one with commissions west of the Mississippi River. Verily, Frank has got to be a power in the land." That power, *The New York Sun* noted, came not just from family influence but also from Blair's courage and character: "Every man in Missouri, whatever his politics, his religion, or his beverage . . . has reason to believe that a braver man than Frank Blair never set foot on Missouri soil or any other soil. No one hereabouts whose hope of eternal life was not well assured, would ever think of drawing a knife or pistol on Frank."

Jo Shelby's personal fortunes, by contrast with Blair's in politics, had declined markedly. The once-thriving Waverly Steam Rope Company had to be sold at a loss in February 1860, along with the warehouse, the farms, and the land where the burned sawmill had stood. (Blair had tried to help Shelby by cosigning notes for his company and ended up having to borrow from his father to pay them off.) World market conditions were partly to blame—the Panic of 1857 in the United States was followed by a steep economic downturn in Europe, a major customer for the South's cotton crop, which, in turn, was closely connected to the hemp trade.

But the primary cause for Shelby's financial difficulty was his indifference to the details of business, formerly so carefully looked after by Howard Gratz. Shelby had spent too much time living the good life of a gentleman farmer—hunting, fishing, attending balls with his pretty young wife; that, and discoursing about politics with the men who had followed him into Kansas and with other admirers, chief among them the young newspaperman John Edwards. He was not poor—he and Betty and their first child, Orville, born in August 1859, still occupied their grand house on Mount Rucker—but Shelby's economic prospects when he received Frank Blair's telegram were dismal.

Shelby arrived in St. Louis on May 10, 1861. It was a city in turmoil, and he was unable to see Blair immediately. While he was en route from Waverly, about eight hundred Confederate sympathizers, members of the Missouri State Guard (as opposed to Frank Blair's Home Guard), had gathered not far from the federal arsenal. They established picket lines around a wooded hill that overlooked the arsenal and called the site "Camp Jackson," after the secession-inclined governor, Shelby's former mentor Claiborne Jackson. Behind the lines were several small cannon sent by Jefferson Davis, the recently announced president of the Confederate States of America.

Anticipating Missouri's secession, Jackson had directed his agents to steal weapons from federal stockpiles around the state, with limited success. A small arsenal near Kansas City had been plundered, but the plum was the arsenal in St. Louis with its million rounds of small-arms ammunition, machinery for manufacturing and repairing weapons, and about sixty thousand old but serviceable muskets.

Thanks to Blair and Lyon, these armaments were already secure.

On April 25, 1861, in the dead of night, they were ferried across the river to Alton, Illinois. The danger to the arsenal was gone, but Camp Jackson remained. On May 9, Lyon learned that a shipment of weapons from the Baton Rouge arsenal, which had been captured by secessionists, had arrived in St. Louis. The armaments included five hundred muskets and two siege guns. On May 10, Lyon surrounded the State Guard volunteers with about three thousand men—federal troops and Blair's Home Guard Germans—and successfully demanded their surrender.

Many of the State Guard prisoners were from prominent St. Louis area families; others were part of the huge local community of Irish immigrants, who sympathized with the South and detested the Germans. A hostile crowd gathered to harass the long double column of Union men as they marched their prisoners down Olive Street to the empty arsenal; there the Southern sympathizers would be held until they gave their "parole," their promise upon release to refrain from further unlawful activities.

Shouting "Damn the Dutch!" and "Hurray for Jeff Davis!" the mob lobbed rocks and dirt clods at Blair and Lyon's men. A drunk was knocked flat when he tried to break into the column. He staggered to his feet with a pistol in his hand and fired; a German member of the Home Guard fell, mortally wounded. A fusillade from the Northern troops into the crowd followed, leaving a score of civilians dead in the street; among them were two women, one holding a dead baby in her arms. Similar outbreaks along the way led to a total of twenty-eight dead civilians—the first blood spilled in Missouri during the Civil War, and a foreshadowing of the fighting between civilians turned guerillas and uniformed Federals that was to come.

Jo Shelby observed some of these scenes in a rage because he could do nothing to help his countrymen. Also watching the carnage in St. Louis that fateful day were two men whose names would soon be inextricably linked as saviors of the Union. One was a short and shabby harness-shop clerk from Galena, Illinois, who had lost his commission in the U.S. Army for being a drunk. After failing earlier in 1861 to regain his regular army status, he was now spending a few idle days in town while waiting to join an Illinois regiment. His name was Ulysses S. Grant, occasionally twisted by his detractors to "Useless Grant."

The other future luminary was, like Grant, a West Point graduate—though at the top of his class rather than, like Grant, near the bottom—who had left what seemed to be a stalled military career to become a businessman. William T. Sherman, now a railway executive living in St. Louis, had just two days earlier turned down a temporary military commission from Frank Blair. Sherman told Blair that he would rejoin the army as a regular officer or not at all.

The North was scrambling to find and hold good men. Preston Blair had failed to persuade Colonel Robert E. Lee, with whom Frank Blair had served in Mexico, to fight for the Union. Frank Blair had no better luck with Shelby, when they finally met on May 10, 1861. Though it is certain that Blair offered Shelby a commission, neither man left a full account of their meeting. Considering the massacre on Olive Street that Shelby witnessed, the exchange must have been tense. Blair no doubt reminded Shelby that with the exception of John Hunt Morgan, virtually all of his friends, among them B. Gratz Brown and himself, had declared for the Union. So, too, had most of his large family, including his parents and his stepbrothers—Cary Gratz, in particular, would soon become a Union officer. The Union was both overwhelmingly powerful and could claim to be on the side of the angels regarding the slavery issue, which needed to be resolved, at long last. Even the great Lafayette, once a guest in Shelby's house, had vowed at the time that he "never would have drawn my sword in the cause of America if I could have conceived" of helping to found a "nation of slaves."

Blair's objection to the extension of slavery derived, in fact, mostly from his sense that it undercut white workers' wages. He was no abolitionist, as Shelby well knew. He had owned slaves himself until recently, and he had worked hard to protect the social and economic interests of Missouri slave owners. Blair agreed with Emerson and others that the North should compensate the slave holders for their lost property (a proposal that never gained much support in Congress). He also shared in the cultural resistance to assimilation of free blacks into white society, a resistance not limited to the southern part of the country, and argued that the black population should ultimately be forcibly resettled in Central America.

Blair's offer of a commission to Shelby was a generous act of trust in a friend with no experience of military command beyond border raids. Had Shelby taken it, his talents might have resulted in a glorious career with the winning side. At the least, what was left of his fortune and property would have remained intact. It is clear from Shelby's later comments that he knew slavery was doomed and that he was less prejudiced against blacks than were most of his friends.

But Shelby at this moment in time, even before the massacre on Olive Street, was well launched into his hothead phase. He was not just a slave owner (or former owner: most had been sold, along with his failed business) whose livelihood was at risk; he was a states' rights patriot who believed his homelands in Kentucky and Missouri were being bullied by a distant and hostile power in Washington.

In fact, Shelby had never intended to accept the offer he had presumed Blair intended to make. His real purpose in coming to St. Louis was to help out his friend, John Hunt Morgan. In a letter Shelby had received in Waverly shortly before he got Blair's telegram, Morgan had said that he was forming a cavalry unit to fight against the Union if it invaded Kentucky. He needed one hundred thousand percussion caps for his men's old muskets. Could Shelby get these for him in St. Louis and figure out a way to get them to Kentucky undetected? Shelby could and did. He bought the caps from an arms dealer and hid them in pots of roses and lilacs for shipment to his hometown of Lexington, where they arrived safely and were quickly put to use by the soon-to-be-legendary Morgan's Raiders.

Shelby returned to Waverly and quickly raised about a hundred men from Lafayette County for the Missouri State Guard. As the elected captain of his company, he saw his first significant action in mid-August 1861, at the Battle of Wilson's Creek. It took place near Springfield in the southern part of the state, following Governor Jackson's defiant decree that Missouri was now an independent republic. The redoubtable Nathaniel Lyon, who had recently jumped in rank from captain to brigadier general, led a reckless assault on a larger Confederate force. Despite being twice wounded, he was on the verge of a brilliant victory when he was killed. The Confederates failed to capitalize on the Union retreat that followed, however, losing their chance to control the state. Missouri would remain loyal to the Union, but the loss of such a gifted leader was a calamity: General Sherman later blamed the power vacuum left by Lyon's death for the vicious guerrilla warfare of the ensuing years in Missouri.

Personal tragedy for Jo Shelby was another consequence of Wilson's Creek. His stepbrother Cary Gratz led a company of the First Missouri Volunteers against the Confederates. He fell dead in the same charge that killed Lyon, not half a mile from Shelby's company. Shelby's grief upon learning the news of his stepbrother's death later that day was reflected by his young friend—soon to be his adjutant— John Edwards, who said that "in life," Cary "had been tender and true." In death, he was a hero.

Shelby and Cary's aunt Rebecca wrote to console Anna and Benjamin Gratz. Now in her eightieth year, Rebecca expressed her anger as vividly as she did her sorrow: "The outrages perpetrated by kindred on each other" were "too appalling to be realized." She could only "lament as among the horrors of war" that "some so near to me in blood & affections" had "raised arms against the hearts and the bosoms of those who have cherished them." A month later she wrote to Frank Blair to ask for his help in seeing that Cary's body was recovered and properly buried in Lexington. And she commiserated again with Anna over the dreadful misfortune that her son Jo was a part of "the Southern Army, so fatal to our Beloved Cary."

Over the next four years Jo Shelby became an important part of that Southern army, a player in the most compelling drama of American history. That epic would be acted out on three huge stages. The first was the eastern theater, with its opposing capitals of Washington and Richmond, which got the most intense press coverage by the big newspapers of the Atlantic seaboard cities. The second was the vital western theater, between the Appalachian Mountains and the Mississippi River, where Grant would turn the tide of the war by taking Vicksburg in the summer of 1863.

Shelby's war was in the third theater, by far the largest in area but remote and sparsely settled—that half of the Confederacy that lay beyond the Mississippi. The "Trans-Mississippi Department," as Richmond called it, was four hundred thousand square miles in size, and included Missouri, Arkansas, Texas, Indian Territory (today's Oklahoma), and western Louisiana. There were only a few cities, none worthy of the name when compared with St. Louis, which had 160,000 people—the largest, San Antonio, had a population of only 10,000. Most of the area's two million white inhabitants lived on farms in eastern Texas, Missouri, Arkansas, and Louisiana—an area itself nearly twice the size of Great Britain and the locale of most of the action in the department during the war.

There was hardly a hint of the network of railroads, highways, and telegraph lines that crossed the North and even large parts of the Old South. Confederate commands in the third theater were variously located in the frontier towns of Shreveport, Little Rock, and Galveston. Far from one another and a thousand miles or more from Richmond, they often operated independently and with minimal coordination or oversight.

Abraham Lincoln saw from the beginning the significance of the Trans-Mississippi region. Its eastern portions bordered the Mississippi River—the nation's spinal column, in Sherman's apt phrase. That great river could only be captured and controlled if the Confederates' Trans-Mississippi Department was neutralized. An added complication for the Union concerned its blockade of Southern ports, which was partly effective on the Atlantic coast. The blockade in the Gulf of Mexico, however, was endangered by the shared border between Texas and Mexico and the international waterway of the Rio Grande. Cotton, the lifeblood of the Confederacy, was easily smuggled into Mexico in exchange for food and munitions bought from England and France. The tricky relations between French-controlled Mexico, the Union, and the Confederacy would have a significant bearing on Jo Shelby's future career, and on that of many other Southerners as well.

Despite its size, geographical importance, and wealth of resources—food and cattle in particular—the department was largely ignored by Richmond. Unlike Washington, Richmond's war office initiated a divided command, leaving the department to operate on its own. Confederate officers who protested that the divided command endangered the Mississippi River, and thus the Confederacy itself, were ignored. The Trans-Mississippi Department itself became a dumping ground—a "salvage yard," as one Shelby scholar has put it—

for senior Confederate officers in the eastern and western theaters deemed malcontents and incompetents.

The forces these generals commanded were small by comparison with those in the other theaters. The entire department could muster only twenty-two thousand men in late 1862, as well as many Indians "upon whom," as one Confederate officer said, "no reliance can be placed." A report in April 1863 indicated there were about thirty thousand men sprinkled throughout the department, but many of these would be summoned by Richmond to defend Vicksburg in 1863 or to supplement other Confederate forces, and never did return.

Union military strategy was to field enough men in the region to control rather than to occupy it. Once the Mississippi River was in hand (as it would be after Vicksburg fell), the department would be cut off and irrelevant. This meant that both sides were fairly matched. The North had more men but also the more difficult military assignment of attacking an enemy on its own ground. Though this was true in the two other theaters as well, the longer lines of supply in the region, plus the ability of Southern forces to live off the land, made Union operations there particularly difficult.

In the Trans-Mississippi Department there were about a dozen pitched battles; some, such as at Wilson's Creek, were as intensely fought as any in the war, though were less costly in terms of lives lost. Shelby took part in half a dozen of these. The last and biggest was a defeat—the Battle of Westport in October 1864, a rout that effectively ended the Southern threat to the Union west of the Mississippi. But most of his time was spent in skirmishes and lightning attacks on stronger Union positions, followed by exhausting retreats under conditions of extreme privation.

Shelby's greatest fame came from his Iron Brigade's extended raid out of Arkansas into Missouri in the autumn of 1863. He found most of the people in the region sympathetic to the South's cause and willing to share what little they had, but the brigade of nearly 1,500 men had been forced to live on what they had captured from the enemy because, he said, so much of the countryside was "desolated." "In many places for forty miles not a single habitation is to be found, for on the road we met delicate females fleeing southward, driving ox teams, barefooted, ragged, and suffering even for bread." In his summary report, Shelby wrote that his brigade covered 1,500 miles, attacking and destroying ten Union forts, killing or wounding about 600 Federals, and paroling another 500.

Northern commanders belittled Shelby's excursion as merely a nuisance, but it was more than that—not least as a propaganda coup for the Missouri Volunteers: "Shout, boys and make a noise; the Yankees are afraid," ran the refrain of a popular song in his honor. "There's something up and hell's to pay when Shelby's on a raid." He was not only their Stuart, he was better: "You've heard of J. E. B. Stuart's Ride around McClellan? Hell, brother, Jo Shelby rode around *Missouri!*"

Such raids extracted a price, often requiring the men to travel a hundred miles at a stretch without rest or food. John Edwards tried to explain what going without sleep felt like. Some men heard "exquisite music" and saw the "radiant beacons" of distant cities beckoning them. Others imagined bugle calls to battle, or shied away from drooping tree branches on the open, treeless prairie. By the middle of the third night "stolid stupor generally prevailed," and led to an insensibility to pain. Men slid from their horses and lay unconscious until pricked by a saber point to remount. Some went "incurably mad" from the strain.

Shelby's example on these marches inspired his men to do more than they thought they could, as it did in battle. In one such engagement, he rallied his men, John Edwards recalled, "riding four horses to death—two falling shot beneath him—his hat off, his face black with perspiration, his shirt open at the throat and his long hair blowing back in the cool autumn wind, he seemed inspired with the very mania of battle; he was the embodiment of calmness and desperation, of great resolves and terrible execution."

When he was finally wounded, on July 4, 1863, at the Battle of Helena—the first and only time, despite having at least five horses shot from under him—Shelby's reaction was remarkable. A minié ball entered at his right elbow and exited through his wrist. "I was near him," an aide recalled, "and he did not even draw in his breath." Billy Hunter, Shelby's friend and slave from childhood, now his manservant, was beside him and recalled that Shelby was waving his saber when he was shot. Hunter himself took a bullet through the leg that day.

Shelby's genius as a commander showed itself both on the attack and in his execution of the fighting retreat—a frequent necessity by virtue of the North's superiority in numbers. Known since ancient times but seldom employed successfully because it required exquisite timing and implementation, the fighting retreat became Shelby's trademark. Shelby had designed the tactic and worked out its execution earlier, in particular the communications techniques between company commanders and himself. He first used it to stun the capable Union general James Blunt in November 1862. Blunt's two brigades of some five thousand men outnumbered Shelby by five to two as they pursued him into the Boston Mountains of northern Arkansas. Taking advantage of the steep and thickly wooded terrain, Shelby deployed his thirty companies every two hundred yards. The first company fired on the Federals' advance unit, then broke off and quickly retreated to the end of the defensive line. The next company did the same, then the third, and so on down the line, preventing the enemy's main body from getting close enough to do real harm. The Federals could lay claim to terrain that Shelby's men gave up in this manner, but at considerable costs in terms of soldiers killed and wounded—and above all, in time lost.

Throughout the war there would be lighter moments to leaven the dark ones. One such was Shelby's first coup, the capture in October 1861 of the Union paddle wheel steamer *Sunshine*. Shelby was returning to Waverly from the east when he spied the steamer, a splendid four-decked packet boat. The captain of the *Sunshine,* observing a large cannon poised on the bluff forty feet above the boat and pointing directly at it, docked at Waverly. Shelby and twenty of his men greeted the captain, according to John Edwards, and inspected the steamboat. The cargo included a hundred army wagons and a thousand sacks of flour. Nearby on shore were stacks of firewood, which would be used to burn the goods, Shelby said—meaning the Federals should not waste time on a retaliatory raid to get them back. The boat was released unharmed to its indignant captain, Shelby having a soft spot in his heart for paddle wheelers.

The *Sunshine*'s captain would have been even more indignant had he known that the menacing cannon that had so frightened him was merely a harmless wooden replica, painted black. As the *Sunshine* steamed on its depleted way to Leavenworth, the gleeful citizens of Waverly divided up the flour and foodstuffs and new wagons—which were never destined for burning. For his part, Shelby enjoyed a rare night at home with Betty and Orville, and the newest member of the family: Joseph Boswell Shelby, born in June a few days before his father marched off to war.

There could even be humor in the usually fraught context of dealing with Union sympathizers. Short on winter clothing, the Confederates had no qualms about wearing captured blue uniforms. One cold day in mid-Missouri a local physician "mistook us for Federal soldiers," a private named Salem Ford recalled, and was "encouraged" in his misapprehension. The doctor invited the false bluecoats to help themselves to forage for their horses and gave them bacon, beef, and chicken, "even to extravagance." Shelby cautioned his men not to molest the doctor or his family. When a messenger in Confederate gray arrived the following morning to see Shelby, the doctor finally realized his mistake: "You could have knocked his eyes off with a stick," Ford wrote. "We thanked him for his kindness and liberality and promised to call again if we should ever again visit that section, to which," Ford added wryly, "he did not insist."

The romantic patina of these tales, whether light or dark, stems partly from the time and the nature of the war. For John Edwards, the Civil War was a contest between chivalric knights of old against an ignoble, uncultured, and materialistic invader. "It was a war of races," he wrote. "It was Puritan against Cavalier; Patrician against Proletarian; grim fanatics who, like Cromwell's followers, carried bibles in their belts and iron pots on their heads, against the descendants of those men who died for Charles the First, and shed blood like water rather than forgo a rollicking song or sing psalms through their nostrils."

It follows that, in Edwards's book about the war, *Shelby and His Men*, Shelby is compared to both Lancelot and King Arthur, his men are Shakespeare's "band of brothers," and all are "knights" or "cavaliers." When one of those cavaliers lay dying, his "features, wan and worn with pain, were lighted up with a tenderness and joy inexpressible, as his loved leader bent over him with a heart too sick for words."

Shelby murmured a "few words of hope he did not feel; a few tears hot and scalding from eyes unused to weep—a long, lingering, fond good-bye, and Shelby rode swiftly away, not daring to look back upon the spot where he had left his flower of chivalry."

Edwards was hardly alone in his romantic view of war, as his story of the impetuous Alonzo Slayback shows. Slayback was a former schoolteacher who had met both Edwards and Shelby while he was studying law at a small college in Lexington, Missouri, in 1856. A handsome young man with a dramatic pompadour, and a "most dashing and gallant officer," according to Edwards, Slayback one day "concluded to try an adventure thought of many centuries ago when knights wore greaves and visors." He challenged an opposing force to send forward a champion to engage him in single combat. "Quick as lightning," a Captain Wilhite "came boldly forth to within twenty paces and fired at Slayback, who returned fire immediately." They both missed, but "upon the second shot, Slayback's bullet inflicted an ugly wound in his antagonist's leg, and Wilhite retired. Two other champions dashed out for the honor of their dishonored regiment." A comrade, "brave as a lion," went gallantly to Slayback's rescue, when another round was fired without additional damage. A third officer rode down from the federal lines, and yet another friend of Slayback's joined him in support, "chivalrous as Bayard." As the firing continued, "another Federal fell, and the two others retreated."

"Strange and true," none of the Confederates "received a scratch." Reprimanded by the more practical Shelby for his foolishness, Slayback would survive to write his own romantic postwar poem, about the burial of the Confederate flag in the Rio Grande.

But Shelby himself could be courtly. He wrote in July 1861, to a Union officer in Waverly to say, "My family states to me that they were kindly treated by your command. Allow me Sir, to say it is a debt I cannot soon forget . . . and nothing will afford me more pleasure than to reciprocate in kind."

And his grandiloquence could match that of Edwards, as in his published appeal for support to the "Freemen of Missouri" the following summer. Could you, he said, "turn your back on this your country in this her dark hour of peril and grief and see the mad waves of anarchy and despotism sweep away all the vestiges of family ties, sacred firesides, and everything that makes life worth life? . . . Wave Missouri, all thy banners wave and charge with all thy chivalry." Concluding, he echoed, perhaps unconsciously, Ulysses's call to his timid mariners in Tennyson's "Lotos-Eaters": "Close up, comrades! Close up, Missourians! Land is ahead; day is breaking. One more effort, one long pull, one strong pull, one pull altogether, and the day is ours."*

Beneath the politesse of Shelby's letter and his fustian call to arms (which may, indeed, have been written by Edwards) lurked a hard and ugly reality—the four years of insurgency bloodshed in Missouri that Sherman blamed on Nathaniel Lyon's death at Wilson's Creek were already well launched. The war in Missouri was not so much "Puritan against Cavalier," but Missourians who considered themselves part of the Union against those who wanted to leave it. To a degree unequaled elsewhere during the Civil War, the conflict in Missouri was neighbor against neighbor, in and out of uniform.

Thus the second part of Shelby's pleasant letter to the Union officer warned him to get out of town while he still could, and the call to arms ended with a threat to Union loyalists and Jayhawkers. "One great aim with me," Shelby said, "will be to give quietude and repose to the neighborhood around my headquarters." Accordingly, "all Negroes and suspicious persons caught after sunset within my lines will be dealt with in the severest manner." Additionally, "Union men too old for service in the ranks, who make their age a pretext for spying and newsbearing, must cease all communications with the Federal commanders or suffer the just punishment of an outraged and violated country."

Even this early in the war, Shelby was addressing two of its most troubling aspects. One was the difficulty of telling friend from foe, and in determining appropriate rewards and punishments for each. The second was what to do about black men, both former slaves and freedmen, who chose to fight for the North. The first of these questions was linked with the status of men who fought usually at their own direction—"guerrillas" who sometimes attached themselves to recognized Confederate units such as Shelby's and operated under their direction, usually as scouts.

---

* "The Lotos-Eaters" begins, " 'Courage!' he said, and pointed toward the land, / 'This mounting wave will roll us shoreward soon.' "

The guerrillas, called "bushwhackers" by the Federals, quickly earned a reputation for murderous determination. The most notorious of them was William Quantrill, a former schoolteacher from Ohio; Shelby despised Quantrill but did not hesitate to use his followers. In early November 1862, about 150 volunteers under William Gregg, who commanded the group in Quantrill's absence, joined Shelby's brigade. Among them were several who would earn postwar fame as train and bank robbers: Dick Yager, Cole Younger, and Frank James, who was lean, saturnine, and intense. Frank's superficially more amiable younger brother Jesse, then just sixteen, may also have been with the group.

A few weeks later, during the Battle of Prairie Grove in early December 1862, Shelby and a few of his men were surprised and surrounded by a company of the federal Seventh Missouri Cavalry. A larger Confederate contingent quickly rescued Shelby and dispersed the Federals. Among those who saved him from capture—and perhaps execution—that day, Shelby later said, was Frank James.

Shelby's association with the guerrillas was more than casual. A key study of the guerrilla leadership identifies two dozen men, half of whom were actively involved in Shelby's brigade—to the point where his staff "seems, at times, to have been virtually interchangeable with the guerrilla movement." This closeness created a problem for him both during the war and afterward. The guerrillas' reputation was forever tarred by the August 1863 attack on Lawrence, Kansas, during which Quantrill and his men killed scores of unarmed men and boys and burned the town. As bad as Quantrill, or worse, was William "Bloody Bill" Anderson, so called because in 1864 he murdered twenty-four disarmed Union soldiers during a train robbery.

Operating independently, for the most part, of Shelby or any other Confederate units, the guerrillas controlled vast areas of Missouri and Arkansas. They were a huge factor in tying down state militia forces that could have been put to better use elsewhere. According to one estimate, there were at least three hundred guerrillas in Jackson County alone, where Kansas City is located. There and elsewhere hundreds of the Union militiamen and Union soldiers were forced into a posture of "static defense" of such points as railways, telegraph lines, storage depots, and towns.

Shelby's receptiveness to the guerrillas was no doubt influenced by their usefulness, but he may not have had to hold his nose as much as their unsavory reputation would suggest. A recent revisionist study of the border wars challenges the familiar characterization of the guerrillas as semiliterate, psychotic white trash (progenitors of those scary backwoodsmen in James Dickey's *Deliverance*), operating entirely outside the Confederate chain of command and without its permission. To the contrary, Donald Gilmore argues: They were legitimate "instruments of the armed forces of the Confederate States of America, operating under general Southern directives, orders, and guidance." Their leaders—though not the execrable Quantrill or Anderson—were "predominantly young men who were the sons of affluent slave owners—the landed gentry of the border—who were subjected to extraordinary circumstances." These young men, according to Gilmore, were a "rural elite" who were "roused into violent action by the repeated incursions into Missouri of marauding Kansans from 1858 onward."

The guerrilla leadership as the region's "rural elite" sounds a good deal like Jo Shelby. It follows, then, that he would suffer directly, as well as benefit, from guerrilla actions. On August 21, 1863, four days after Quantrill's raid on Lawrence, Union general Thomas Ewing, Jr. (General Sherman's brother-in-law, as it happened), issued an order affecting all citizens living in four large Missouri counties that shared the border with Kansas. Those who would not swear fealty to the Union would have to leave their homes. If they stayed in the area they were to report to federal detention sites. Ewing meant his Order No. 11, as it was called, to inhibit local support for the guerrillas, who needed the backing to carry out their depredations. The order was widely opposed, even by staunch Union men such as the Missouri painter George Caleb Bingham.

Like most Missourians, Bingham had friends on both sides of the conflict (he has been credited with doing the very fine painting of Jo Shelby in his Confederate uniform late in the war, now owned by the University of Missouri). Upon learning of Ewing's forthcoming decree, Bingham told the general it was an "act of imbecility." "If you execute this order," he promised Ewing, "I shall make you infamous with pen and brush." (The finished painting, *Order Number 11*, dramatizes the terror that Ewing unleashed. It was praised when it appeared in 1868 by none other than Frank James—"This is a picture that talks," he said—who had been a part of the Lawrence raid that prompted Ewing's harsh directive.)

Among the families dispossessed by Order No. 11 was Jo Shelby's. His treasured mansion on Mount Rucker had already been torched by Kansas redlegs—so called for the red leather bindings they wore— along with much of the town of Waverly, earlier in the war. Betty and the children were living with Rebecca Redd, the mother of one of Shelby's men, on a farm near Waverly. Betty later wrote:

> Myself and children were left under the protection of a high-spirited woman who had sent several sons to the southern army, and when taxed by the Federals with furnishing altogether too many rebel soldiers, she boldly retorted that if she had a hundred sons they would all be there. Many threats were made to burn out this nest of rebels. Frequently as many as twenty-five soldiers would appear and order a meal of the best we could produce, which we dared not refuse, else our smokehouses would have been raided and nothing left to us. My aunt provided a cot and nursed for several weeks, in the brush, one of our men who had been badly wounded. A surgeon came surreptitiously in the night and set a broken bone. My aunt went every day and dressed the wound and sent him food. On another occasion two of our men were secreted under a dormer window in the top of the house. They had been traced there, and the Federals threatened to burn down the house if they were not produced. Had they carried out their threats our friends would have been shot down in endeavoring to escape. Soon, however, we had to leave our homes, and finally when General Shelby's raids became more frequent had to leave the state.

Caleb Bingham took experiences like Betty Shelby's and wrote a word picture of the expulsion as compelling as his painting. The Kansas redlegs abused the Missourians mercilessly, he said. Men were

> shot down in the very act of obeying the order, and their wagons and effects seized by their murderers. Large trains of wagons,

extending over the prairies for miles in length, and moving Kansasward, were freighted with every description of household furniture and wearing apparel belonging to the exiled inhabitants. Dense columns of smoke arising in every direction marked the conflagrations of dwellings, many of the evidences of which are yet to be seen in the remains of seared and blackened chimneys, standing as melancholy monuments of a ruthless military despotism which spared neither age, sex, character, nor condition. There was neither aid nor protection afforded to the banished inhabitants by the heartless authority which expelled them from their rightful possessions. They crowded by hundreds upon the banks of the Missouri River, and were indebted to the charity of benevolent steamboat conductors for transportation to places of safety where friendly aid could be extended to them without danger to those who ventured to contribute it.

When Shelby learned what was happening, he was hundreds of miles away in Jacksonport, Arkansas. He turned to Frank Blair for help. "I am surprised [sic]," he wrote indignantly, "that any set of men should resort to such means as to vent their feelings on some innocent women." He trusted—no, he *demanded*—that Frank should make amends for the vile policies of Ewing by seeing that Betty and the children were safe. He also sent his love to Blair's wife, Appoline, and said that he looked forward to calling on her soon—once his Confederate forces had returned to St. Louis and taken it under their protection.

Soon afterward, Benjamin Gratz journeyed from Kentucky to Waverly to escort Betty and the children, along with Mrs. Redd, to St. Louis, where, Betty wrote, they "were somewhat protected because of the relationship between General Shelby and Frank Blair, but the authorities feeling that Shelby's raids would be less frequent if his family was out of the state, we were completely banished." She and the boys then traveled to Lexington, Kentucky, passing through Union lines with authorizations issued by Frank Blair from Washington. They would stay with Jo's parents until 1864, when they felt compelled by local hostility to Confederate loyalists to leave for Arkansas.

Shortly after Shelby's family was rescued an incident demonstrated how intermingled the opposing forces could be and how ruthless he was becoming. In October 1863, he took part in the capture of about two hundred outnumbered Union troops in Neosho, Missouri. So many of his men wore captured blue Union tunics that they took care to identify themselves as Confederates by tying bright rags around their arms. The Union would charge Shelby with deliberate violations of military law and convention in wearing the blue, but a rare complaint by Shelby around this time to his superior provided a defense of his actions. He said his men lacked not only uniforms but warm clothing, and half of his horses were unfit: "We have no iron or time to shoe" them and they "are beginning to die pretty fast," having gone for about forty hours without forage on a recent trek. Only 1,068 of 2,319 troops were ready for duty. A hundred soldiers per day were falling ill from cold and lack of "blanket, overcoat, shoes, or socks." To remedy these lacks, notes one of his biographers, Shelby "would come to rely on the Union as his quartermaster," as he did in this instance. His men gathered up the Federals' four hundred horses as well as their revolvers and rifles, medicines, blankets, and clothing, paroled the prisoners, and marched northward, all dressed in warm blue overcoats.

Passing on through a German settlement called Cole Camp, Shelby was hailed by a rough-looking civilian, "a tall, lank, kill-dee sort of fellow," according to an observer, who was glad to see the blue-coats. He said he had heard that Shelby was in the area and hoped to get a shot at him. He boasted about killing Rebels, including four men just the day before. Shelby asked, "Did these men make resistance, and were they lying out in the brush?"

"No, not exactly that," was the smirking reply. "But they were Rebels, you know."

"So are we Rebels," Shelby said, outraged. "You are a common murderer." He ordered Ben Elliott to take the man into the woods and shoot him.

Occasional encounters with raiding parties of Indians and renegades from the sanctuary of Indian Territory resulted in a number of deaths and very few prisoners. In one typical instance, Ben Elliott took a company out after a band of "Pin Indians"—Cherokees loyal to the Union—and found them all drunk. Elliott's group killed an unspecified number of the Indians, perhaps fewer than Elliott would have liked after he found what appeared to be the scalps of a dozen white victims in the camp. After that, Shelby's men refused to treat Indians as legitimate combatants; whenever they caught them, they shot them on the spot. Blacks did not fare much better.

Official Confederate policy encouraged brutality against blacks, especially after Lincoln authorized enlisting former slaves and freed black men as armed combatants in the Union army in 1863. In May of that year, the Confederate Congress approved of an earlier proposal by Jefferson Davis to regard all former slaves enlisted in the Union army as strayed property. They would be returned to slavery or executed, along with their white officers. The Confederate secretary of war James Seddon went even further, saying that field commanders "ought never to be inconvenienced with such prisoners . . . Summary execution must therefore be inflicted on those taken." Several notorious incidents followed, including one at Fort Pillow, Tennessee, where Nathan Bedford Forrest's men murdered dozens of defenseless black soldiers who had surrendered.

The new commander of the Trans-Mississippi Department, Lieutenant General Edmund Kirby Smith, chided an officer for capturing "negroes in arms," insisting on "giving no quarter to armed negroes and their officers." Shortly afterward, in April 1864, Shelby participated in an engagement in Arkansas, Marks' Mills, that would be compared to the atrocities at Fort Pillow.

The battle was a consequence of Lincoln's directive in early 1864 that the Union should invade Texas. One goal of the invasion was to demonstrate Union strength and resolve to the French in Mexico, thereby keeping Napoléon III from recognizing the Confederacy. The largest Union push of the war in this region—ultimately a failure—would follow: Seventeen thousand men under General Nathaniel Banks, plus ten thousand of Sherman's soldiers under General Andrew Jackson Smith, and thirteen ironclads under Rear Admiral David D. Porter were to meet at Alexandria, Louisiana, on the Red River, and go south from there to Shreveport. There they would be met by General Frederick Steele's fifteen thousand men from the Department of Arkansas.

Shelby's brigade was part of a major Confederate effort to prevent

Steele from getting to Shreveport. On April 15, 1864, Steele's main body found itself entrapped in the village of Camden, Arkansas, with both his men and animals suffering from extreme hunger. On April 25, at Marks' Mills, about thirty miles from Camden, Shelby attacked a federal supply wagon train that was on its way to the beleaguered Steele. From Shelby's perspective, it was a legitimate attack on a strong and capable enemy unit consisting of 1,500 men, and a difficult one, lasting more than three hours. The federal commander, Colonel Clayton, minced no words in his after-battle report: "The attack upon our train at Marks' Mill resulted in its entire capture. We have lost 240 wagons, five pieces of artillery," and all 1,500 men, captured or killed. Among those captured were about 150 black soldiers, and another 100 blacks were killed.

The significance of the Confederate capture of the wagon train was profound, according to the military historian Joseph Hanson: "It was one of the most substantial successes gained by the western Confederates during the war. It forced General Steele to abandon Camden and retreat to Little Rock," and was instrumental in the humiliating failure of the Union's Red River expedition.

Marks' Mill was a triumph for Shelby. However, anecdotal testimony by Union soldiers afterward suggested that his men had violated the laws and customs of warfare in the heat of battle. An Iowa infantryman said, "They shot down our Colored servants and teamsters and others that were following to get from bondage as they would shoot sheep dogs." Another Union soldier said, "A large number [of] negroes . . . were inhumanly butchered by the enemy, and among them my own negro servant." A third, who was captured, said, "The Rebs pointed out to me [a] woods where they told me they had killed eighty odd negro men, women, and children. . . . I fully believe they are heartless enough to do any act that wicked men or devils could conceive."

One Shelby biographer, Dallas Cothrum, claims that at Marks' Mills "the Iron Brigade had committed one of the greatest atrocities of the war—one that was as depraved as the activities of William Quantrill or 'Bloody' Bill Anderson—and further stigmatized Shelby as an irregular and diminished his stellar victory." In another account of the battle, Gregory Urwin cites an account by an Arkansan who said, in Urwin's paraphrase, that he saw Shelby "bring a clubbed rifle down on the head of a frightened slave. He then calmly dispatched the man with a shot from his revolver."

The origin of the specific charge against Shelby is a hagiographic biography published in 1959, *Sterling Price: The Lee of the West*. The author was an Arkansas postmaster, Ralph R. Rea, whose grandfather, George Rea, was a young private during the war. George Rea, in his grandson's words, was walking beside Shelby when "suddenly a large negro infantryman jumped from the brush in front and leveled his rifle on the General. Quickly Shelby lunged at the negro, grabbing his rifle barrel, and with a twisting motion seized the gun from the soldier's grasp, then brought it down with a bone-crushing thud on the negro's head. As the soldier fell to the ground Shelby jerked his pistol from his belt and shot him to death."

The description of the incident by George Rea does not reflect as badly on Shelby as does Urwin's later paraphrase of it—there is a difference between disarming and killing a soldier who wants to shoot you and murdering a terrified and defenseless slave. But the incident is implausible in any event. Shelby's right arm was so crippled from his painful wound nine months earlier that he could barely use a pen, let alone wield a rifle or even a pistol—much less use "a twisting motion" to wrest a weapon from anyone. No other evidence of such behavior on Shelby's part exists, and much to contradict it does.

The larger charge by Cothrum—that Shelby's actions were as "depraved" as any by Quantrill and Bloody Bill Anderson in that he permitted and encouraged the atrocities described by the Union soldiers—is more troubling, but there is no evidence to support it. John Edwards admitted that the general battle scene was "sickening to behold," but largely because the soldiers, not the officers, were out of control: "No orders, threats, or commands could restrain the men from vengeance on the negroes, and they were piled in great heaps about the wagons, in the tangled brushwood, and upon the muddy and trampled road." Assuming, as seems likely, that Shelby deplored what his men were doing, he has to bear some part of the blame for their actions, just as he deserves credit for the successful capture of the wagon train. That does not mean that Shelby was guilty of war crimes simply for being present at an action beyond his control.

General Edmund Kirby Smith, not surprisingly, saw nothing to complain about in Shelby's performance. On May 27, 1864, Shelby was appointed Confederate commander of cavalry north of the Arkansas River. His main assignments were to harass the Union supply line between Little Rock and DeValls Bluff, and to conscript recruits for the Confederate army in the wilderness known as the White River Valley—a "deserter's paradise and the coward's retreat," in the words of John Edwards, where mob rule prevailed and thousands of malingerers lived by pillage and selling blacks back into slavery in Texas.

Shelby sent out a stern warning to the area, saying he wanted "no more smuggling, no more stealing cotton, no more dodging conscription and harboring deserters." He would not "condemn or bully," but he would "rather act than talk" and promised "to strike": "All who refuse to rally to their country's flag shall be outlawed, hunted from county to county, and when captured hung. . . . I come with veterans to fight for your homes, but you must fight too, or the homes will be desolate and your blood shall be spilt upon the door-sills." He did not recognize the possibility of neutrality: "Come up like men, or go to General Steele like men," he said, adding not to expect mercy if they tried to avoid commitment. By the end of July he had raised a force of five thousand men—many of them without weapons or shoes, admittedly, and not always the most willing of fighters, but enough to swell the ranks for the trials to come.

In September and October 1864, Shelby's battlefield abilities were tested to their utmost in the Confederacy's last-gasp effort to wrest control of Missouri from the Union. Three men with whom his fortunes in Mexico would be closely intertwined were responsible for this attempt. The first was the politician-turned-general Sterling Price, recently promoted to commander of the newly designated Army of Missouri. The second was General Edmund Kirby Smith, a professional soldier out of West Point and commander of the enormous Trans-Mississippi Department. And the third was a scholar and schemer named Thomas Reynolds, governor-in-exile of Confederate Missouri.

Sterling Price was a figure seemingly destined to command. Born in 1809, he moved to Missouri in 1831, served in the state legislature, and was elected to Congress. He resigned his seat in 1846 to raise a regiment to fight in the Mexican War. He was assigned instead to command the Territory of New Mexico, where he crushed an uprising in Taos of Indians and Mexicans and subsequently captured the Mexican city of Chihuahua. A farmer and slave owner in Missouri after returning home in 1848, Price was a popular governor of the state from 1853 to 1857. In the spring of 1861, Price was a "conditional Unionist"—he opposed both secession by the South and coercion of Missouri by the North, declaring that his primary goal was to protect his beloved Missouri from harm.

On the day of the Camp Jackson shootings in May 1861, which had been witnessed by Shelby, Grant, and Sherman, Sterling Price was also present, meeting with others who hoped to keep Missouri neutral. So stirred was Price by his observation of the day's events that he gave up all hope of a safely neutral Missouri and declared for the Confederacy. After some hesitation, he agreed to command the newly re-formed Missouri State Guard, with the encouragement of then lieutenant governor Thomas Reynolds.

Price's greatest coup came early in the war, in September 1861, when he captured the Union garrison at Lexington, Missouri, after a seven-day siege. In 1862, he became a major general in the regular Confederate army. An admiring fellow officer described Price as a strikingly handsome and impressive man:

> He was over six-feet two inches in stature, of massive proportions, but easy and graceful in his carriage and his gestures; his hands and feet were remarkably small and well shaped; his hair and whiskers, which he wore in the old English fashion, were silver white; his face was ruddy and very benignant, yet firm in its expression; his profile was finely chiseled, and bespoke manhood of the highest type; his voice was clear and ringing, and his accentuation singularly distinct.

Shelby's impression of Price was less favorable by the time he came to know him well, late in the war. He disapproved of the luxury in which Price lived, with a private chef who served him kidneys stewed in sherry, and of his self-induced physical limitations. Now tipping the scales at about three hundred pounds, often troubled by gout, Price found it hard to sit on a horse for very long and often appeared in battle in a softly sprung ambulance wagon. With his long, flowing white hair, his gift for oratory, his imperial manner, and his earlier undoubted courage under fire, Price generated a degree of fondness in his men, who liked to call him "Old Pap." (A hint of that affection, and of Price's limitations, surfaces in the fat, lazy old cat called "Sterling Price" owned by John Wayne's character, Rooster Cogburn, in the movie *True Grit*, based on the 1968 novel by Charles Portis.)

Shelby had begged Price in the summer of 1864 to let him take a small and highly mobile cavalry division of 5,000 men on a recruiting raid into Missouri. The state was vulnerable to attack, he wrote to Price's adjutant, "stripped of regulars for Grant and Sherman." He was sure he could raise another 5,000 recruits. "With permission, then, I could sweep through Missouri and return to your command with 10,000 well-mounted, well-clothed, and well-armed men."

Shelby had no hope or intention of capturing territory with such a small force but believed he could disrupt Union forces significantly. But Price, Reynolds, and Kirby Smith instead decided that a much larger cavalry force of 12,000 men should try to capture St. Louis. Only state militia were left to defend the city, and George Todd, Bloody Bill Anderson, and other guerrillas were stronger than ever in much of the countryside of north-central Missouri. If Price could not take St. Louis, he was to retreat in an orderly fashion westward along the Missouri River and then into Kansas, appropriating whatever livestock and supplies he found there.

Disaster was the result of all their planning. The army never reached St. Louis—if it had, Shelby would have had to fight his friends B. Gratz Brown and Frank Blair, sent home by Lincoln to campaign for his reelection. Following a series of missteps by Major General Price, his army had retreated in a confused and meandering path toward Kansas City. By October 23, 1864, it had been routed at Westport, south of Kansas City, and was fleeing southward. Shelby was leading his division at the head of Price's column, moving toward Fort Scott, Kansas, when a courier from Price arrived with a desperate cry for help: "Tell General Shelby that he alone can save the army."

Shelby reached Price in time to hold off Union forces long enough for Price to escape, but the Federals under General James Blunt continued their pursuit. By the time Price had reached the Carthage, Missouri, area, 150 miles south of Kansas City, Shelby was called on again to save him. On October 28, 1864, he interposed his reduced division of some three thousand men between Price and the Federals, which were twice his number and led personally by the formidable Blunt.

There was no subtlety about Shelby's tactics. He dismounted his troops and had them form a line of battle on the open prairie far from their horses—they would stand fast and fight until they were killed or captured, or the enemy was turned back. As Shelby's subordinate commander M. Jeff Thompson said in his report, "There was no chance for science, no occasion for skill, and the only thing needed was just what each of these men had, and that was PLUCK." There were, Thompson continued, many "acts of courage that should be described by the pen of the poet, and severe suffering that should be painted with gloomy shades; but this 'unvarnished tale' is sufficient for Shelby's brigade, for its reputation is established."

Twenty of Shelby's men died that day—half as many as Blunt's—and fifty were wounded, but they bought enough time for Price to escape again, this time to safety in Arkansas. A small affair by Civil War standards, this Second Battle of Newtonia, as it came to be known—but a critical one in terms of preserving what was left of the Trans-Mississippi Department's mauled cavalry. It would also be the last battle of the Civil War west of the Mississippi River.

THREE

Rebellion Against Surrender

As the war progressed, the Blair family continued to grow in Abraham Lincoln's esteem. Frank had served ably as one of Sherman's key commanders on the march through Georgia, and Postmaster General Monty Blair was one of his most reliable cabinet ministers, though some of his enemies tagged him as "the meanest man in Washington." Lincoln also valued the usually calmer judgment of Francis Preston Blair, Sr., tempering as it did the frequent excesses of his hotheaded sons. Chatting one day with his secretary, John Hay, about the Blairs, Lincoln recalled once hearing a conversation in a bar in rural Illinois about an old man who had been "tricked in a trade." Couldn't be true, was the response: "Why, the old man aint so easy tricked. You can fool the boys but ye can't the old man."

Lincoln's regard for the elderly but still spry Preston Blair—he was now seventy-three years old—had only increased since their first meeting years earlier. That fondness may explain why, in December 1864, he entertained from Blair a suggestion so outlandish that it would have earned another man a derisive dismissal.

Blair proposed that the Union and Confederate armies, rather than fighting each other, should unite to throw the French out of Mexico— and to take their place as rulers of a nation that would then stretch from Canada to the Isthmus of Panama. Presumably the experience of fighting and conquering as comrades in arms would bring the two sides together and end the four years of internecine bloodshed that had ruined the country.

William Seward, Lincoln's secretary of state, had provided some precedent for at least a part of the idea. When the French had invaded Mexico in January 1862, after the government of Benito Juárez defaulted on its international bond payments, Seward toyed with the idea of a unified North-South front against the French, but it was never given serious consideration.

The continued presence of the French—now three years along and enhanced by the arrival in 1864 of the Austrian Archduke Maximilian as "emperor"—was a flagrant violation of the Monroe Doctrine. The larger war at home had prevented Seward and Lincoln from launching military action to expel the French after diplomatic remonstrances had failed; fearful that Louis-Napoléon would recognize the Confederacy if pressed too hard by the Union, Washington had contented itself with giving Mexican patriots such as the embattled former president Juárez whatever unofficial aid and encouragement it could. "One war at a time," Lincoln said.

Lincoln authorized Blair to travel to Richmond and present his proposal to Jefferson Davis, hoping Davis's response would tell him something about how long the South could hold out. He handed the old newspaperman a pass dated December 28, 1864, that said, "Allow the bearer, F. P. Blair, Sr., to pass our lines, go south and return." Blair then wrote two letters to Davis. The first was an official ruse, to be made public, if necessary; it concerned the return of private papers that had disappeared from his house in Silver Spring when it was occupied earlier by General Jubal Early (Monty Blair's nearby house was burned at the same time). In the second letter, the private one, Blair said his "main purpose" was to "unbosom [his] heart frankly & without reserve," in the hope that the two of them could talk about the affairs of the country in a useful way.

January 11, 1865, was a cold day in Richmond, but Blair received a warm welcome. "Oh you Rascal, I am overjoyed to see you," Davis's young wife, Varina, said as she threw her arms about him. Davis, too, was cordial, as Blair had anticipated. Born in Kentucky in 1808, Davis had attended Transylvania University in Lexington in the 1820s before graduating from West Point. When Blair reminded Davis that "every drop" of his own blood, and of his children's, came from "a Southern source," Davis said he would never forget how kind the Blairs had been to himself and his family, and that they would "be remembered in his prayers."

Seated companionably before a fire in the library of the Confederate White House, Davis and Blair talked through the afternoon. Together, Blair told Davis, they could frustrate "the designs of Napoleon to subject our Southern people to the 'Latin race.' " Blair pulled out all the rhetorical stops, declaring that Davis would become part of the grand tradition established by Washington and Jefferson, Monroe and Jackson. Not only would he expel foreign powers but he would further the expansion of America's manifest destiny to include all of Mexico.

" 'There is my problem, Mr. Davis,' " Blair recalled saying to his host in John Nicolay and John Hay's *Abraham Lincoln: A History.* " 'Do you think it possible to be solved?' After consideration, he said: 'I think so.' I then said, 'You see that I make the great point of this matter that the war is no longer made for slavery, but monarchy. You know that if the war is kept up and the Union kept divided, armies must be kept afoot on both sides, and this state of things has never continued long without resulting in monarchy on one side or the other, and on both generally.' "

Given the great decline in the fortunes of war for the Confederacy by January 1865, Blair's statement has to be read as an ominous prediction for the South, if not an outright threat. But as a sign of his good faith and fellowship, perhaps, Blair suggested that his son Frank be one of the generals leading the combined Confederate and Union armies into Mexico, along with a general of Davis's choosing.

Davis seemed to be enthusiastic about the plan—the key element of which involved colonizing a neighbor under the guise of rescuing it. So was everyone else to whom Blair talked over the next few days. They were all "convinced," John Hay noted, "of the hopeless condition of the rebellion, and even eager to seize upon any contrivance to help them out of their direful prospects."

Montgomery Blair did his bit to further his father's plan, according to Alfred and Kathryn Hanna in their definitive study, *Napoleon III and Mexico.* On January 15, 1865, Monty told the talented young chief of the Mexican legation in Washington, Matías Romero, that he thought "the Confederates would be willing to settle with the Lincoln government by undertaking an expedition to Mexico. . . . He urged Romero to involve Confederate troops in a move against Maximilian." Benito Juárez told Romero that he would consider authorizing an expeditionary force; he would appoint an American commander in chief who would, in turn, become a general of a division of the Mexican army. The Americans would consider themselves as Mexicans during their service, which would end with the defeat of the French. Officers would be allowed afterward to remain in the Mexican army, and soldiers would be encouraged to become colonists. The commander in chief would be paid 100,000 pesos in money or land. The American corps would fund itself for six months and provide its own arms and equipment. No more than a third of the men would be Southerners. Juárez also cautioned Romero to insist on a "specific guarantee that Mexican independence and territorial integrity would not be violated"—or at least to get a "moral commitment" to that effect.

Nothing came of what John Hay called Blair's "wild scheme of military conquest and annexation." But that scheme must have appeared at least plausible enough for Frank Blair to write to Jo Shelby sometime in the following weeks—another surprising instance of the interaction between two generals on opposite sides of the war, and of their ongoing mutual affection. In that letter, according to Shelby's later reminiscence, Blair outlined the possibility that Lincoln might look favorably on Confederate soldiers entering Mexico to act in opposition to Maximilian.

When Shelby heard from Blair, he was in no position to consider the possibility of going to Mexico. He and his men were recovering from the hardships that followed his rescue of Sterling Price at Newtonia the previous autumn. The three-hundred-mile slog through rain and snow into the sanctuary of northwestern Arkansas and eastern Texas had been grueling. Food, even flour and salt, was in such short supply that they had to slaughter some of their horses and mules. There was no medicine for fevers, and dysentery was raging. Shelby shared in the hardships, while still suffering from the effects of his wound. One of his soldiers recalled him "mixing around among the men trying to cheer them up," adding, "even when he felt the pangs of hunger himself it never changed his pleasant demeanor to his men."

Conditions improved by late November 1864, when Shelby reached Clarksville, Texas, a pleasant town about a hundred miles northwest of Shreveport that had become a haven for Confederate refugees from Missouri and Arkansas. For the next four months the brigade would respond to various orders from Kirby Smith's headquarters in Shreveport that sent them on what proved to be pointless and frustrating missions. By mid-April, Shelby was stationed near Pittsburg, Texas, forty miles south of Clarksville.

Although frustrated with the lack of activity and the confusion of the time, Shelby had one considerable consolation: Betty and their two boys came to Clarksville from Kentucky around the turn of the year. Though his mother and stepfather had welcomed Betty into their home in Lexington, Kentucky, their opposing loyalties had inevitably caused tension—particularly after Shelby's friend John Hunt Morgan attacked his hometown, now a federal stronghold, in early June 1864. The Gratzes were not directly affected, but a member of the distinguished Clay family lost $25,000 worth of fine horses, and the Branch Bank of Kentucky gave up $3,000 in gold and $25,000 in greenbacks to Morgan's raiders. Union sympathizers like the Gratzes were gratified when Morgan died in battle that September—though a fine statue of Morgan on horseback is one of Lexington's main tourist attractions today.

Accompanied by the wife of one of Shelby's men, Betty and the boys, now five and three years old, had made their way to Memphis by steamboat and then traveled overland to Clarksville. As Betty later recalled her trip, they "suffered untold trials getting through the lines at all as there was fierce fighting raging around Little Rock and vicinity. We were finally in company with other refugee families from Missouri, placed at Clarksville, Tex. where we remained until the close of the war."

Betty omitted the final trauma of her trip to rejoin her husband, which was described by one of Shelby's men, William Whitsett. While crossing the flooded Sabine River near the village of Pittsburg,

Betty found that "the bottom was badly overflowed," Whitsett wrote. Betty "had 4 mules to the Ambulance and an old negro driving and some miscreants overtook them and took the mules out from the ambulance, leaving her and her children sitting in the vehicle and it axle deep in Mud and Water. He [Shelby] never got any trace of the marauders or the mules, if he had found them or ever caught up with them they surely would have died on the spot."

During the winter and early spring of 1865, the critical events of the war were happening a thousand miles away, as Sherman pressed northward from Georgia through the Carolinas against General Joseph E. Johnston, and Lee's once-formidable Army of Northern Virginia was shredded. Sterling Price's cavalry, with little to do other than speculate what kind of disaster lay ahead for them, became mutinous and sullen. Price himself was under attack from one of the two men who had sent him into Missouri, and who had accompanied Shelby and his brigade, even though he was a civilian: Thomas Reynolds. The quarrel between Price and Reynolds—who were both closely tied to Shelby at the time and, later, in Mexico—helps to explain the Confederacy's decline and fall. It was vicious and pathetic in its expenditure of time and energy—and not a little dangerous.

The roots of the quarrel lay several years in the past, in 1861, when Reynolds was lieutenant governor of Missouri under Claiborne Jackson as the war broke out. Reynolds, like Shelby, was a comparatively recent arrival in Missouri. Born to a wealthy family in Charleston, South Carolina, in 1821, he graduated from the University of Virginia. He then earned a law degree from the University of Heidelberg in 1842; competing with Germans studying in their own language, he graduated summa cum laude, a remarkable intellectual feat. He married a French woman, after which he received a diplomatic appointment in Spain, thereby adding fluency in French and Spanish to his command of German.

Reynolds's brilliant mind served him well after he moved to St. Louis in 1850. After opening a law practice, he became prominent in the Democratic Party. He was a handsome man with a pleasing manner when he chose to exert it, and his experience in Heidelberg earned him strong support from the local German immigrants until his pro-slavery views turned them against him. Among those whom Reynolds came to consider his personal enemies were the Germans' particular favorites, Frank Blair and B. Gratz Brown, Shelby's stepcousin and childhood friend.

In 1853, Brown's political attacks on Reynolds in his free-soil newspaper provoked Reynolds to challenge him to a duel. Brown tried to rebuff Reynolds with a joke: Knowing that his opponent was near-sighted, he chose "the common American Rifle with open sights, round ball not over one ounce, at eighty yards." Reynolds rejected those terms and canceled the duel, but goaded Brown a few years later into issuing his own challenge. This time Reynolds could choose the weapons—traditional dueling pistols—and he consequently left Brown with the limp that he would suffer for the rest of his life.

A friend of Jefferson Davis's and a true son of the Old South, Reynolds had mistrusted Sterling Price since Price's initial hesitance to take up arms against the Union. Price's trouble, in Reynolds's view, was that he was too much of a Missourian and not enough of a Con-federate. They became uneasy allies after Claiborne Jackson died in office in late 1862 and Reynolds, then living on his family estate in South Carolina, became the new governor-in-exile of Missouri—an empty honor but one in which he took great pride. Price had been called to fight in the east after his initial successes in 1861 but hoped to return to the war in Missouri. In January 1863, Price and Reynolds went to Richmond together and persuaded Jefferson Davis to send them both to Missouri. Price would have an independent command, and Reynolds would hold an ambiguous post as adviser—despite his lack of military experience—to the Trans-Mississippi Department commander, General Edmund Kirby Smith.

By the time he and Kirby Smith were planning the Missouri inva-sion, in the summer of 1864, Reynolds had come to doubt Price's ca-pabilities. He regarded him, according to Price's biographer Albert Castel, as "devious, insincere, petulant, and arrogant" and "impulsive, tactless, and prone to indiscreet and exaggerated language." Kirby Smith concurred with Reynolds, saying Price was "good for nothing."

In December 1864, while Price and Shelby established themselves in Clarksville, Reynolds traveled south about sixty miles to Marshall,

Texas. He had earlier designated that small town, thirty miles west of Shreveport, as the government-in-exile of Missouri. In his governmental office—a one-story cottage that belonged to a judge—Reynolds spent several weeks writing a screed against Price that was published on December 23 in the Marshall newspaper. As Albert Castel says, it is "without doubt one of the most vicious assaults ever made in print on a military commander."

Reynolds charged Price with gross incompetence and malfeasance of every kind, and of displaying an imperial indifference to the opinions of his men. "His regular course was to sit in his ambulance at the head of his train on the march, rarely mounting his horse; to sip his copious toddy immediately after going into camp, and in view of the soldiers passing by, and soon after to take a nap," Reynolds wrote. Indeed, so marked was Price's "somnoloncy" that one day "he stopped the whole command for about half an hour and took a nap on a carpet spread out under a tree."

Edwards, too, had little use for Price, who he said had "the roar of a lion but the spring of a guinea-pig." But for him—and, we have to assume, for Shelby—the issue was less a matter of Price's character or military competence than it was his training and temperament: He was simply not a cavalryman, which "requires a peculiar fitness and schooling." He was also too old. Unlike Shelby, he could not march forty miles and then fight for six hours.

Price asked to be court-martialed, certain that he would be found innocent of Reynolds's charges. They were no more than "a tissue of falsehoods," he said, but they needed to be exposed as such in a formal proceeding. Knowing his opponent's vanity, Price tweaked Reynolds as an imposter "who pretends to be, and styles himself in it, the Governor of the State of Missouri."

Kirby Smith stalled on Reynolds's request, finally choosing to hold a court of inquiry rather than a formal court-martial, because Reynolds, as a civilian, could not testify at the latter. Reynolds objected that the vindication of his charges by a mere court of inquiry would be construed as politically motivated and meaningless. Kirby Smith held his ground. Finally, in late April, the court of inquiry convened in Shreveport. Several prominent officers testified for Price. Shelby was scheduled to testify but did not do so; if he had, it would probably have been to the detriment of Price. Reynolds was Shelby's friend and had helped him gain his promotion to brigadier general in December 1863 through his good connections in Richmond. Moreover, Reynolds was undoubtedly echoing complaints he had heard Shelby and Edwards make about Price while he was with them during the Missouri campaign. When one of Price's supporters publicly claimed that Reynolds had been a "deadhead" in Missouri who merely stayed behind the lines and "therefore knew nothing of the campaign," Shelby praised Reynolds for his courage and "untiring energy for good." The most that Shelby could say in Price's defense concerning the Missouri campaign, in his official after-battle report, was that Price "had elements in his command, so helpless, so incongruous that no human hand could control them."

Kirby Smith, for his part, had been less than eager to see Price pilloried because of incompetence—after all, he had not only chosen Price as commander but had accepted and commended Price's overblown accounts of his success. "The movement of General Price," Kirby Smith reported to Richmond, "accomplished all the objects for which it was inaugurated by me." That is, it committed thirty thousand Union troops that were "en route for Sherman's army"; it also aided in the defense of Mobile, hampered Union general George Thomas's campaign against Confederate general John B. Hood in Georgia, and allowed Nathan Bedford Forrest to raid Tennessee. In Kirby Smith's eyes, only the unfortunate conclusion of the campaign (the near-entrapment of Price's army at Westport and its pell-mell retreat afterward) had compromised the complete success of the Missouri raid.

Shelby had, until now, been restrained in his criticism of Kirby Smith. Certainly, of all the men who went with him into Mexico, or whom he encountered there, Kirby Smith had been the most professionally accomplished. He had graduated from West Point with Jefferson Davis, who admired him for his able service in the Mexican War and on the Texas Indian frontier. Intellectually able, he had taught mathematics at West Point from 1849 to 1852. He resigned his U.S. Army commission after Fort Sumter and was enrolled in the Confederate army as a lieutenant colonel. He became a brigadier general in June 1861 and was seriously wounded soon afterward at the

First Battle of Bull Run. Successes followed. He played a key role in the invasion of Kentucky in 1862, under General Braxton Bragg, and saw heavy action at the battles of Perryville and Stones River.

Kirby Smith was a devout Episcopalian who had once hoped to become a priest. Austere, gaunt, heavily bearded, with piercing blue eyes and a somber manner, he seemed much older than his years. He was also ambitious and was said at one point to be in line for command of a corps under Lee, along with Thomas "Stonewall" Jackson and James Longstreet. Instead, he became Jefferson Davis's last hope for reviving the Trans-Mississippi Department, which he took command of in early 1863. He soon established a successful system for running the Union blockade and later earned Davis's gratitude by turning back the Red River expedition led by General Nathaniel Banks in 1864. So thoroughly did he put his stamp on the department, making himself its virtual dictator, that it became known as "Kirby-Smithdom." But once Vicksburg fell in July 1863, the department became a vast, echoing shell, devoid of real significance, and the last place in the world for a man once regarded as worthy of inclusion in the pantheon of Lee's great lieutenants.

An inquiry into the competence of Sterling Price, his chosen commander for a disastrous campaign, was not, then, something that Kirby Smith could have looked forward to, even if Price had been vindicated. As it happened, two important events soon overshadowed the inquiry: Lee's surrender to Grant at Appomattox on April 9, 1865, and Abraham Lincoln's death on April 15.

It took two weeks for the news of the surrender and the assassination to reach Shreveport, an indication of how completely fractured all lines of transportation and communication were. Shelby's men cheered at the news of Lincoln's death, but Shelby reprimanded them, saying it would be a disaster for the South. Modern readers might consider his reaction merely reasonable—how else could he have responded? But it needs to be set against more typical Southern opinions, such as that of one Kate Stone, who lived on a ranch in Tyler, Texas, and kept a diary of the war years. A courageous, intelligent, and usually sweet-tempered young woman, Kate's reaction upon learning that John Wilkes Booth had died was far more typical than Shelby's of Southern feelings about Lincoln's death: "Poor Booth, to think that he fell at last. Many a true heart at the South weeps for his death. Caesar had his Brutus, Murat his Charlotte Corday, and Lincoln his Booth. Lincoln's fate overtook him in the flush of his triumph on the pinnacle of his fame, or rather infamy. We are glad he is not alive to rejoice in our humiliation and insult us by his jokes."

Shelby's measured response to Lincoln's death is particularly striking, given his heated insistence upon hearing of Lee's surrender that he would never live under Yankee rule. "No! no!" he said. "We will stand together, we will keep our organization, our arms, our discipline, our hatred of oppression, until one universal shout goes up from an admiring age that this Missouri Cavalry Division preferred exile to submission, death to dishonor." Others agreed. On the evening of April 29, 1865, a large meeting of Confederate officers and officials took place in the Shreveport town square. Fiery orations ensued, many urging continued armed resistance. Price and Kirby Smith, though they concurred, did not speak, nor did Shelby or Reynolds.

As the torchlights dimmed and the speakers finally dwindled away, word came that Union colonel John Sprague, representing General John Pope, hoped to present Pope's terms for General Kirby Smith's surrender. Sprague was waiting on a steamboat a hundred miles to the southeast, where the Red River joined the Mississippi. Kirby Smith prepared to sail down the Red River the following day to meet Sprague, but a colonel on his staff claimed that Kirby Smith's boat was loaded with valuable cotton—the general, it was thought, intended not to negotiate but to surrender outright and to leave the field a rich man. The charge was baseless, as it happened. But Price, Shelby, and several others discussed it and agreed that Kirby Smith should not go to see Sprague. He should, instead, invite Sprague under a flag of truce to come to Shreveport. If Kirby Smith "proved troublesome"—that is, if he tried to go downriver, presumably to surrender—Shelby would arrest Kirby Smith and seize Shreveport.

Price asked Shelby to approach Kirby Smith's chief of staff, General Simon Bolivar Buckner, to seek his support. Buckner reportedly assured Shelby that he would seize command if need be from Kirby Smith and "fight it out." Buckner, however, was loyal to his senior officer, not to the conspirators. He informed Kirby Smith of the Price plot. Kirby Smith told Thomas Reynolds that he had no intention of surrendering to the Yankees, and that he would die before he would submit to any effort to displace him. He got rid of Price—who now really had done something meriting a court-martial—by transferring the still-pending court of inquiry proceedings concerning Reynolds's charges of incompetence to the tiny town of Washington, Arkansas, some fifty miles away. Apparently Kirby Smith was unaware of Shelby's willingness to aid Price, as there were no repercussions for Shelby.

Kirby Smith did, however, prudently stay put in Shreveport. On May 8, 1865, Sprague arrived and gave him the devastating news of General Joseph E. Johnston's surrender to Sherman on April 26 in North Carolina. At the same time, Sprague described Pope's generous terms for Kirby Smith's own surrender. Kirby Smith put off the patient Sprague. He said he needed first to confer in Marshall, the new Confederate capital, with the rest of his command and the several state governors who would be affected by a surrender. At the Marshall conference that immediately followed, around May 10, Kirby Smith was authorized to surrender what was left of his army, now much depleted by desertions. Reynolds, also now reconciled to defeat, pressed Kirby Smith to continue stalling Sprague and Pope long enough for the Missourians to prepare for an escape into Mexico.

Kirby Smith readily agreed with Reynolds's request, as it coincided exactly with his own plans. Months earlier, in February, he had sent a message to Maximilian saying that he planned to seek asylum in Mexico should the Confederacy fall, and that he could bring with him "intelligent and daring soldiers" who would help him preserve Maximilian's empire. On April 19, he wrote again to Maximilian to say that nine thousand Missourians and ten thousand men from other Southern states "would gladly rally around any flag that promises to lead them to battle against their former foe."

According to Kirby Smith biographer Joseph Parks, General Pope told Sprague to let Kirby Smith know that he would "offer no objection but sign no written permission . . . if organized bodies wished to march to Mexico, taking their materials of war with them." (Pope said nothing about the Confederates volunteering to fight for Maximilian.) As another communication from Pope to Kirby Smith reveals, the Union general was anxious to secure the final surrender: "The duty of an officer is performed and his honor maintained, when he has prolonged resistance until all hope of success has been lost," Pope wrote. Beyond that, "wisdom and humanity alike" dictated an end to resistance costing more bloodshed.

Despite this welcome information allowing his passage to Mexico, Kirby Smith continued to press for more time; he told Sprague on May 15, 1865, that Pope's terms were not acceptable. Sprague had to return to St. Louis to confer with Pope, delaying further talk of surrender for at least a week.

A second meeting of the generals who had suspected Kirby Smith's intentions, including Shelby, took place a day or two later in Marshall. Reynolds was also present. Major General Shelby—he had received his long-delayed promotion on May 13, 1865—spoke first, according to Edwards. He said, "The army has no confidence in General Kirby Smith," who should be replaced by a leader who was fit to command. Under that leader, the last Confederate army, augmented by "fugitives from Lee and Johnson" who would join them in the thousands, would fight their way southward and across the Rio Grande, where they could join forces either with Juárez or with Maximilian, depending on who would make them the best offer (though Shelby's unstated preference was Juárez). Buckner, at Shelby's recommendation, agreed to be their leader.

Shelby then met with Kirby Smith alone at his quarters in Marshall, according to Edwards. It was a typical soft spring evening in the South, redolent with the scent of jasmine and magnolia, but the talk was harsh and brutal. Shelby said, "The army has lost confidence in you." Kirby Smith agreed and asked what the army wanted. His resignation as its "direct commander," Shelby said, and the appointment of Buckner in his place. "The astonished man rested his head upon his hands in mute surprise," then asked Shelby what he advised. "Instant acquiescence," was the response.

This account is disputed by Joseph Parks, who complains that Edwards "apparently built his story around a few facts told him by Shelby." Only someone "whose attraction to the dramatic was stronger than his love for truth" could have concocted such a scene, he says. But the fact remains that Kirby Smith did leave on May 18, 1865, for Houston. Although he retained command of the Trans-Mississippi Department, he ceded control of the army to Buckner, as Shelby demanded. Of course, Shelby was unaware that Buckner was playing a double game as Kirby Smith's agent among the conspirators, Price and Shelby. Buckner had no intention of betraying Kirby Smith, who he assumed wanted to surrender but was consumed with dithering. If Kirby Smith did put his head in his hands when Shelby said he had to give Buckner command of the army, he might have done so to hide a smile.

In the end, both Kirby Smith and Shelby were undone by Buckner, who saw more clearly than they did how hopeless further resistance was. "The troops were deserting by divisions," Buckner wrote to his wife in explaining his actions, "and were plundering the people as well as the government property." On May 26, 1865, on his own authority, Buckner signed a surrender treaty in New Orleans; he made General Price go with him to the ceremony, hoping thereby to discourage the Missourians under Price from fighting on.

Shelby was the leader of those holdouts. Still looking to engage the enemy, he prepared to attack federal troops on the Brazos River. He was near Dallas when he learned of Buckner's surrender. Smelling treason, Shelby recalled that Buckner had been Ulysses S. Grant's roommate for three years at West Point and that he had commanded Fort Donelson when it surrendered to Grant in 1862—the occasion of Grant's first major victory and his first demand for "unconditional surrender." Enraged, Shelby addressed his troops: "Soldiers, you have been betrayed. The generals whom you have trusted have refused to lead you. Let us begin the battle again by a revolution." He reversed direction, launching the division on an attack on Shreveport, nearly three hundred miles to the east. There, he vowed, they would seize the Confederate munitions and supplies and attack all Federals with as much strength as they could muster.

But the elements conspired against Shelby. Torrential rains washed out scores of bridges across the many streams and rivers that course through eastern Texas, stopping him almost in his tracks. He had barely reached the town of Corsicana, about sixty miles from Waco, when he met troops who had stacked their arms in Shreveport and fled into Texas.

Among these soldiers was a courier from Kirby Smith with orders for Shelby to return to Shreveport and surrender to General Pope. On that very morning, June 2, 1865, Kirby Smith himself surrendered the hollowed-out administrative carapace of the Trans-Mississippi Department to Pope at Galveston, sealing Buckner's earlier surrender of its body, heart, and soul, the army. Thus June 2, 1865, rather than the more familiar date of Lee's surrender at Appomattox on April 9, may be said to mark the true conclusion of the Civil War.

PART TWO

EXILES IN MEXICO

1865–67

FOUR

Shelby Pacifies Texas

Jo Shelby finally had to admit that he was finished. He calmed his men, who had followed his lead and reviled Kirby Smith for betraying them. Despite his anger, Shelby did not think Kirby Smith was a villain—he thought he was merely a weak and indecisive man who, in the words of John Edwards, was "slow, nerveless, indifferent; more of an Episcopalian preacher than a revolutionary leader." Kirby Smith could do as he liked. But surrender, as Shelby had said repeatedly, was not a word in his vocabulary. He "formed his men around him on the open Prairie," wrote one of them, Thomas Westlake, "and made a Speech to them recounting many of the hardships and Struggels of the four years past. He said he was not going to surrender but was going to Mexico and requested all that would to go with him."

Westlake said about 150 men chose to go with Shelby, or one in ten; Edwards put the number at 500, no doubt an exaggeration born of his distress and unwillingness to admit that the end had come for Shelby's division as "a living, breathing, terrible body" of horsemen. "I do not desire to dwell upon the leave-takings, the tears glistening in strong men's eyes, the last, long embraces among comrades who had shared the same blankets for weary years." A private named Sam

Box echoed Edwards, recalling that the men took "formal leave of each other," sending "messages to absent friends and relatives," all suspecting they would never meet again "this side of the judgement bar."

Shelby's shrunken division reorganized itself the following day as an independent regiment—though it was really no larger than a battalion. Including some of the men who had fled Shreveport and other stragglers, the total number was about three hundred men. Shelby was elected to lead the regiment, assuming the rank of colonel. Some of the officers who had been critical to his success remained: John Edwards, who continued to record his impressions of Shelby's character and his adventures; the irrepressible Alonzo Slayback, who had survived his chivalrous battlefield encounters; Ben Elliott, a Virginia Military Institute graduate just a few months older than Shelby (known as "the iron colonel," Elliott was famous for once rallying his men during a fierce fight by challenging them to follow his lead and catch the bullets in their hats); D. A. Williams, who had been a hard-bitten farmer and a "border ruffian" before the war and became a battalion commander under Shelby and one of his most ruthless men (he was charged with murder by the Union army for shooting seven soldiers who had killed his brother); Yandell Blackwell, now twenty-seven, who had been a pharmacist in central Missouri and was with Shelby from the beginning of the war; and another pharmacist, Ben Gordon, at forty-one the oldest of the inner circle, who had assumed command of Shelby's brigade when Shelby took command of the division that spring.

All capable men, all resourceful and stubborn, the leaders of the new regiment soon solved the problems that had plagued them throughout the war: shortages of food and weapons. Near Waco they came upon a wagon train that had been en route from Brownsville to Shreveport and abandoned when news of the surrender at Galveston reached its drivers. Intended to feed Kirby Smith's headquarters staff of "gold-laced tapeworms"—as Edwards called them—the wagons were full of everything from salt pork, bacon, and lard to jellies, cakes, and dried fruit. And not least, a plentiful selection of wines and whiskeys.

As for arms, the whole of east Texas was a weapons park, dotted with deserted arsenals begging to be plundered. Shelby helped himself to arms and ammunition bought by the Confederates from dealers in England and France and smuggled across the border with Mexico: ten Napoleon howitzers with 600 shells; 6,000 new British Enfield rifles, still marked with the queen's arms; 40,000 rounds of small-arms ammunition; a wagon load's worth of gun caps and pistol cartridges; 500 dragoon sabers. Each man was now a small moving fortress, the proud possessor of an Enfield; a Sharps carbine; four heavy-caliber revolvers, with 120 rounds of ammunition for each; plus one or two bowie knives and a saber. So excited was Shelby by the unexpected windfall of weapons that his men had to talk him out of dashing back to Shreveport with a pair of the Napoleons and unloading a barrage on the occupying Yankees.

Well fed, well armed, and well mounted on horses bought from ranchers with bartered weapons, Shelby's men had never had it so good. They needed everything they had, because they were not the only band of hard cases on the prowl and bristling with weapons from abandoned arsenals. Many of the others were Texans, released from service when Kirby Smith surrendered. Pendleton Murrah, the governor of Texas, issued a warning in mid-May that all the structures of an orderly society had broken down. "The voice of the law is hushed," he said. "Murder, robbery, theft, outrages of every kind against property, against human life, against everything sacred to a civilized people, are frequent and general. The rule of the mob, the bandit," is supreme. "Foul crime is committed, and the criminal, steeped in guilt, and branded by his own dark deeds with eternal infamy, goes unwhipped of justice."

In the absence of any kind of authority, Shelby declared martial law in the various cities he passed through or close to en route to San Antonio, which was more than two hundred miles from his starting point at Corsicana. His concern was for his own safety—more precisely, for that of Betty and the children—as much as it was for the citizens of Texas. After many discussions with Betty over the months since she had joined him in Clarksville, Shelby had decided that it would be safer to have her and the boys with him than to send them back to Lexington—the lawless looting that Governor Murrah complained about was not limited to Texas but widespread throughout the parts of the country through which she would have to travel. For now, most of the battalion, including Shelby, would stay together with the half-dozen wagons bearing women and children. They would follow a fairly direct route through Waco to Austin, and from there via New Braunfels to San Antonio.

Shelby sent trusted men in small detachments to deal with troubles as he learned of them in other towns. The first of these rescues occurred at Tyler, about seventy-five miles from Corsicana, as Shelby was beginning his trek. An arsenal in that city was under attack by a gang of "desperate deer-hunters and marauders" and "shirking conscripts," in the words of John Edwards. Shelby sent Yandell Blackwell with forty men to guard the arsenal and to put the fear of God into the "boldest in all that band." Four of Blackwell's men were on watch at a separate structure containing rifles and gunpowder when a score of hostile Texans ordered them to step aside. Each of the four men then carried a keg of gunpowder toward the gang, leaving a trail of powder behind them leading to the arsenal. Asked what they had in mind, one of them, James Kirtley, said they planned "to blow you into hell if you're within range while we are eating our supper." They were tired after a long day's ride and in no mood for talk. The bandits were buffaloed into flight, aware that "one spark would have demolished the town."

A larger, more distant encounter took place west of their line of march, in Houston, where renegade soldiers were gathering to besiege and loot a major Confederate arsenal. Shelby sent about fifty men under James Meadow and James Wood to seize and hold the munitions and supplies until they could be distributed lawfully. Still wearing their butternut uniforms and loaded down with revolvers, Enfield rifles, Sharps carbines, and boot-sheathed bowie knives, Meadow and Wood's men arrived to find the arsenal occupied by an undetermined number of men—probably not the "two thousand greedy and clamorous ruffians," drunk, belligerent, and armed, that Edwards claims, but certainly enough to intimidate a normal contingent of police. Their leader responded to Wood's order to disperse with cool effrontery: "The war's over, young fellows, and the strongest party takes the plunder." Wood answered that he and his men were Missourians with nothing left but "our orders and our honor." Without a written order from Jo Shelby "not so much as one percussion cap" could leave the arsenal. Cowed into submission—"such was the terror of Shelby's name"—the would-be robbers backed off and slunk out of town.

The most lurid story associated with Shelby's Texas journey, and one in which he was directly involved, occurred in Austin in mid-June. His men were camped outside the city, hunkered down in the rain, when word came that a gang of freebooters under a "notorious Captain Rabb" was trying to rob the Confederate subtreasury. As Shelby's men rode into town they saw scores of citizens carrying torches and rifles gathered in front of the subtreasury. The robbers had broken open several large safes with sledgehammers and cold chisels. Alerted by his pickets, Rabb and most of his men had grabbed what they could and escaped, their pockets filled with gold coins and worthless Confederate specie. One man remained, "too far gone in whisky" and too greedy to flee. Shot down when he refused to surrender—either by Shelby's men or by the citizens' posse—the robber was discovered to have "a king's ransom about his person," according to Edwards. "He had taken off his pantaloons, tied a string around each leg at the bottom and had filled them. An epicure even in death, he had discarded the silver" in favor of gold. Afterward, a trail of gold coins was found outside of town, having leaked through a hole in the blanket one of the thieves had used to carry it.

Governor Murrah credited Shelby with saving the bank from Rabb's gang and pressed him to take at least some of the money with him; Shelby's honor led him to decline the offer, saying, according to Edwards, "We are the last of the race; let us be the best as well."

Shelby acquired a new volunteer, or rather, another dependent, as a result of this experience. Murrah had battled for four years to keep a balance between the demands of the Confederacy and the independence of Texas as a state and as a former republic in its own right. His primary antagonist during much of this time had been the imperious general John Magruder, the Confederate commander at Galveston, who had made constant demands on Texas for men and supplies that Murrah had regarded as excessive and impossible to meet. Even so, Murrah had been firm in his support of the goals set in Richmond, and he now feared that the advancing Union forces would jail him for that loyalty, so he decided to join Shelby's regiment on their journey. He may also have hoped that his absence would help to prevent the burning of the capital, as he understood—mistakenly—had been the case elsewhere as the defeated Confederate states were occupied.

Murrah was a young man, just four years older than Shelby, but he was dying of tuberculosis. He was a sad figure among the strong and virile soldiers he rode with toward San Antonio: All the "insidious and deceptive approaches were seen in the hectic cheeks, the large, mournful eyes, the tall, bent frame that quivered as it moved," Edwards observed. Broken-hearted and defeated, he nonetheless "put on his old gray uniform, and mounted his old, tired war horse, and rode away dying to Mexico."

Austin was also eventful in that Shelby made the difficult decision to send Betty and the boys home. The relatively easy part of the journey southward lay behind them. East Texas was flat, laced with streams and dotted with ranches and farms and villages, but beyond San Antonio their path would take them through blistering deserts and expose them to new and sterner hardships. Billy Hunter would go with them, Shelby said; he would send for them as soon as he was settled in Mexico.

As John Edwards frequently noted, Shelby was not given to complaint, and neither he nor Betty left any record of how wrenching this decision must have been. Perhaps the bookish Edwards tried to comfort Shelby by quoting Francis Bacon's observation that a man with wife and children has hostages to fortune. It was certainly true that Shelby could hardly continue to function effectively as a military leader so long as he was encumbered by his family.

The wisdom of Shelby's decision to send Betty home became apparent once he reached San Antonio, on June 16, 1865. Wealthy from four years of the cotton trade and untouched by the war, it had been swarming with speculators, profiteers, gamblers, draft dodgers, and deserters even before the war ended. Now it was occupied by desperadoes who, as Edwards writes, "had taken possession of the city and were rioting in royal fashion, sitting in the laps of courtesans and drinking wines brought through the blockade from France." When the mayor learned that Shelby was camped twenty miles north of the city, he rode out in the middle of the night to ask for help. Within the hour Shelby had positioned his men, under D. A. Williams and Alonzo Slayback, on opposite sides of the river that bisects the city. Shelby and the rest of his men then scoured San Antonio's bars, boardinghouses, and whorehouses, rousted the troublemakers, and drove them from town. They were encouraged on their way by Slayback and Williams. Those who resisted were shot on the spot.

Among those for whom the mayor had sought protection were a number of eminent visitors, all residents of the comfortable Menger Hotel adjacent to the Alamo. Until very recently, these men had held the lives of thousands in their hands. They were Confederate generals, judges, legislators, governors, and others driven by approaching Yankees to this last sanctuary. Sterling Price was there, as was his enemy Thomas Reynolds. John Magruder, who had signed the surrender papers for his command in Galveston just two weeks earlier, was there as well.

Also present was Thomas Hindman, who Shelby had known and admired during the early years of the war. Hindman had served in Mexico in 1846 as a lieutenant and had then been a rising young politician in Arkansas. Barely five feet tall but famously combative, he survived both a shootout with a man who had knifed his brother, as well as gunshot wounds inflicted during a street fight with Know-Nothing adherents. He used a cane and wore a modified boot with a thick heel as the result of the fight, but he was also a dandy, favoring snug uniforms, ruffled shirts, and patent leather boots. By 1862, he was a major general in command of the Trans-Mississippi Department. His stringent military edicts, including conscription of citizens into the Confederate army and requisition of supplies from local populations, as well as his authorization of guerrilla activities and some of Shelby's excursions, led to his reassignment in the east in August 1862.

Shelby had applauded Hindman for his aggressive style during the war; he regarded Hindman's successors, including Kirby Smith, as fatally lacking in that key quality. About Kirby Smith himself nothing had been heard directly since May 30, 1865, when he had delivered a final address to his troops that was "remarkable for its bitterness," according to his biographer. Kirby Smith apologized to Colonel Sprague of the Union army for the riotous and ill-disciplined behavior of his men, who had left him "mortified" and "humiliated," and he told his men they were "unpatriotic." The rampaging Texans whom Shelby had been forced to fight and kill from Waco to San Antonio were among those soldiers chastised by Kirby Smith as the Confederacy had collapsed in upon itself.

Shelby took a room at the Menger Hotel in order to plan the march to Mexico with Reynolds, Hindman, and Magruder. His men were camped just outside of town. The next day, as he was seated on his balcony above the plaza, Shelby observed the arrival by carriage of an old man, bent over and white with road dust. Though the man kept his hat low and his head down and signed the register as "William Thompson," Shelby easily recognized Kirby Smith.

Shelby went out to the street and looked up to the second-floor window of Kirby Smith's room in time to see him pull the blinds and the curtains. Considering that the last time he had seen Kirby Smith was the day he had told him that he and his men no longer supported him, Shelby's subsequent actions are surprising. He rode to the edge of town and called out the unit's band leader, telling him to get ready to perform a serenade. The rest of his men, all three hundred of them, were ordered to assemble in formation before the Menger Hotel. Shelby pointed to the closed window and ordered the band to play "Hail to the Chief." There was no response. Then he told it to play "Dixie"—no Southerner could resist that tune. Still no response. That "old man up there is Kirby Smith," Shelby said at last to his men. "I would know him among a thousand. Shout for him until you are hoarse."

At last the weary, dejected Kirby Smith stepped onto the balcony. His former soldiers, who had criticized him for surrendering to the North, applauded and cheered lustily. Shelby, who had previously led the criticism, now praised Kirby Smith for joining them in their exile and said he was still their commander. Together, they were to begin anew, south of the border, Shelby said, concluding, "We bid you good morning instead of good night, and await, as of old your further orders."

A week later, on June 25, 1865, a large part of the core of the leadership of the old Trans-Mississippi Department—Generals Price, Magruder, Reynolds, and Hindman, joined the next day by Kirby Smith, along with Governor Murrah and a score of lesser lights—set out for Eagle Pass under the protection of Jo Shelby, the youngest, boldest, and most capable field commander among them.

FIVE

"Shall It Be Maximilian or Juárez?"

For men who had grown up in the green river valleys and fertile farmland of Missouri, the scorched landscape of southern Texas had all the charm of a den of rattlesnakes—desolate, arid, and hot beyond belief, it was festering with desperadoes. They trailed after the battalion like wolves hoping to pick off strays from a cattle herd, waiting for a moment's inattention. Despite some grousing from the men, Shelby determined that the only way to frustrate the outlaws, since he could not waste time chasing them down, was to maintain the same pattern of watches and patrols that had kept them alive for four years of roaming cavalry excursions and semi-guerrilla warfare.

On the second night out of San Antonio, D. A. Williams was returning with ten men from a provisions foray to rejoin the regiment. With him were seven mules laden with grain purchased from a nearby ranch. Williams sent one of his men, George Cruzen, ahead on point. Alone on the rutted path, under a blazing full moon, Cruzen heard a stallion whinny. The noise came from a dry streambed in an arroyo that the road crossed—a defile perfectly designed for an ambush. Cruzen dismounted and led his horse back a hundred paces, tying him loosely to a chaparral bush. Dropping down to the streambed, he crept forward until he saw, around a bend, about thirty armed men waiting silently. Cruzen returned cautiously to his horse and walked it back toward Williams.

Williams pondered what to do. The ambushers were situated between him and Shelby. He could not retreat, and if he tried to go around them, he would probably be discovered and attacked. He might send Cruzen to get Shelby to attack from the other side of the arroyo, but that would take too long. So he did what he had seen Shelby do so often during the war: He attacked, leading his small band back to the dry gulch where the outlaws waited, and creeping up on them silently. His men were spotted at the last moment. Both sides opened fire. Within minutes the outlaws were dead, as were five of Williams's men.

What is remarkable about this episode is that only weeks earlier most of the antagonists had been on the same side, fighting against the Yankees. The ferocity and brutality of the encounter is all the more stark for the quickness with which it, like the dead men, is dispatched by John Edwards, whose account this is. Subsequent encounters south of the border with Indians, Mexican bandits, and followers of Benito Juárez would follow the same pattern: explosive action, no quarter given, and a heap of bodies on whom no sympathy or tears are wasted. In this instance, the result was worth the cost—there were no further attacks on the Missourians by renegade Texans.

Shelby's response the following day to another challenge, this one from a pursuing federal detachment, was just as intransigent. He was aware, in a general way, that the Union was pouring troops into Texas—more than thirty thousand men, the size of Kirby Smith's army at its largest during the war. They were led by General Philip Sheridan, after Grant and Sherman the Union's most popular and most capable cavalry officer—it was Sheridan who had neutralized the Confederate cavalry superiority in the eastern theater, killing Jeb Stuart in the process. Grant ordered Sheridan to establish order in Texas and to secure the border from Confederate forces like Shelby's that refused to surrender and tried to cross into Mexico. Sheridan gave that assignment to General Frederick Steele, who brought a special zeal to the task: Shelby's success the previous year in preventing him from linking up with General Banks had resulted in the Union's failure to conquer Texas and had blighted Steele's promising career. By May 31,

1865, Steele had reached Brownsville, and on June 20 he was a hundred miles up the Rio Grande, in Roma. His goal was to reach Eagle Pass, another two hundred miles to the northwest, and seal the border.

The morning after the fight with the renegade Texans, two scouts who had been covering the rear of Shelby's column confirmed his anticipation of federal pursuit: A cavalry brigade, including a six-gun artillery battery, was about seventeen miles behind them. Shelby sent for Jim Moreland, a poised and articulate young officer. He handed Moreland a note to give to the Union brigade commander: "My scouts inform me that you have about three thousand men, and that you are looking for me. I have only one thousand men, and yet I should like to make your acquaintance. I will probably march from my present camp about ten miles further today, halting on the high road between San Antonio and Eagle Pass. Should you desire to pay me a visit, you will find me at home until day after tomorrow."

The Union commander, a Colonel Johnson, received Moreland "with all the courtesy of a wartime adversary," and the young officer delivered Shelby's insouciant challenge—"at home," indeed—with appropriate punctilio. Johnson appeared ready to accept it; by nightfall he was camped just five miles from Shelby. He had an overwhelming advantage in numbers and artillery—Shelby's boast of a thousand men was hugely exaggerated, and he had long since dumped all but two of the field pieces he had found earlier as too cumbersome to haul around. But despite a few feints the following morning, Johnson held his fire and did not pursue the Confederates as they re-formed their column and continued their march. The war had been over for more than three weeks now, and Shelby assumed that Johnson was unwilling to shed his men's blood in order to stop a former enemy from leaving the country. There is no record of General Steele's reaction to his lost opportunity to exact revenge for his forced retreat from Camden the previous year.

General Kirby Smith may have applauded Shelby's defiant response to Colonel Johnson, understanding that he could hardly have done otherwise—the pace of Shelby's journey southward was dictated by his slow supply wagons and the two field pieces. But either because he was alarmed at the proximity of Union troops, or simply impatient, Kirby Smith announced that he planned to go ahead with three of his friends to Eagle Pass and risk the trip to Mexico City alone. Shelby sent Maurice Langhorne with half a dozen men to escort the party to the border. When they parted at the Rio Grande, Langhorne told Shelby afterward, Kirby Smith said that if all his men had been up to the standard set by Shelby's, he would not now be going into exile. The unforgiving John Edwards, when he heard this story, said that if Kirby Smith himself had been up to Shelby's standard, all of their fates might have been vastly different.

The former commander of the Trans-Mississippi Department, the austere and dignified ruler of "Kirby-Smithdom," was then ferried across the river into Mexico. Aboard a mule, he wore baggy flannel trousers and a calico shirt with the sleeves rolled up, and a silk bandanna tied around his neck "a la Texas," he recalled later. He carried a revolver in his belt and a shotgun across his saddle. Everything else he had left behind, he wrote to his wife, "except a clear conscience and a sense of having done my duty." With "a light purse but a heavy heart" he entered the scorching desert of an alien nation. As he did so, he was surprised by a "feeling of lightness and joy" at being no longer the commander but just "plain Kirby Smith relieved from all cares and responsible only for my own acts."

Shelby had both more and less freedom of action than did Kirby Smith. As the elected leader of his men, he could be confident that they would follow his commands on the field, as they had when they waited obediently for Johnson's charge. But decisions beyond the tactical—such as to whom they would offer their services in Mexico, or even if they would stay together as a unit—were up to the men. Those decisions had yet to be made as they reached the dusty Texas town of Eagle Pass, on about June 29, 1865. Shelby wasted no time in displaying the Confederate flag that he had been presented two years earlier by the ladies of a small Arkansas town: "Let it ever be on the crest of battle," John Edwards had said then. Now it flew over the battalion as it formed a menacing line along the bluff overlooking the Rio Grande. Shelby placed his howitzers so that their shells could easily land three hundred yards away in the middle of the Mexican town of Piedras Negras, named after the black shale that lined the river.

Shelby thus presented his visiting card to General Andreas Viesca, governor of the state of Coahuila. More than two thousand Mexican soldiers were stationed near Piedras Negras. If Viesca chose to deny him entry into Mexico, Shelby would have to fight his way across or return to face Sheridan's army. He sent a man under a flag of truce across the river to request a meeting. Viesca agreed, and the two men sat down that afternoon in the town square under the watchful eyes of Shelby's artillerists.

Viesca and Shelby each carried the burden of his country's history and character. Viesca was bilingual in English and Spanish, polished, and opaque, more politician than soldier; Shelby was, according to Edwards, "blunt, abrupt, a little haughty and suspicious." Though Viesca had the power to stop Shelby from entering Mexico, Shelby could reduce the adobe huts of Piedras Negras to rubble from the safety of Eagle Pass. As a man on the run from the United States, he need not feel bound by its rules against violating international borders. Viesca, however, knew that Benito Juárez, hoping for continued support from Washington, would certainly forbid any incursion by Mexican forces into Texas, even to silence Confederate guns.

Shelby's threat was an effective way to make the point that he was a force to be reckoned with, but it may have been unnecessary. As a highly placed Juárez official, Viesca was probably aware of Preston Blair's plan for a united Confederate-Union force that would evict the French from Mexico, and of Juárez's approval of that idea in principle. The Confederacy was no more, but the French were still very much a presence in Mexico. Viesca could have had no doubt that Shelby was dangerous but must have hoped that he could persuade him to side with Juárez rather than Maximilian.

For Viesca, as for many Americans, it was clear that Benito Juárez was Mexico's only hope for freedom from French oppression—an oppression that was particularly galling because Mexico had only recently, after three centuries of Spanish rule, won its independence by force. That proud year was 1821, about the time of Viesca's birth. By 1835, Mexico had become nearly as large as the United States in territory, claiming a third of today's contiguous forty-eight states— Texas, Arizona, New Mexico, and California among them. But the country's population was small and impoverished: About seven million mestizos and Indians were ruled by a tiny minority claiming

Spanish blood. These privileged few were the rich landowners, the hierarchy of the Roman Catholic Church, and a military claque so corrupt that it fielded nearly as many officers as ordinary soldiers. Opposing this cabal were various reformers, idealistic but disorganized and given to quarreling among themselves, who championed the cause of the illiterate peasants.

Beset for decades by violent internecine strife, the Mexicans were incapable of governing the vast regions of the north. In Texas, particularly, they ruled in name only—in 1836, when Texas declared its independence, there were ten Americans (about thirty-five thousand) for every Mexican living in the state. The rest of what would become the American Southwest and California were also soon peopled by Americans eager for land and convinced of their "manifest destiny" to create a nation that would sweep from sea to shining sea.

In 1846, war between Mexico and the United States erupted over Texas and California. An American expeditionary force quickly defeated the Mexican army; the result was the forced sale by Mexico to the United States of half its territory, two-thirds the size of the immense Louisiana Purchase of 1803. (The emotions roused both in the United States and in Mexico by this reordering of two huge nations are still hot today; a 2008 ad in Mexico for Absolut vodka that featured a map of the United States and Mexico as they looked before the war of 1846 delighted the Mexicans as much as it outraged American conservatives.)

Washington paid the Mexicans the equivalent of $300 million in today's currency for their northern territories, a generous act by the standards of international conquest. But the money was quickly stolen or squandered. The Mexican government then sold high-yield bonds on the international market to stay afloat and by 1860 was mired in debt to England, France, and Spain. Benito Juárez became president in 1858; in 1861, after winning reelection, he declared a moratorium on interest payments to the bondholders, who threatened to collect the debts by force, if necessary. England soon backed away from that idea, as did Spain, nearing the last stages of its own collapse. But Napoléon III saw an opportunity for France to re-create and even to expand its once-grand overseas empire, this time in Latin America. In

January 1862 he landed about 2,500 troops at Veracruz. It would take the French many thousands more men and a year and a half of fighting before the Mexican army backing Juárez was defeated.

Juárez escaped to the northern state of Chihuahua—and then eventually, for a time, to New York City. Thousands of his men, now called Juaristas, Liberals, or republicans, remained to fight a war of attrition against the invaders, many of them as loosely organized guerrillas. They controlled vast areas of the countryside, leaving the cities to the French. In 1864, Maximilian, younger brother of the Austro-Hungarian emperor Franz Josef, was named emperor of Mexico. But the power behind the throne was the French army, including a large detachment of international troops belonging to the French foreign legion.

Official Washington policy as well as President Lincoln's personal sympathies had long favored Juárez over both his Conservative opponents in Mexico and his imperialist creditors abroad. Now that the Civil War had ended, Lincoln's secretary of state William Seward, who had been retained by President Andrew Johnson, was able to devote more attention to getting rid of the French. The last thing he wanted to see was huge numbers of Americans, former Confederates especially, heading into Mexico and propping up the European interlopers.

All of which meant that Shelby had strong reasons for wanting to accept the proposal Viescas now made him. It was an attractive offer: Shelby was to remain in Piedras Negras for two or three months, drawing other Americans to serve under him against Maximilian. Shelby assured Viesca that he could recruit twenty thousand men within that period. He would then march two hundred miles due south to the French stronghold at Monterrey, manned by about two thousand foreign legionnaires and Zouaves, and attack and defeat them. His reward would be military control of Coahuila, Tamaulipas, and Nuevo Leon—all of northeast Mexico, including two hundred miles of the Gulf Coast down to Tampico, ensuring virtually complete control of shipping between the United States and eastern Mexico.

In return, Shelby would have to swear his allegiance, and that of his men, to Juárez. Shelby told Viesca he would reply to his proposition the following day; first he had to meet with his men and secure their agreement.

The last time Shelby had received such an intriguing offer was from Frank Blair, just as the Civil War was beginning in May 1861. Partly as a result of having turned down the chance to become a Union officer, he was now being given a chance to begin his life again, at thirty-five. John Edwards speculated that visions of conquest danced before his old friend's eyes: "After he once got a foothold in the country," Shelby would rule not just these desolate eastern provinces but could perhaps move west to capture the fabled gold mines of Sonora, and eventually—why not?—all of Mexico. The French had taken it with fewer men than Shelby would be able to raise.

These dreams were probably better suited to the romantic Edwards than to Shelby, who was more hardheaded. But Shelby did do his best to persuade his battalion that Viesca's offer was one that they should all think seriously about accepting: "If you are all of my mind, boys, and will take your chances along with me, it is Juarez and the Republic from this time on until we die here, one by one, or win a kingdom. We have the nucleus of a fine army—cannon, muskets, ammunition, some good prospects for recruits."

But the boys were emphatically not "all of his mind." Though Shelby was less prejudiced than most of his class, he was surrounded by others who cherished a white, midwestern, Anglo-Saxon contempt for blacks, Mexicans, and all those other dark-hued people whom Tennyson had called "lesser breeds without the law." How, they asked him, could they trust Viesca, or any Mexican, to keep his word? Why should they side with Juárez, who had supported Abe Lincoln and been supported in turn by the Union? Who did they have more in common with—the French, who had fought side by side with their ancestors against the British, or a bunch of greasers no better than niggers? And even if they did throw in with Juárez, how likely was it that they could raise more men, with Sheridan closing down the border?

In the end, it was Shelby's admired Virginia Military Institute comrade Ben Elliott, four times wounded during the war, who summed up the feelings of the rest: "General, if you order it, we will follow you into the Pacific Ocean. But we are all Imperialists, and would prefer service under Maximilian."

Shelby was stunned by the almost unanimous opposition to Viesca's offer. He tried to make the men see sense, arguing that President Andrew Johnson would surely direct General Grant to expel the French by force if they did not soon commit to leaving Mexico under their own steam. If the Missourians now took up arms for the French, they would be enlisting for another lost cause, this one more hopeless than the Confederacy had ever been—and this time not fighting on and for their own sacred soil but a thousand miles from home.

But when the men stood firm, Shelby said their decision would be his, too. They would march directly to Monterrey to tell the French of their willingness to serve the emperor Maximilian: "Let no man repine. You have chosen the Empire. Your fate shall be my fate, and your fortune my fortune." He promised to inform Viesca of their unanimous decision the following day.

But to Edwards, as they returned to their tent, he said: "Poor, proud fellows. They would rather starve under the Empire than feast in a Republic." They would all be lucky to escape death by famine if not "by fusillade" against a wall.

In the meantime, still thinking ahead like a good cavalry officer, Shelby devised a way to avoid such a disaster. He would take his men all the way across Mexico to the Pacific coast city of Mazatlán, about four hundred miles southwest of Monterrey. There the Juarist forces were weaker than elsewhere and would pose less of a threat to his men. If Maximilian sent him word in Mazatlán accepting his offer of military assistance, he could raise more volunteers from among the thousands of ex-Confederate soldiers who were already fleeing westward. If Maximilian said no thanks, Shelby and his men could easily return to the United States by way of Arizona or California without having to face the kind of strong federal troop presence that lurked north of the Rio Grande.

The next morning, July 1, 1865, Shelby gathered his senior officers in the shallows of the Rio Grande to bury the flag. Edwards recalled the flag's origins in Arkansas and how it had "gleamed grandly through the smoke and sorrow" of scores of battles. Now, faded and torn, "it was displayed once more to its followers before the swift waves of the Rio Grande closed over it forever." Alonzo Slayback, described by Edwards as a "beau sabreur," tried afterward to catch the moment in poetry, in a requiem that ended:

> *They buried then that flag and plume in the*
> > *River's rushing tide,*
> > *Ere that gallant few*
> > *Of the tried and true*
> *Had been scattered far and wide.*
> *And that group of Missouri's valiant throng,*
> *Who had fought for the weak against the strong—*
> > *Who had charged and bled*
> > *Where Shelby led,*
> *Were the last who held above the wave*
> *The glorious flag of the vanquished brave,*
> *No more to rise from its watery grave!*

By noon, Shelby had his men, horses, mules, wagons, and artillery across the river and encamped just outside Piedras Negras. After telling Elliott and Slayback to come for him with guns at the ready if he was not back within an hour, he left to give Viesca the bad news— that his men preferred to fight on the side of the French, and he was bound to join them despite his own preference for Juárez. Viesca simply shrugged and said Shelby was free to do as he chose; he could do nothing to hinder him. The French were doomed if they tried to stay, and Shelby was a fool to join them.

But if he did insist on going to Monterrey, Viesca said, Shelby should be aware that there were only two routes to follow. One was a good road, but it was controlled by Juaristas far more aggressive than Viesca was. The other route was less a road than a path, winding through the low and high deserts before it led to a difficult series of mountain passes. It was infested with bandidos and Apaches, so dangerous that the Juaristas and the French alike stayed clear of it. In neither case could the Americans be bogged down with a wagon train and artillery. Would Shelby sell him the supplies and munitions he did not need?

Shelby sent a man back to tell Slayback and Elliott he would be delayed and settled in for an afternoon of haggling with Viesca over money and terms of sale. Luckily for Shelby, Piedras Negras was not a poor town, for all its bedraggled appearance. There was a new customs house built to handle the wartime cotton and arms trade that until a few months ago had been collecting more than $50,000 a month in duties. The town abounded in cantinas and shops of every description, whose owners could be pressed by the authorities to contribute to a worthy cause. The upshot was that Shelby sold Viesca everything his men could not carry themselves and on pack animals: the artillery pieces, the extra Enfield rifles and ammunition, the superfluous exotic food and wine that they had found in Texas, and the wagons and mules. It all went for $16,000 in silver and the promise, never fulfilled, of an equivalent sum in Juarist scrip. Most of the money was deposited for safekeeping overnight in the customs house, but some of it was divided immediately among the men. One of them, Thomas Westlake, recalled being handed sixty silver dollars; though he never knew how much the artillery sold for, he was always "satisfied that General Shelby saw to it that all were delt fairly with."

The merchants from whom Viesca had extorted the money got some of it back that afternoon as the men relaxed in the cantinas and flirted with the señoritas. As the tension from months and years of constant fighting relaxed, so did the discipline that had held the men together. Their coherence as a unit had already begun to fray. Though they still numbered about three hundred men, scores of these were refugees and deserters who had attached themselves to Shelby for their own convenience.

Three of the men who had only recently joined the expedition were a rough-looking lot even by the standards of the Iron Brigade. They claimed to have fought under Lee in Virginia but otherwise offered little information about their backgrounds or why they wanted to go to Mexico. Edwards noted that the strangers seemed to have a high degree of curiosity about the dozen fine horses Shelby had purchased from a ranch near San Antonio. Most of the horses bore several brands, including some indicating Mexican ownership, but that was not uncommon. Shelby had the bills of sale in his saddlebag and could prove the horses were legally acquired. He was determined, he told his men both in Texas and Mexico, to stay within the law, and to prove to

any legal authority who questioned them that they had paid for whatever they needed.

Ike Berry was the newest proud owner of one of these animals,
which were all confined to a makeshift corral under an acacia tree just
off the central square. A farmer from central Missouri, Berry was the
biggest man in the battalion, well over six feet tall and weighing about
240 pounds. He needed a big horse like the sixteen-hand roan on
which he now sat casually, with one leg crooked around the saddle
horn, smoking a pipe and combing the horse's mane. Eight or ten
other men were grooming their horses nearby.

None noticed the three men supposedly from Lee's army, or the
squad of armed Mexican soldiers behind them, until one of the Americans walked up and put his hand on Berry's horse's bridle. "This is my
horse," the man claimed. Pointing to an old brand that had been par-
tially obscured by a more recent one, he said that all the horses were
stolen, and the Mexican army was here to help him get his property
back.

Berry peered quizzically at the stranger and said he must be mistaken. No, said the other, he was not mistaken: "Dismount!"

In a flash, Berry drew his saber from its scabbard and brought it
down on the arm that clutched the bridle, severing it near the shoulder. The man fell backward, blood spurting from his stump. The two
friends of the injured man and the Mexicans fanned out as Berry and
his comrades drew their revolvers and crouched behind their horses.
One of them darted through the back fence of the corral to find
Shelby, who was enjoying a beer with a young Englishman at a nearby
cantina. Shelby shouted for his bugler, Martin Kritzer, to sound the
rally as he raced down the street to the corral. D. A. Williams led a
dozen men to scatter the Mexican guards around the artillery and
wagons they had just been sold, and Maurice Langhorne dashed to
the customs house to secure the battalion's silver. A third group
headed for the river to seize the boats there. Still others raged through
the town, certain that they had all been betrayed. By the time the
shooting stopped, more than a dozen members of the Mexican squad
that had backed up the three Americans were dead; of those three, the
only survivor was the man who had lost his arm. None of Shelby's
men was injured.

Governor Viesca hastened to the scene to mollify a furious Shelby, who pointed to his howitzers and threatened to shell the Mexican army barracks if he was attacked in force. He showed Viesca his bills of sale for the horses and demanded an apology for the insulting charge that his men were thieves. Viesca acquiesced, promising to restrain his men and to pay the rest of the money owed to Shelby for the supplies and munitions when the Americans left in the morning.

At dawn, while Piedras Negras still slept, guns were traded for money and the remnants of the Iron Brigade set out for Monterrey. They chose the more difficult route described by Viesca, hoping to avoid further encounters with the Juaristas on the main road and confident that they were more than a match for the Apaches who claimed the land as their own.

SIX

"Beware of the Sabinas!"

On a high ridge a dozen miles south of town, the column halted for a last look back, across Piedras Negras to Eagle Pass. A lone horseman loped toward them, a mile away, but otherwise the landscape was deserted. With the field telescope that he had owned since the early days of the war, Shelby could see that a Confederate flag flew briskly from the parade ground at the deserted Fort Duncan in Eagle Pass, raised by some anonymous admirer. "Some memories of home and kindred"—of Betty and the boys, of his parents in Lexington, of his burned home in Waverly—might have flashed through his mind then, John Edwards imagined. As for the rest of the men, "some voice may have spoken even then to ears that heard and heeded, but the men made no sign. Their bronzed faces never softened."

The horseman reached the head of the column as Shelby resumed the march. He called out "Amigo!" Did he want to join them, Shelby asked cautiously? Did he need help? No, the man said, he needed nothing: not money, not horses. Just the American's ear for a moment to warn him of danger ahead. Shelby thanked the man and asked why he should want to help them. Because, the Mexican said, an American in Texas had once saved his life. Now he would repay that favor with four words of caution: "Beware of the Sabinas!"

The Sabinas was a river valley three days to the south—the first oasis in a landscape more desolate than anything they had seen in Texas. On July 3, 1865, Shelby slowly scanned, by ten-degree segments, the wide valley from a ridge a mile away. His exhausted men filed by on foot, leading their even wearier horses. At noon the sun was a dazzling, molten ball, the sky a pallid blue, the temperature well over a hundred degrees. Heat waves shimmered and danced over the stony path, the ragged clusters of prickly pear and saguaro cactus, and the frequent little heaps of rocks with white crosses that marked earlier travelers' graves—luckless victims of accident or murder, reminding Shelby of the warning he had received.

The river looked more inviting than dangerous. Broad and deep, it meandered through the far end of the valley for several miles, then narrowed before vanishing into a canyon to the south. Irrigation ditches from the river watered fields of yellowing maize. In their midst was a tiny village with a dozen flat-roofed adobe huts. It was siesta time, Shelby supposed; that would explain why the fields were empty and the village was so still—there were no signs of life aside from a few wisps of smoke. The circling vultures over the village were not particularly ominous—called *zopilotes,* they were everywhere in Mexico, and functioned as nature's garbagemen.

The thirsty horses pricked up their ears, and their pace, at the distant scent of water. Shelby sent Edwards ahead to halt the column's advance and to lead a scouting party of ten men into the village. Edwards's flag signal shortly afterward that the way was clear did not prepare the battalion for the horrors that lay before them. The farmers and their families had been massacred, about forty people in all. A few of the men had fought back and were lucky enough to die quickly. Others had been tortured: "Men hung suspended from door facings literally flayed alive," Edwards wrote. "Huge strips of skin dangled from them as tattered garments might hang. Under some a slow fire had been kindled, until strangulation came as a tardy mercy for relief." Women and children had been speared and slashed.

Shelby and Edwards had been through years of war together and yet had never seen anything so terrible. Ben Elliott, who had fought Indians in Texas, said this kind of torture was the work of the Lipan

Apaches—the Plains branch of the Apache nation that had been harried out of Texas into Mexico by the Comanches in the 1840s. Nomadic raiders, they lived only for plunder. In recent years, they sometimes made common cause against the French with the bandits and the Juaristas, most of whom were of mixed Indian and Hispanic blood. The French were the Apaches' greater enemy, as they regarded all Indians, especially Apaches, as vermin to be exterminated without mercy. Shelby and his men, who proposed to aid the French, would be equally hated by the Indians.

But why torture and slaughter the villagers? Long-suffering peasants provided discriminating raiders a reliable source of grain and food, but only so long as they were allowed to live and work. Shelby decided that the massacre was a warning to him to turn around and go home. He was still only a few days south of the American border, hundreds of miles from his goal of Mazatlán, with no assurance of a welcome once he arrived. The ruined village was just a taste of the scorched earth and ruin that lay ahead for Shelby's brigade. The Apaches' message read: "Yanquis, go home!"

Shelby was poised, as the classically inclined John Edwards frequently said, between Scylla and Charybdis (though Shelby would have said between a rock and a hard place). The still-hot fires in the village suggested that the attack had taken place only hours earlier, which meant the enemy was close at hand—waiting, no doubt, to ambush them at the Sabinas, as their mysterious friend outside of Piedras Negras had perhaps foreseen. Unable to stay where he was, and unwilling to retreat, Shelby moved his brigade along the Sabinas River to confront the Apaches.

But first, needing rest, the regiment camped that night in a secure clearing by the river. The men caught catfish and roasted a few cattle that had strayed from the village. It was their first decent meal in days. They were joined, after dark, by two Austrian soldiers, French foreign legionnaires who had deserted and were heading for Texas. Shelby had little time for deserters of any stripe, but he was taken aback by their stories of French military discipline, as translated by the former Missouri governor Thomas Reynolds. Even those who deserted, then changed their minds and returned for duty, were routinely shot. How could such an army expect to hold its men in line? And how bad must it have been for these two legionnaires to hazard death at the hands of the Apaches rather than stay with their unit?

As it happened, the deserters said they had crossed the main ford downriver a day earlier without incident—no sign of Juaristas or Apaches. They thought it would be safe for Shelby's brigade to cross there as well.

Shelby thought otherwise. He had made hundreds of river crossings in hostile territory, and made it a rule never to take the easy fords—especially in the morning when the opposite banks were obscured by river mists and fog. Instead, he chose difficult crossings, less likely to be heavily defended. The pattern had been set during his first major battle, at Carthage in 1862; there Captain Shelby had routed the Union commander, General Franz Sigel, by crossing at a difficult but vulnerable position and flanking the enemy. Audacity, John Edwards said, always carried the day for Shelby, as it had for Frederick the Great: "L'audace, l'audace, toujours l'audace."

Shelby's scouts discovered a crossing in the canyon a hundred yards to the south of the main ford. It was dangerous—the water was swift and deep, and the crossing was located just above rock-strewn rapids and a fifty-foot waterfall. If the crossing was competently defended, the expedition would be lost. After conferring with his commanders, Shelby decided to take his chances that afternoon.

The advance was done in carefully planned stages. First, twenty men under D. A. Williams were sent to reconnoiter the east side of the Sabinas and to draw fire if they could from the west bank. Shelby then asked for ten volunteers to lead the preliminary move across the rocky ford, once Williams had determined the number of Apaches on the other side. These ten would then harry the enemy from the rear. At that point, the whole brigade would charge, with Shelby in the lead.

Dozens of men stepped forward, each eager to be one of the chosen ten. Among them, Shelby was surprised to see, was old John Clark. Born in 1802, Clark had been a lawyer in Fayette and a major general in the Missouri state militia before the war. He had resigned his seat in Congress to become a brigadier general in the Missouri State Guard when war broke out and had been wounded at Wilson's Creek,

Shelby's first battle. Most of the other senior officers and important persons who had thrown in their lot with Shelby at San Antonio had stayed well in the background during their adventures since then—either because they were emotionally exhausted or because they knew that Shelby had enough on his hands without tending to a bunch of prima donnas. Even such tempestuous characters as Reynolds, Hindman, and Magruder kept their opinions to themselves and gathered around their own campfires each night—though Magruder did volunteer that according to his chronometer, the date of their coming engagement at the Sabinas was portentous indeed: July 4.

Clark was different. He had seen little action during the war after his early wound and was eager now to be of help, even volunteering for late-night guard duty. Shelby had grown fond of the old man but had no hesitation in telling him he was not needed. There were "younger and less valuable men" to make the risky charge. "Get out of the ranks, General," he ordered. "The column can not advance unless you do."

Ben Elliott was selected to lead those who drew the shortest straws. The regiment marched in column formation toward the river and drew up just out of sight of the other side. Williams returned from his forward position, saying he had drawn some fire. There were perhaps four hundred men across the river, most clustered north of Shelby's chosen crossing point. They were armed with single-shot muskets—not repeaters. "Good," Shelby said. "Take your place in the front ranks. Elliott goes ahead with his men. I will lead the column."

Ten abreast, the midafternoon sun hot on their faces, Elliott and his men spurred their horses into the rushing water, beyond rifle shot of the easy shallow ford where most of the enemy waited. Covering fire from the battalion distracted the Apaches until Elliott's squad was halfway across, all but submerged in the water. Two or three men were wounded, but they all reached the bank safely and charged into the brush with sabers drawn.

A flare blazed from the west bank, telling Shelby that Elliott had accomplished his mission. Shelby ordered the bugler to sound the charge, and more than two hundred cavalrymen followed Elliott's path into the Sabinas. They rode with reins in their teeth and pistols in both hands, firing in response to the puffs of smoke that betrayed the positions of the invisible enemy.

Despite their distance upriver and Elliott's harassment to their rear, the Apaches could hardly miss hitting a few Americans. A dozen riders flew from their saddles and floated, dead or nearly so, over the waterfall, some never to be found. Others would die in the battle that followed. But for the enemy it was, Edwards said, a "hurricane." Surprised and trapped as a result of Shelby's tactics, they were hewn down with sabers and shot where it was safe to use pistols. After what the Americans had seen in the village, no quarter was given. About two hundred Indians were killed and left unburied, a deliberate insult to a dishonored foe. The rest escaped, taking with them yet more dead.

The victory was not cheap. In addition to the men lost in the river, six others died and thirty-seven were wounded, one mortally. This was one of the "less valuable" volunteers, in the sense that he was not an original member of the group: the nameless young Englishman with whom Edwards said Shelby was talking "about cognac and Catalan" when the fracas over the horses erupted in Piedras Negras. Witty and charming, the Englishman had often joked about his recurrent nightmare of dying in a train wreck, and how he would be safe here, far from any train. Edwards suspected that he had carried his own demons with him into battle, where his reckless bravery during the fight at the river astounded the Americans. When his horse was killed, he grabbed another; when his leg was shattered by a musket ball, he continued his charge until he was hit in the chest.

As he lay dying that evening, the Englishman gasped out a peculiar final confession—in French, to Thomas Reynolds, because he was too ashamed to tell his story in English. "I was the youngest son of an English baron," the story began, as recalled by the enthralled John Edwards. Rejected by the girl he loved for his best friend, he had killed his friend in a duel and fled the country. Consumed by remorse, he had been seeking absolution by means of a heroic death ever since. Edwards claimed that Reynolds gave him a "free translation" of the confession, which he later turned over to the British minister in Mexico. It must be said that it is a remarkably full and detailed account, especially for a man with a hole in his chest and speaking a foreign tongue. It ended when the young man spoke his final words: "It is so dreary to die in the night. One likes to have the sunlight for this."

Among the surviving wounded, in the real rather than the romantic world, were Ben Elliott, who had almost been crushed under his dead horse, and four of his men. Amazingly, none of the ten had died. Weary and saddened by their losses, the battalion recuperated for a week by the river—a couple of miles upstream and upwind from the gory remains of the enemy's rotting bodies—before resuming its southward march.

Their intermediate destination was the town of Lampazos, seventy-five miles southeast. Their pace was slowed to a walk as they entered the foothills of the Sierra Madre Oriental, the horses slipping on the loose shale, sick and wounded men lurching painfully in their saddles. Every few miles they would pass a cluster of adobe farmhouses where well water allowed enough grass and grain to sustain a family, but in the higher elevations to the north, west, and south the landscape was deserted, as stark and lonely as the moon. At night, though, roving bands of thieves and Apaches continued their harassing attacks, sniping at the men as they sat around their campfires and trying to steal their horses. It was everything Shelby could do to restrain the men from pursuing them and taking reprisals on anyone hapless enough to cross their path, Indian or Mexican, innocent or not.

The attacks diminished as the battalion reached the passes that led between the ragged peaks of the Sister Mountains, the Sierras de Hermanas. The passes were not high by the exacting standard of Maurice Langhorne, one of Shelby's most adventurous officers—he had made his way to the California gold fields over the Sierra Nevada range in 1850, and had seen where the Donner party had suffered and died. But at four thousand feet the temperature at night was cool enough to cause chills and fevers in horses that had never known high elevations. John Tisdale, a bluff and hale doctor in his fifties who had been a brigade surgeon, now added ailing horses to his list of patients. He told the men to give up their own blankets to their mounts, reminding them that they could hardly expect to survive long on foot.

At last they stumbled into a balmy oasis about twenty miles from Lampazos. It was a quiet, narrow valley with a rushing stream surrounded by lush grasses and palm trees. The grateful horses were staked out to graze as the men settled in for their first comfortable night since leaving the Sabinas. Guards were assigned to watch the ends of the valley. As the campfires dimmed and the evening mists rose, John Edwards ruminated on the peculiar nature of the palms hovering over him, so different from the pines of Missouri. "Strange and shapely, and coldly chaste," they seemed to him, somehow "human and desolate, standing all alone in the midst of luxurious nature." The palm was a "pensive tree," he thought, and vaguely sinister; its softly rattling leaves, sad and solemn, suggested "the sound of ruffled cerements when the corpse is given to the coffin."

Edwards's artful foreshadowing was borne out by the sharp single crack of a revolver at midnight. Shelby was awake instantly, as was the Quantrill guerrilla John Thrailkill, next to him. They listened intently, raised on their elbows, then sensed rather than saw ghostly forms moving among them in the mist—Apaches and bandits had infiltrated their lines, slipping around the guard posted at the north pass whose belated warning shot came almost too late. Barefoot and half-naked, Shelby and his men rolled out with their revolvers and knives to repel the attack, stumbling through the boulders and cacti toward the pass. When it was over, a scant few minutes later, eleven Americans were dead and seventeen wounded—adding to the toll at the Sabinas. The survivors counted about seventy dead among the enemy, including their leaders—a "renegade priest" named Juan Anselmo and "Antonio Flores, a young Cuban who had sold his sister to a wealthy haciendado and turned robber."

Lampazos was a poor but appealing refuge when they finally reached it, bloodied and exhausted, two days later. A hundred miles north of Monterrey, it was founded in the seventeenth century, as the Spanish pushed their trade and colonization efforts northward. The town was nestled comfortably between a high mesa, formerly an Indian stronghold, and the white crest of the Eastern Cordilleras. It was alive now with the seasonal fiesta; the sounds of trumpets and guitars and the overwhelming scent of wild pigs roasting on spits over mesquite charcoal wafted through Shelby's encampment. He gave firm orders to his men to stay put—he had no idea how many of the villagers might have been involved with the attackers to the north. They would wait for an invitation, not barge in uninvited, Shelby said.

No invitation came. The Mexicans had too much experience with wandering bands of well-armed men to rush to make the acquaintance of a new one—so after a time three men slipped out of camp and joined the fiesta. Seeking to reassure the villagers that they meant no harm, they left their guns and knives behind. There were a few dances, a few beers, no *problemas*. As they were making their unsteady way back to camp, one of them, a rawboned and handsome lad named Crockett—he claimed to be kin of the famous Davy—stopped to talk to a pretty girl standing in an open doorway. According to Edwards, she drew back as Crockett bent over to kiss her. Her shawl was pulled away, "leaving all her bosom bare, the long, luxuriant hair falling down upon and over it." She screamed. Armed men rushed from the house and attacked the Americans. One of them, Thomas Boswell, was slashed three times, and Reuben Walker took a bullet in the face that passed through both cheeks and his tongue. Crockett was not injured. The attackers scattered. Boswell, whose wounds were superficial, helped Crockett carry the semiconscious Walker between them toward their camp.

As they reached their guards, a young Mexican, one of those who had attacked them, appeared and demanded to see the commanding officer. Shelby arrived and looked at the wounded men with a mixture of concern and disgust. He did not need an interpreter to understand the young Mexican's demands: "Satisfaction."

Crockett had insulted his sister's virtue. He could have killed him in town but had chosen the honorable course of waiting until the American could be armed. Shelby asked Crockett if the charge was true. "Partly," Crockett replied, adding that he had meant no harm. Shelby asked coldly how many times he had to say that men who behaved as Crockett had were not fit to ride with him. From the beginning of the war, Shelby had promised to expel any man who survived a duel under his command. To do so in Mexico was tantamount to a death sentence. Yet to allow a duel would be to violate one of his most basic rules. He tried to convey to the young man that he had already had his revenge in the form of two injured Americans. The Mexican was adamant; he wanted blood. Would Crockett fight?

"Willingly," Crockett said, reaching for his gun belt. No, the Mexican said: knives, not pistols. Crockett agreed, though it should have been up to him to choose the weapons, as the other man had challenged. Crockett was an accomplished brawler, though usually with his fists, not knives. He was also still recovering from the last of three wounds he had received during the war, a bullet in the calf of his right leg, and he was half-drunk.

A circle formed around the combatants. A dozen men held torches, the flames dancing in the night wind. The fight was quick and short, a chiaroscuro of shapes and shadows by the light of the ascending moon and the torches. The Mexican youth was lithe and poised, darting forward and back with incredible rapidity as he sought an opening. He struck at Crockett's heart. The American threw up his left arm and took the knife in his shoulder, buried to the hilt. But with his right hand he found the Mexican's heart. The boy was dead before he hit the ground.

Shelby was sickened. Four years of war, of comradeship and sacrifice, had come to this, a Roman circus of gladiators surrounded by spectators cheering them on to their glorious deaths. All his efforts to keep from rousing the Mexicans to action against him had come to nothing. His decision to allow the duel to go forth would poison any possibility of rapprochement with the Mexicans. It remained to be seen whether his earlier decision in Piedras Negras to sell his artillery to Viesca would have a similar effect on the French.

SEVEN

Shelby Reaches Monterrey

Colonel Pierre Jeanningros, commander of the French outpost at Monterrey, was a thirty-year veteran of countless campaigns who had learned the value of patience. Upon learning that a group of Confederate soldiers under a certain Shelby had sold weapons to the Juaristas in Piedras Negras, his junior officers were eager to take a thousand men northward to intercept and destroy the Americans. "Wait awhile," Jeanningros said. First they would catch them, and then they would hang them.

Shelby had learned of the French authorities' displeasure with his actions from the two Austrian deserters who had stayed with him on their way to Texas, but there was no way for him to avoid Monterrey; besides, he needed permission from the French to continue his journey to Mazatlán. He halted his men a mile north of the city and dictated a note to John Edwards that Thomas Reynolds translated into French. John Thrailkill and Rainy McKinney then carried it into the city under a white flag of truce, through the public square to the Palacio Municipal. Admitted without delay to see Jeanningros, they handed over Shelby's note and waited for the response.

"I have the honor," Shelby's note began, "to report that I am within one mile of your fortifications with my command. Preferring exile to surrender, I have left my own country to seek service in that held by His Imperial Majesty, the Emperor Maximilian. Shall it be peace or war between us? If the former, and with your permission, I shall enter your lines at once, claiming at your hands that courtesy due from one soldier to another. If the latter, I propose to attack you immediately. Very respectfully yours, J. O. Shelby."

Jeanningros smiled at the notion that Shelby's two-hundred-odd ragged, half-starved, and badly mauled adventurers would attack two thousand French legionnaires. The American's audacity tickled the tough Frenchman's fancy. "Tell your general to march in immediately," he said to Thrailkill and McKinney in faultless English. "He is the only soldier that has yet come out of Yankeedom."

Jeanningros himself was a soldier of extraordinary ability who understood how fickle the fortunes of war could be. He had arrived with the first elements of the French army in Veracruz in March 1862. Two months later, on May 5, a ragtag and undermanned Mexican band of defenders in the mountain city of Puebla repelled a French assault and sent six thousand soldiers of Europe's finest army reeling back toward the coast. The Cinco de Mayo triumph—today celebrated as one of Mexico's most joyous holidays—so invigorated Juárez's Liberals that it took the French another year and more to capture the capital city, only a hundred miles away. Once they finally did overwhelm and occupy Mexico City, in June 1863, they considered the conquest complete. During the next two years, the European expeditionary force had gradually extended and solidified its hold on large sections of Mexico.

At this time it appeared as if the grand ambitions of Napoléon III to rival the first Napoléon, the great Bonaparte, were about to be realized. Although he had nothing of his uncle's military genius, the younger Napoléon did enjoy the advantage of an extended liberal education in many countries. He was born Louis-Napoléon in 1808, in Holland, which was at the time ruled by his father, Bonaparte's brother. Educated in Germany and Switzerland, he spoke French with a German accent—a foreigner, in effect, like his Corsican uncle.

In his twenties, Louis-Napoléon was exiled from France for political activism, taking up liberal causes such as Italian unification, and he lived for long periods in New York and London. Following the revolution of 1848, he exploited France's continuing fascination with the legacy of his famous uncle, who had initially, at least, brought order out of chaos, and was elected president. In 1851, denied a second term in office by the constitution, he staged a coup and had himself declared Napoléon III, the leader of the new Second Empire. (Napoléon II, the first Napoléon's only son, died in 1832, too young, at twenty-one, to leave his mark on history.)

Obsessed with a vision of reconstituting abroad a facsimile of the first Napoléon's grand empire, Napoléon III set out on a series of international adventures in the 1850s and 1860s. He sided successfully with the English in the Crimean War, won control over Algeria and much of western and central Africa, established French rule in what was called Cochin China—later South Vietnam—and participated in the Opium Wars that opened China to Western trade. But his greatest and most ambitious gamble was the one he undertook in Mexico—the one that would become known as his very own Waterloo.

Napoléon III's "Grand Scheme" involved not just Mexico but Central and South America. The corrupt and decadent Spanish-American republics were to be "regenerated" into monarchies. Along with Brazil, and under the guidance of France, the Latin race, as Napoléon III conceived of it, would outstrip the combined political power of England and the United States. Paris would be recognized as the cultural hub of the world, and Rome as its religious center—a prospect that entranced the religious conservatives in Mexico and won their strong support for Napoléon III's ambitions.

A *New York Times* article in 1863, which was based on a French pamphlet known to reflect the emperor's views, revealed that Napoléon fully intended to recognize the Confederacy as an independent nation. On one level, he was engaged, in the words of the historians Alfred and Kathryn Hanna, in the most "sinister project" ever to challenge the Monroe Doctrine. On an even deeper level, he hoped to "consecrate the final separation and secession of those states from the American Union." The sentimental affection that many in the United States had for France based on its aid during the American Revolution mattered not at all to the emperor; nor did the fact that the United States had given him shelter in New York as an exile for four years. His deepest conviction was that the first Napoléon had erred greatly in selling the Louisiana Territory to the Americans in 1803; by so doing, he had created what his nephew termed a "political Frankenstein," a monster whose democratic example and economic power now threatened to destroy not only France but the idea of monarchy throughout Europe. French imperial triumph in Mexico would make amends for creating that monster, and its support of the Confederacy would contribute to rending the arrogant United States into two lesser halves.

And the Monroe Doctrine, which forbade European interference in American affairs and those of its neighbors? That was "nothing more or less than a policy of insurance against civilization," represented by "the regeneration of the Latins" that the French intended to bring to Mexico. Napoléon III believed that "the Confederate States will be our allies, and will guarantee us against attack by the North." If the North were to win, thousands of Yankee adventurers "would simply fling themselves into Mexico, and all that we have gone so far to secure would be lost" to them. If the South were to win, on the other hand, Napoléon could realize his greatest goal: to reshape "the Union, Confederacy, and Mexico into geographic divisions forming a confederation similar to that of the German states."

For all of Napoléon's talk about establishing an exalted civilization in the New World, he revealed in an 1862 letter that money, or commerce, was his primary motive. The United States, if unhindered, would become "the sole dispenser of the products of the New World. Mistress of Mexico, and consequently of Central America and of the passage between the two seas, there would be henceforth no other power in America than the United States." A Mexico made strong "by the arms of France," however, would be an "insuperable barrier" to American expansion. French influence would then "radiate northward as well as southward," creating "immense markets for our commerce" and guaranteeing "the materials indispensable to our industry."

Napoléon's instrument of conquest and rule in Mexico was Archduke Maximilian of Austria, an ambitious young man who felt stifled by his domineering brother, Franz Josef, and unlikely ever to achieve a position of real power within the Austro-Hungarian empire. Two years of complicated maneuvering over paying the costs of his new Mexican empire and dividing its spoils were concluded in April 1864 when Napoléon and Maximilian signed the Treaty of Miramar.

Most objective observers thought Napoléon had hoodwinked the young archduke. He would get most of the immediate profits generated by the conquest, in return for agreeing to keep twenty thousand French troops in Mexico for at least three years. Eight thousand of those would be foreign legionnaires, who would stay as long as Maximilian needed their protection. But Maximilian had to pay the costs of the French troops. Moreover, his brother, Franz Josef, insisted that he sign away any rights to succession to the throne in Vienna. If Maximilian failed in Mexico, he would have nothing to come home to in Austria other than life as a useless dilettante.

Napoléon initially kept his part of the bargain, preparing the way for Maximilian's safe arrival in Mexico from Trieste in May 1864. French forces eventually numbered about thirty thousand. There were three regiments of Zouaves, five regular infantry regiments, and two regiments of Chasseurs d'Afrique, colonials from North Africa—light cavalry called "Cazadores de Caballo" in Maximilian's dispatches. Augmenting these troops were various artillery units, engineers, military police, and reconnaissance troops. A battalion of Egyptian soldiers, including many Negroes, was added later, on the assumption they would be better able to handle the tropical climate.

The Austrians and Hungarians were also represented by an elite force of seven thousand men: three infantry battalions, one regiment of Uhlan lancers, and one regiment of Hungarian hussars, as well as artillerists, engineers, and even a military band. Finally, there was the Belgian contribution: Maximilian's young wife, Charlotte, was the daughter of King Leopold of Belgium, who, despite his doubts about the whole enterprise, sent two thousand of his troops to serve in Mexico. All of these forces were eventually gathered under the command of the highly competent Marshal Achille-François Bazaine.

At the time of Maximilian's grand entry into Mexico City, in June 1864, Bazaine controlled a third of Mexico, an area about the size of France—though a British diplomat noted drily that large parts of these regions were virtually deserted: "possibly inhabited by two Indians and a monkey." In the northeast, which was more populous, the emperor's control extended two hundred miles east of Monterrey to

Matamoros, just across the Rio Grande from Brownsville, Texas. The Juaristas, unable to stand up to the French in open battle, fought as guerrillas, attacking army outposts and towns that had acknowledged French authority, then fleeing into the hills. Juárez himself had retreated northward along the same route of march that Shelby would finally follow to Mexico City, from San Luis Potosí to Monterrey to the Texas border.

Confederate agents operating in London and Paris from the beginning of the Civil War were encouraged by events in Mexico. The British, like the French, wanted to see the United States hobbled and were actively sympathetic to the Confederacy well into the war. Tangible evidence of British support was unmistakable in British Honduras, on the Yucatán peninsula, where the port of Belize allowed Confederates to break the Union blockade for the first two years of the war.

Early in 1864, before Maximilian's departure from Trieste, Jefferson Davis had sent General William B. Preston to Mexico with a plan to stir up trouble between Union forces on the Rio Grande and the French army in Mexico. The result, Davis hoped, would be war between the two nations. Additionally, once Maximilian was in power, Davis hoped the French and the Confederates could raid the gold cargoes coming out of California and sailing along the coast of Mexico en route, via Cape Horn, to the East Coast. It was claimed that these cargoes would contribute $40 million a year to Maximilian's treasury, and at least that much to Richmond's.

Preston's plan came to naught, largely because Lincoln and Seward managed to convince Maximilian that the Union might, after all, recognize him—but only if he, in turn, refused to recognize the Confederacy. But the mutual sympathy between Maximilian and the Confederates remained in place nonetheless.

Unfortunately for the ambitions of both Napoléon III and Jefferson Davis, the French army's triumph over Juárez's army in June 1863 virtually coincided with the Confederate defeats in July at Vicksburg and Gettysburg. Eventual Union victory now appeared certain in London and Paris, a year before Maximilian arrived to claim his throne in Mexico. The French foreign minister hastily assured Washington that Maximilian would not be heading a puppet government ruled from

Paris, saying "the strings would be too long to work." One American suspected that Napoléon was already wondering how he might dislodge "that incubus of Mexico off his shoulders." A European observer thought a different part of Napoléon's anatomy was threatened—he was sitting on the sharp end of a bayonet. And in France, liberals who had opposed the Mexican adventure from the outset warned of the mortal danger of Prussian aggression against France itself—this while Napoléon had a large part of his army in Mexico, plus another twenty thousand men in Italy and forty thousand in Algeria. Small wonder, then, that Napoléon's support for Maximilian was fast eroding, even as the American Civil War drew to its conclusion, freeing the Americans to cause what mischief they could for the French in Mexico.

In January 1865, Preston Blair's scheme to mount a joint invasion of Mexico with Confederate troops to oust the French was soon scotched. But after Lincoln's death, the border started boiling with plots hatched by various Union generals, including Ulysses S. Grant, John Schofield, and Philip Sheridan. The most tangible affront to the French came in the form of Sheridan's taking thirty thousand muskets from the federal arsenal in Baton Rouge and leaving them unguarded for the Juaristas to "steal" in Brownsville. At about the same time, on June 16, 1865, Grant asked Secretary of State Seward to send "one of our general officers for the purpose of going to Mexico to give direction to such immigration as may go to that country," as well as permission to sell arms openly to the Juaristas. Seward refused. When Sheridan pressed for permission to cross the border in pursuit of Shelby and to confront the French, Seward refused again, fearing that to do so would cause the French to declare war on the United States.

Then Grant startled Washington with a revised version of Preston Blair's plan. He wanted to put his wartime western theater commander John Schofield in charge of an army of two divisions. One would be commanded by Frank Blair—as Preston Blair had suggested—and the other by former Confederate general Joseph E. Johnston. The army of forty thousand armed immigrants would be capable not only of expelling the French but of taking over all of Mexico for the United States.

Seward was appalled by Grant's idea, but he had to proceed with caution against the popular general. He flattered the eager Schofield, whom he regarded as an intellectual lightweight, by inviting him to his summer house at Cape May, New Jersey. He had in mind a special mission to Paris, Seward said, that only a man as subtle, clever, and trusted as Schofield could undertake: "I want you to get your legs under Napoleon's mahogany, and tell him he must get out of Mexico." Once in Paris, the hapless Schofield had to wait for weeks before he saw Napoléon, who evaded any commitment—long enough for the air to go out of Grant's invasion balloon. Grant was furious that Seward had killed his plan and complained that nothing good would happen in Mexico as long as Seward was secretary of state.

Grant's own motivation remains obscure; perhaps he wanted to finish the job he had started as a young officer during the Mexican War of 1846. He may also have been afflicted with the same demons that drove Shelby and so many other Confederates to continue their struggle. One of his biographers suggests that Grant was impelled not so much by further military conquest as by a simple inability to "let go of war" because without it he had "no life to lead." Whatever the truth of that may be, Seward's decision to be patient and allow the French to save their honor and pull out on their own terms would be fully justified.

Much of this scheming was known to Marshal Bazaine from French intelligence agents in Washington and Paris. Colonel Jeanningros was thus well informed of American plots, even before he began to hear rumors and stories from the steady stream of exiled Confederates who had preceded Shelby to Monterrey. Some of those men had already gone on to Mexico City, but others remained. Truth be told, it was probably less Shelby's audacious note to Jeanningros that saved him than the intercession of three old comrades whom he had protected earlier in his journey: Edmund Kirby Smith, Thomas Hindman, and John Magruder had arrived in Monterrey just a few days before Shelby.

Still others had already arrived and departed, their stories rivaling Shelby's for adventure. Among these was the tale of Alexander Watkins Terrell, a Texas attorney and politician who had been promoted by Kirby Smith to brigadier general in the last days of the war. Terrell persuaded Texas governor Pendleton Murrah to give him a letter of introduction to Maximilian. With a dozen other former officers and men, he crossed the Rio Grande at Roma, between Laredo and Brownsville. Their crossing was several days earlier than Shelby's, on June 25, 1865, and considerably more difficult. The river was flowing too swiftly and was too cold for the horses and mules, and the men feared the animals would cramp and drown if they tried to swim it. Spying a raft on the other side that was large enough to carry horses, Terrell and the others stripped and swam across to retrieve it. As they loaded the last mules for the third and final trip across the river, a lookout warned Terrell that one of Sheridan's cavalry units was approaching. They made it across just as they began to hear bullets whizzing past their ears.

A few miles south of the border a new danger presented itself. A party of thirty men, a "rough looking set of scoundrels," in Terrell's words, stopped the group and ordered them to give up their guns. The leader identified himself as General Juan Nepomuceno Cortina, in the service of his excellency Benito Juárez. Terrell knew the name. Long famous as the "Red Robber of the Rio Grande," Cortina was, according to the Texas historian J. Frank Dobie, "the most daring as well as the most elusive Mexican bandit" in the region. Terrell drew his men up in a circle. Each had a rifle and two Colt revolvers at the ready. Terrell said he would surrender his weapons at the nearby Mexican army post in Mier, but not to Cortina. Unwilling to risk a shoot-out, Cortina escorted the Americans to Mier and rode on to seek less combative prey.

Mier was not much of a haven, as Terrell knew. It was notorious as the site of an 1842 massacre of Texans who had ventured too far below the border. The natives there were hardly more friendly to this new crew of Texans than Cortina was, but Terrell's spirits lifted when a man called out his name and "threw himself in true Mexican style on my bosom, calling me his 'amigo.'" Their savior was Narcisco Leal, who had worked as an interpreter for Terrell when he was a judge in San Antonio before the war. Leal assured the townspeople that the Americans had come as guests, not invaders, and should receive the hospitality of the "magnanimous Mexican nation." It was agreed, after much discussion, that the visitors should allow their weapons to be stored for the night in the city hall. They could have them back in the morning, after a good night's sleep in the stone barracks on the town square, and be on their way.

The Texans slept badly in the barracks—the men who were murdered in 1842 had been held in these very rooms. Terrell and the others had been boys then, but their families had known the victims. They rued their decision to surrender their arms; Leal could be trusted, but Cortina might come back at any time. After midnight, by the bright light of a full moon, the men made their way quietly to the city hall. It took only a few minutes to break in and retrieve their weapons. Their horses and mules were safe in a corral next to the barracks, behind which was an arroyo. Shielding their horses' and mules' heads with their coats to keep them quiet, and muffling their hooves with rags, the men stole silently through the arroyo. Once safely away, they put the spurs to their horses and ran for their lives. At dawn they felt secure enough to shoot a few rabbits for breakfast; a week later they were enjoying the hospitality of Colonel Jeanningros at Monterrey; and in late August, General Terrell was volunteering his services to the emperor Maximilian.

Good luck played a role in Terrell's survival, as it did in Shelby's. Bad luck of the worst kind befell General Mosby Parsons, a friend of Shelby's from Jefferson City who had been the attorney general of Missouri before the war. For three long years he had been one of Sterling Price's best officers. Hoping to join Shelby in Mexico, he arrived in Piedras Negras a few days too late. Around July 10, 1865, while Shelby's men were recuperating at the Sabinas, Parsons and his friends were caught near Matamoros by none other than General Cortina.

Too few to resist Cortina, as Terrell had, the Parsons group had allowed themselves to be disarmed by what they thought was a legitimate military unit. Four of the five were then shot down in cold blood, not all at once but one by one, in order to prolong the agony and let those who remained anticipate what was coming to them. The fifth, General Parsons, was at first treated differently, according to John Edwards: "Clad in the showy and attractive uniform of a Confederate major general, having the golden stars of his rank upon his collar, magnificently mounted, and being withal a remarkably handsome" soldier, Parsons seemed likely to bring a good ransom from the Yankees in Brownsville. However, riding back toward Matamoros, Parsons challenged his captors to a horse race. He won, and escaped as he had planned, but was soon recaptured. His stripped and bullet-ridden body was subsequently found in a ditch by a French patrol.

Shelby and the others, especially Sterling Price, vowed revenge when they heard this story in Monterrey, but Jeanningros warned them to wait until they could attack in force. He had seen many wars, from North Africa to the Crimea to China, and this guerrilla insurrection was one of the ugliest. Stories about Mexican brutality and fatalism on both sides—for and against the emperor—were legion, and later collected by Jack Autrey Dabbs in his book *The French Army in Mexico, 1861–1867.*

There was, for example, the incident involving the imperialist general Lozada. A full-blooded Indian, Lozada had lived as a poor farmer until the Mexican government tried to force him to join the army in 1850. When he fled to the countryside, the police whipped his mother in retaliation. Lozada became a bandit. After capturing the man who had abused his mother, he slashed his feet and made him walk over hot coals before hanging him for the buzzards to eat.

When the French arrived, Lozada volunteered his services and his band of outlaws. For most of his men—those recently recruited by the French, not his tried and true *bandidos*—Lozada had neither regard nor affection. Once, when he was attacking the Juarist guerrilla Gutierrez's well-entrenched five-hundred-man force, he ordered thirty of his soldiers to make a suicidal frontal charge. Asked why by the French, he responded that they were bad soldiers and this was the easiest way to rid himself of them. The result was as expected, as a French officer recalled: "All the bodies were naked, and had their eyes eaten out by the birds, and they bore signs of mutilations impossible to describe. Those who were hanging too near the ground had their legs and insides eaten away by the foxes. . . . The soldiers promised to give no quarter to the Gutierrez band if we ever met up with it."

The atrocities of Gutierrez, Cortina, and others like them, along with the questionable nature of their own Mexican allies, drove the

French high command to demand carte blanche in the form of retaliatory measures. On November 3, 1864, Maximilian issued a draconian decree virtually condemning all captured Juaristas to death. Henceforth, the law said, "all the armed bands that still rove some parts of our beautiful country . . . should be considered *cuadrillos de bandidos* and fall consequently under the inflexible and inexorable severity of the Law. We order all officials, magistrates, and military leaders of the Nation to pursue them with all their forces, to annihilation."

Bazaine issued a tongue-in-cheek warning to his officers, saying, "Do not have any summary executions. You have a court-martial at your disposal; it is always available to you, and in all cases have it pronounce the sentence, and it will save your responsibility." But all this meant was a twelve- or twenty-four-hour delay in carrying out the sentences. Scores of captured prisoners were shot after drumhead trials. Juárez himself was subject to execution if he was caught, though the emperor insisted that he be notified before any such action was taken. The Juaristas responded in kind, murdering French soldiers out of hand.

Ernst Pitner, a young Austrian lieutenant, wrote candid letters home explaining in practical terms how the enemy was sometimes dispatched. He had heard that in one instance some four hundred men were captured and shot, "which is truly fortunate." As for the enemy's practice of attacking isolated detachments of the emperor's forces, the solution was "to leave the fellows undisturbed so long that they feel safe in some place or other and then to surround them completely, catch them and string them up. In this way one rids oneself of this rabble most easily and with the least bloodshed." Another effective technique was to visit villages that announced their republican or Liberal allegiance. This "problem" was usually resolved "quite peacefully by the installation of new village chiefs, the arrest or shooting of a few people and the demolition of one or two houses whose occupants have gone over to the enemy."

At the more remote army outposts, the men and tactics employed by the French were brutal in the extreme. At Monterrey, Colonel François Achille Dupin commanded the contre-guerrilla regiment, authorized by Bazaine to track down and exterminate the guerrillas.

Dupin at this time was sixty years old, "straight as a rapier," according to John Edwards, "with a seat in the saddle like an English guardsman, and a waist like a woman's." His beard and hair were snowy white and framed a lined, deeply tanned face. Decorations for bravery and battle citations gleamed on his broad chest. Those decorations had been stripped from him some years before, in 1861, for looting the Chinese emperor's palace. Caught "staggering under the weight of rubies and pearls and diamonds," Dupin protested during his trial that he could have taken much more: "By God, I am astonished at my own moderation!"

Dupin had been reinstated and his medals returned by Napoléon III when his services were needed in Mexico. In describing the man's predatory nature, the literary John Edwards summoned up a passage from Victor Hugo's novel *Toilers of the Sea* that alludes to a piece of silk stolen from the Chinese emperor. The scarf perfectly reflected Dupin's philosophy, showing "a shark eating a crocodile, who is eating a serpent, who is devouring an eagle, who is preying on a swallow, who is in his turn eating a caterpillar. All nature which is under our observation is thus alternately devouring and devoured. They prey, prey on each other."

Less poetically, Dupin was notorious for his policy of amputation. "When you kill a Mexican," he said, "that is the end of him. When you cut off an arm or a leg, that throws him upon the charity of his friends, and then two or three must support him. Those who make corn cannot make soldiers. It is economy to amputate." The result of Dupin's policy was a legion of maimed men throughout northeastern Mexico, and his designation by the Juaristas as "the tiger of the tropics."

Jeanningros, who had been wounded thirteen times during his career, was as battle-scarred as Dupin. But he was a smoother, more polished man—"one of the handsomest soldiers in France," as *The New York Times* would note in 1881, after he had become a renowned lieutenant general. He began his military career as a common soldier, rising from corporal to captain of a Zouave regiment in Algeria to his present assignment, commanding a foreign legion regiment on the outpost of an empire. Four battalions of the Second and Third Zouave regiments were in Mexico, one of them stationed at Monterrey.

The Zouaves' distinctive North African uniforms—including a fez and turban, huge baggy trousers, leggings, a vest, and a short cutaway jacket, all in bright blues and reds—were familiar to some of the Confederates who had seen variations of them worn by Union troops from Pennsylvania and Illinois. The Zouaves were renowned for their bravery on the field and their insubordination off of it, both admirable qualities in the eyes of Shelby's men. Most were French citizens from North Africa and spoke no English, though some of the legionnaires did.

The former Confederates were shown what there was to see of Monterrey by the French soldiers. The old cathedral, severely damaged during the war of 1846 by the Americans when it was used as a powder magazine, had been restored and was worth a visit, as were the hot springs north of the city where a daughter of Montezuma had bathed. Some of the men explored the Garcia Caves while others made their way to the top of a fine waterfall from the mesa overlooking the city. But most of their time was spent carousing and trading war stories with their new compatriots.

The most compelling of these tales was that of the one-handed hero of Camerone. It happened during the lengthy French attack on the city of Puebla in the spring of 1863, almost exactly a year since the Cinco de Mayo disaster there. The French commander at the time, General Élie-Frédéric Forey, ordered Jeanningros to protect the supply lines between Veracruz and Puebla. On April 29, Jeanningros sent a company to convoy a caravan carrying munitions and a fortune in gold, to be used for paying the troops in Puebla. The company had been riddled by disease; its strength was reduced to only sixty-two men, and its four officers were all volunteers from other units. The officer in command, Captain Jean Danjou, was nevertheless confident that his legionnaires could handle anything the Mexicans might throw at them.

Captain Danjou was normally a staff officer; having lost a hand earlier in his career, he was regarded with special affection by his men for his dash and for his wooden hand, which he had designed and wore encased in a white glove. On the morning of April 30, 1863, the legionnaires had passed through the ruins of a village called Camerone when they spied what turned out to be 800 Mexican cavalry on the ridge above them. Beyond the ridge, though they could not yet know

Wedding picture of Jo Shelby
(1830–1897), 1858. "He was
the finest looking man I ever
saw, black hair and handsome
features," an acquaintance recalled.
State Historical Society of Missouri

Wedding picture of Elizabeth
"Betty" Shelby (1841–1929),
eleven years younger than her husband, when she was seventeen. She
joined her husband in Mexico and
ultimately bore him eight children.
State Historical Society of Missouri

Frank Blair (1821–1875), Shelby's childhood tutor and lifelong friend, despite their taking opposite sides during the Civil War. Blair became a Union general and close Lincoln advisor who told Shelby in early 1865 that Lincoln would not object to his going to Mexico.
Battles and Leaders of the Civil War, **vol. 1**

John N. Edwards (1838–1889) wrote two books about Shelby's life and adventures, most of which he observed firsthand. A prominent newspaperman after the war, he disagreed openly with Shelby's later admission that the southern cause had been blighted by slavery.
John N. Edwards: Biography, Memoirs, Reminiscences and Recollections, **1872**

Painting of General Jo Shelby, attributed to Caleb Bingham, c. 1864.
State Historical Society of Missouri

Ben Elliott (1820–1911), Shelby's "Iron Colonel," went with him to Mexico and stayed there for more than ten years as a farmer.

Virginia Military Institute Archives

Lt. Gen. Edmund Kirby Smith, CSA (1824–1893), the last commander of the Trans-Mississippi Department. Shelby demanded his resignation in April 1865 for being willing to surrender to the Union, but later saw to his safe crossing into Mexico.

Civil War Battles, courtesy of civil-war.net

Lt. Gen. Sterling Price, CSA (1809–1867), Shelby's senior officer during the latter part of the war, and leader of the Carlota colony in Mexico. Shelby saved Price's army from destruction at Westport but despised him as an incompetent blowhard.

Library of Congress

Maj. Gen. John B. Magruder, CSA (1807–1871). Known as Prince John for his regal bearing, he met Shelby in San Antonio and traveled with him to Mexico. Maximilian subsequently appointed Magruder to a government position to encourage Confederate emigration to Mexico. **Library of Congress**

Maximilian (1832–1867), seen here with his young wife, Carlota (1840–1927), was emperor of Mexico from 1864 until his execution by Benito Juárez in 1867. Both were sympathetic to the Confederate cause and receptive to Shelby's presence in Mexico, though Maximilian declined to use him as a soldier. **Huntington Library**

Matthew Fontaine Maury (1806–1873), Confederate loyalist and oceanographer known as the Pathfinder of the Seas. Maury persuaded Maximilian to create an immigration bureau, which he then headed, and hoped to found a "New Virginia" colony in Mexico. *Journal of American History*, vol. IV, 1910

Benito Juárez (1806–1872).
A full-blooded Zapotec Indian,
Juárez is revered today in Mexico as
the founder of the modern state and
for his resistance to French occupation.
Although frequently compared to
Lincoln as a man of the people, he was
more ruthless. He denied worldwide
requests for clemency for Maximilian,
considering his execution a necessity
for the country's defiled honor.

General Philip Sheridan (1831–
1888), famed Union cavalry leader
to whom Shelby was often
compared. Sheridan was convinced
that the Confederates were hoping
to prolong their rebellion in Mexico
in collusion with the French. In
1882, over dinner and drinks
together in New York, Sheridan
told Shelby that his failing to
stop Shelby from going into
Mexico was "was one of my
bitterest disappointments."
National Archives

Alonzo Slayback (1834–1882). A key Shelby officer, in the Rio Grande Slayback wrote a long poem based on his own experience, "The Burial of Shelby's Flag," that became famous in the South. He later gave the Emperor Maximilian English lessons and was dubbed "The Knight of Oaxaca." He died relatively young, shot by the editor of the *St. Louis Post-Dispatch* in a dispute over Southern honor.
Deanna Adams Holm

Frank James (1843–1915), some years after the time of his trial for murder in 1883. Frank James once saved Shelby from capture during the war. Shelby gave him and his brother Jesse haven when they were on the run in the 1870s as bank robbers, and he testified as a character witness in Frank James's trial. The absence of a statue to Shelby (until 2009) is said to be the consequence of his support of the James brothers.
Jesse James Farm and Museum, Kearney, Missouri

Jo Shelby, a few years before he
was appointed U.S. Marshal
for Western Missouri in 1893.
Library of Congress

A life-size bronze statue of General Jo Shelby on horseback was dedicated in his
adopted hometown of Waverly, Missouri, in 2009. It was delayed for one year because
the sculptor had to finish a statue of Martin Luther King—an irony that Shelby, who
late in life said that "John Brown was right," might have appreciated.
Sherry Hardage

this, were another 1,200 militiamen on foot. The legionnaires retreated into the ruins of Camerone, losing sixteen men in the process, only to come under fire there as well.

Captain Danjou and his remaining men took cover behind a crumbling wall, where they repulsed a cavalry charge but had to watch helplessly as their mules, carrying their ammunition, were driven into the enemy camp. An hour later the Mexican colonel in command called for the legionnaires to surrender, promising that they would be treated honorably. They were surrounded and outnumbered by more than fifty to one, the colonel said. Danjou responded by reciting legion doctrine, "We'll die before we surrender."

In late afternoon, Danjou was cut down by a sniper as he reassured his men that help was on the way. An hour later, just one officer, Lieutenant Maudet, remained alive, along with five soldiers: one French, one German, one Polish, one Austrian, and one Swiss, nearly a perfect miniature cross section of the legion. Maudet ordered the men to reload, to fire on his command, and then to follow him through the breach in their wall: "We'll end this with our bayonets." As Maudet's men charged headlong into certain death, the Mexican colonel struck his own men with the flat of his sword to save the brave few surviving legionnaires.

Twelve hours later the relief that Danjou had promised arrived, led by Jeanningros and a column of lancers. Danjou's body could not be found, but his wooden hand, within the white glove now covered with blood, was. Jeanningros carried it back to Veracruz with him; from there it was sent to legion headquarters at Sidi Bel Abbès, in Algeria, where it would become, according to the historian Richard O'Connor, "the legion's most sacred relic, the stark symbol of one of its most gallant actions."

Though indisputably brave, legionnaires were not allowed to serve in France itself, where they were regarded as *canaille*—trash swept up from the leavings of foreign armies, criminals on the run, and adventurers seeking their fortunes. Marshal Bazaine, their commander, thought more than a few were opportunists who would desert their posts when they could: "It is quite clear that a good many of them enrolled in the corps to get a free trip, but it will cost them dearly if they are caught." The problem of desertion was especially common,

Bazaine said, in the region around Saltillo, near Monterrey, "where chances of escaping were good."

In Monterrey, Colonel Jeanningros enforced Bazaine's order to shoot all deserters without hesitation. "There was a ghastly wall in Monterrey," according to Edwards, against which many men had faced a firing squad. Jeanningros even declined to spare a young lieutenant who had fled "in a moment of temporary insanity" inspired by drinking absinthe. The lieutenant had reached the Rio Grande, then returned to take his punishment, saying he was a Frenchman and he knew how to die. He asked only one favor. If he was executed, his mother would lose her benefits; if he killed himself, she would keep them. He asked Jeanningros to provide him with a pistol and a bottle of brandy in his cell. This request was granted. Informed the following morning that the prisoner had blown out his brains, Jeanningros remarked that the act was precipitous: "He was entitled to two bottles, instead of one."

A more pleasing aspect of Jeanningros's character was his graciousness as a host. Like Kirby Smith's Trans-Mississippi Department headquarters in Shreveport, Jeanningros's did not lack for good food and fine wine, brought from France at enormous expense. He shared these liberally with his guests at a banquet the night of Shelby's arrival. John Edwards did not describe the mood of the guests he named—Kirby Smith, Price, Reynolds, and Hindman, among others—but it cannot have been festive. The tuberculosis that afflicted Governor Murrah had let him live just long enough to reach Monterrey; his recent death there cast a pall, as did the news of General Parsons's murder. Kirby Smith was bitter and glum. Despite Shelby's generous homage in San Antonio, he wrote to his wife that he was upset about "Confederate censorians, fault finding & dissatisfied," all of them—including his dinner companions?—full of "criminations & selfishness."

Shelby preferred to look forward rather than back. During that dinner and over the course of the next few days, he absorbed all that Jeanningros had to tell him about Napoléon III, about American schemes along the border, about the challenges presented by the Juaristas, and about the enigmatic Maximilian. According to Edwards,

Jeanningros was less than enthusiastic about "the Austrian." Shelby would have to see him to understand. He was "more of a scholar than a king. Good at botany, a poet on occasion, a traveler who gathers curiosities and writes books. A saint over his wine and a sinner among his cigars." He was deeply in love with his young Charlotte—now called Carlota—and an "honest, tender-hearted and sincere" man.

Maximilian felt he had a calling, Jeanningros said. He was possessed of a generous certainty that he could make the lives of his subjects better, and that they would love him for doing so. But he lacked the essential qualities of a ruler—strength, guile, suspicion; an understanding of diplomacy; and, most of all, ruthlessness: "He cannot kill as we Frenchmen do. In a nation of thieves and cut-throats, he goes devoutly to mass, endows hospitals, says his prayers and sleeps the sleep of the gentleman and the prince." The emperor's days were numbered, Jeanningros said, most indiscreetly. "All the power of France" could not help him keep his crown on his head, "if, indeed, it can keep that head upon his shoulders."

Shelby offered a bold alternative to the disaster that Jeanningros prophesied was inevitable if the French had to withdraw from Mexico. "Give me a port as a base of operations," he said, "and I can organize an American force capable of keeping Maximilian on his throne." He noted that the French control of the Gulf ports of Tampico and Veracruz was open to challenge by the United States. In the west, however, the U.S. military had few men and ships to hinder Americans who wanted to cross the border. There were two ports where he believed he could establish a presence and draw in supporters— Confederates like himself as well as others who would come for money and land in return for fighting against the Juaristas. One possibility was Guaymas, on the Gulf of California coast, two hundred miles south of the Arizona border; the other was Mazatlán, farther south on the Pacific coast, and four hundred miles southwest of Monterrey—about the same distance as Mexico City. It was to Mazatlán that Shelby hoped to take his band.

Jeanningros told Shelby he had his "full permission to march to the Pacific," contingent upon the approval of Marshal Bazaine. He thought that Bazaine might favor "the employment of American soldiers in the service of the Empire." This was a marked improvement over Jeanningros's earlier threat to hang the American, and Shelby wasted no time in readying his men to leave the following day. Their route would take them first to Saltillo. From there they would cross the Sierra Madre Oriental to the French outpost at Parras, under the command of Colonel Marguerite Jacques Vincent du Preuil. If du Preuil had received the needed confirmation of Jeanningros's permission from Marshal Bazaine, he would allow Shelby to continue on to Mazatlán. They should be able to reach the city in about three weeks. Once there, he could inquire further about volunteering his service to Maximilian—or returning to the United States.

Shelby's grand plans for drawing thousands of American soldiers and settlers were not without precedent. He had as his dinner companion at Monterrey a model of sorts in the former California senator William M. Gwin, one of the most flamboyant adventurers and would-be empire builders of the crowded nineteenth century.

As would happen so often with Shelby, his family in Lexington was well known to Gwin. Born in 1805 in Tennessee, Gwin had graduated from Transylvania University in 1828 with a degree in classics and in medicine. A giant of a man with a craggy face—a young American woman in Mexico City said it looked as if it was "hewn out of a block with an ax"—and a commanding presence, he found politics more to his taste than medicine. He served a term in Congress, representing a district in Mississippi in the early 1840s, then drifted to California's Sierra Nevada gold country in 1849. He struck it rich with a mine in Paloma, not far from Mark Twain's celebrated Angels Camp.

Gwin's future seemed assured after California's admission to the Union in 1850, when he won a seat as the new state's Democratic senator. But Gwin was self-righteous and quarrelsome, alienating much of his party's hierarchy with his support for the South. He even fought a duel with one rival: rifles at thirty paces, with no injuries reported except (fatally) to a grazing donkey. By 1861, he was flirting with the notion of California as an independent republic. Threatened with arrest, he was allowed by President Lincoln to return to his plantation in Mississippi.

When his plantation was destroyed during the war, Gwin took his family to Paris. He met Napoléon III and persuaded him that he could bring thousands of skilled and energetic Americans into Sonora to work the gold and silver mines there. The French emperor agreed to recommend Gwin and his plan to Maximilian, and even to name Gwin the "Duke of Sonora." In April 1865, the ambitious rebel headed directly for Mexico City to make his case in Maximilian's court.

His success appeared imminent, he wrote to his wife, and essential—he feared a "massacre" when the war ended. "It really makes me sick when I think of the bloody agony that awaits the southern people." A Northern victory "made the blood of every southern sympathizer run cold with horror. No one will be safe in our native country. How I thank Providence that I have cast my lot elsewhere." He closed by saying that his "policy is on every man's lips as the only one that will save [Maximilian's] empire."

In June 1865, even as Shelby was heading for Monterrey, *The New Orleans Times* was certain that "Dr. Gwin will get his project through" and that the immigration he envisioned was to be "strictly southern or Confederate. Ten thousand confederates are to be armed and paid by the empire" to protect the immigrants. "Strategical points are to be fortified and garrisoned on the frontier," the article noted, concluding optimistically that "the southerners are elated and golden visions float before them."

Unfortunately for Gwin, the supposedly naïve Maximilian was a better judge of character in this case than his scheming patron in Paris. He had no intention of approving Gwin's plan, not because it seemed impossible but because Gwin might actually be able to pull it off: "I fear him most of all because of his extreme finesse and the great ability which I see in him." Maximilian could understand why Napoléon would be fascinated by Gwin, but added that "he did not fascinate me" enough to support him. If Gwin succeeded in really becoming the Duke of Sonora, Maximilian would have given a foreigner control of one of the richest states in the nation.

Gwin told Shelby that Maximilian had rejected his plan because he was afraid the United States would invade Mexico if it came to pass. Even though both the emperor and his wife were said to be reliably pro-Confederate, Gwin explained, there was little hope of him using any of them, including Shelby, in a military capacity. As for Gwin, he was on his way out of the country forever; he would take a steamer from Matamoros and surrender to the federal authorities in New Orleans when it landed.

Accompanying Gwin would be the elderly General John Clark, who had been so eager to join the fight against the Apaches at the Sabinas. The more he heard about Maximilian's empire, the less he wanted to do with it, Clark decided; better prison at home than this kind of life in Mexico.

EIGHT

"You Will Turn Aside"

I t was with diminished hopes and a smaller group of men that Shelby left Monterrey for Mazatlán in the first week of August 1865. He did not regret the departure of the spirited but feeble General Clark, nor the absence of the querulous Kirby Smith, who had left earlier for Mexico City with a French escort. But he was troubled by the absence of the redoubtable Alonzo Slayback, who had fallen ill on the approach to Monterrey and had to be left behind, with an attending soldier, until he could regain his health and catch up with them.

And he was saddened by Ben Elliott's determination to strike out on his own, ahead of Shelby, for Mazatlán—a decision that they had agreed upon at Eagle Pass. Elliott had been Shelby's best commander, his "iron colonel," in the words of Shelby biographer Deryl Sellmeyer, and a man "whose nerves were steel," according to a comrade in arms. Shelby and Elliott were within months of being the same age, and had been inseparable for the past four years; now Elliott was gone, taking with him about fifty men, leaving Shelby with fewer than two hundred. They would not see each other again for twelve years.

On their third night out of Monterrey, at the suggestion of his traveling companions Thomas Hindman and John Magruder, Shelby made camp on the site of an old ranch called San Juan de la Buena

Vista. It was the site of the February 23, 1847, Battle of Buena Vista, one of the critical battles of the Mexican War, which was said to have created two presidents, Zachary Taylor and Jefferson Davis. Hindman had been stationed there for a few weeks after the battle. Though he had not seen action, he spent days wandering the battlefield and described the campaign clearly now to John Edwards and the other soldiers who were still boys when it happened. But it was the towering Magruder, not the diminutive Hindman, whose presence and stories most enthralled his tough but respectful listeners. It was here, as an artillery officer fighting beside such storied names as James Longstreet, Braxton Bragg, and Jefferson Davis, that Magruder's reputation for pugnacity and dash was first earned.

Born in 1807, Magruder had attended the University of Virginia, where he once dined with Thomas Jefferson and was a friend and classmate of Edgar Allan Poe. He graduated from West Point in 1830, fought in the Seminole War in Florida, and distinguished himself during the Mexican War not only at Buena Vista but while storming the walls of Chapultepec. In 1862, Magruder, now a major general, fooled the overly cautious Union general George McClellan at Yorktown into thinking he was outmanned and allowing a much smaller Confederate force to escape. His greatest achievement during the war was winning the Battle of Galveston on New Year's Day, 1863. From August 1864 to March 1865, Magruder commanded the Department of Arkansas, working closely with Edmund Kirby Smith during the surrender negotiations.

A gifted singer with a fine tenor voice, Magruder had leavened the tedium of army life between campaigns with amateur musical productions. Now fifty-eight years old, he was still a theatrical presence, easily overwhelming young men such as the San Antonio newspaper reporter who had met him at the Menger Hotel with Shelby. Magruder was a strikingly handsome man who "stood six feet four inches in height," wrote the reporter, "and had a form that the men envied and the women adored. His nickname, 'Prince John,' was fully deserved. His nerves were all iron. Foreign travel and comprehensive culture had given him a zest that was always crisp and sparkling. He could fight all day and dance all night. In the morning a glass of brandy and a good cigar renewed his strength." A stickler for appearance, "he loved magnificent uniforms, magnificent horses, magnificent riders, and magnificent women. Gifted and graceful in conversation, he was a pet in the boudoir and a logician in the barracks."

It did not detract from Prince John's appeal that he had a pronounced lisp when he was in his cups. Once, it was said, an enlisted man wandered into an officers banquet and sat down next to the general. Magruder asked him if he knew with whom he was dining. The soldier replied that he was hungry and, while he "used to be particular" about his dining companions, "it don't make a damn of difference now." Amused, Magruder responded, "Your impudenth ith thublime, thir. Keep your theat, thir!"

Magruder may sound to modern readers a bit like George Mac-Donald Fraser's fictional rogue Harry Flashman. Certainly Shelby seems to have regarded him somewhat askance because of his flamboyant personality as well as his advice to Kirby Smith in April and May to capitulate. But there could not have been a better man to explain the tactics, strategy, and personalities that had made the Battle of Buena Vista so important at the time.

The Mexican War had come about as the result of President Polk's expansionist maneuverings around the Mexican border in 1845. On April 23, 1846, the exasperated Mexican government declared war on the United States and sent troops across the Texas border to attack American soldiers. General Zachary Taylor quickly defeated the invaders, then crossed into Mexico and captured Monterrey in September. When Taylor allowed his Mexican prisoners to go home with their weapons, which were essential for protection from marauding Indians, President Polk sought to shut him out of the war. General Winfield Scott in Washington, Taylor's superior, told him to stay put in Monterrey with his army, composed largely of three-month enlistees whose terms were almost up. Scott himself, Taylor's rival and Polk's favorite, would launch the main attack with twenty thousand men at Veracruz, two hundred miles east of Mexico City, in February 1847.

Zachary Taylor was a blustery and impetuous man—not to say insubordinate. He ignored his orders and marched well south of Monterrey, nearly two hundred miles, to Ciudad Victoria. There he received a directive to send the better part of his force to support Scott's effort in Veracruz. Obeying his orders this time, Taylor dispatched the required forces and withdrew northward with the remainder. Meanwhile, a large Mexican army under General Antonio López de Santa Anna was anticipating Scott's invasion. Santa Anna had more than twenty thosuand men, enough to repulse Scott. If Scott could be turned back, the Americans would have to withdraw and negotiate a peace.

Santa Anna, however, committed a fatal blunder. He learned that Taylor's weakened force of fewer than five thousand men was located far from any supply lines. Scott, the real threat, was barely fifty miles east of Santa Anna, but the Mexican general turned north to pursue and destroy what looked like easy prey. This was consistent with Santa Anna's earlier behavior in wiping out the handful of defenders at the Alamo in 1836 and, even more notoriously, massacring several hundred Texans who had surrendered to him at Goliad.

Taylor reached Buena Vista, with Santa Anna in hot pursuit—so hot that the Mexicans covered forty-five miles without food or rest in twenty-four hours. Under Colonel John Wool, Taylor's second in command, the Americans positioned themselves on the mesas above the road and covered the narrow gap between the mountains through which it ran. Wool blocked the road itself with boulders. The American artillery, fifteen guns under John Magruder and Braxton Bragg, bombarded the hapless Mexican infantry with canister and grapeshot, sometimes mixed with stones, from above. When the Mexicans nevertheless almost broke through the American left, Jefferson Davis's Mississippi Rifles appeared on the run, wearing black slouch hats, white duck pants, and red shirts flapping behind them. They joined the Third Indiana, each forming the legs of a V formation. Facing the V and preparing to attack were two thousand Mexican lancers, dressed in blue uniforms with red trim. The brilliant colors clashed and merged as the lancers were raked by the American columns. Though outnumbered four to one, the Americans held there and elsewhere throughout the long day and night.

Now, nearly two decades later, John Edwards looked out at the "sepulchre" of the battlefield under a harvest moon. With the help of Magruder and Hindman's reconstruction of the encounter, he conjured up a mirage of spectral soldiers rising from their graves: "Pale squadrons galloped again through the gloom of the powder-pall; again the deep roar of the artillery lent its mighty voice to swell the thunder of the gathering battle." The brave Mexican lancers charged once again, "falling there in giant windrows" like summer hay before the scythe. Then the mirage vanished, leaving only "the silent and deserted battlefield" and the "droning katydids sighing in the grasses above the graves."

The relevance of that distant battle for Shelby and his men was more than merely sentimental. According to the military historian Geoffrey Perret, Santa Anna's defeat shattered Mexican confidence and assured a relatively easy victory in the south for Winfield Scott. With Taylor's triumph at Buena Vista, all hope that the Mexicans had of foreign aid from Britain and France—which had been expected— vanished. So, too, did their pride and self-respect. In their place rose an aggrieved Mexican nationalism and anti-Americanism that would condition much of the reaction later to the Confederates who appeared on their doorstep.

A guerrilla attack two nights after Buena Vista provided more proof, if any was needed, that Shelby's presence was unwelcome. It happened at the end of one of the frequent mountain thunderstorms that boiled up in the summer afternoons and evenings. Four of Shelby's men were on picket duty when they saw shadows moving among the rocks on the hill above them. They fired, alerting Shelby at the main camp a quarter of a mile away. By the time Shelby and his men reached them, the pickets were involved in knife fights with the attackers, and all four were wounded. The attackers retreated into the rocks, drawing Shelby farther away from the camp—as they had planned, for this attack was only a diversion. The main guerrilla force of about two hundred men had converged on the dozen men who were guarding the horses. More valuable than gold, the horses meant the difference between life and death to the Americans.

When he heard the shots, Shelby yelled "Countermarch!" In the melee that followed, dozens of Mexicans were killed. According to Edwards, only "close, reckless fighting" saved the expedition from destruction. The cost to Shelby was the lives of half a dozen men, with three times that number wounded.

———

It was with considerable relief that Shelby descended from the treacherous mountains into the Coahuila desert the following day. His destination, the small city of Parras, lay like a green gemstone on a sand table display, an oasis of vineyards and fertile farmland fed by deep springs and a meandering stream. Wine had been the town's raison d'être for two hundred years, and the French fort where Jeanningros had told Shelby to report was manned by happy troopers of the Twelfth Regiment of Chasseurs d'Afrique.

Their good humor did not extend to the commander, Colonel Marguerite Jacques Vincent du Preuil, as Shelby soon learned. The colonel, seated at his desk, glanced up as Shelby entered his office, politely removed his hat, and offered to shake hands. The offer was rudely ignored, as the French officer poured himself a glass of brandy from a half-empty bottle. Shelby waited for an invitation to be seated. When none came, he took a chair and said he wished to have permission to march to Mazatlán. Du Preuil responded shortly: "Such permission is impossible. You will turn aside to Mexico City."

Shelby asked the reason for this change of plans. Ben Elliott and his men had been allowed to pass through, he knew. He said that Jeanningros "had no information to this effect when I left him the other day at Monterrey." Du Preuil did not condescend to explain that the order was not of his making, but came directly from Marshal Bazaine. Instead, according to Edwards, the French officer became abusive. He said, "Let the devil fly away with you and your information." Shelby was playing the same old game the Americans always played, "robbing today and killing tomorrow, plundering, always plundering." He said Shelby could not stay in Parras and could not go to Mazatlán, adding, "Whatever you do, you shall obey."

Shelby stood and very deliberately put on his hat. He said that he must have been mistaken in assuming that a French officer would behave like a gentleman. Du Preuil was unworthy of his office, Shelby continued: "You are a slanderer and a coward."

Du Preuil rose and reached for his sword. Shelby unbuttoned the flap of his holster. Both men's aides, including Edwards, flattened themselves against the office walls. Du Preuil pointed to Shelby's hat, and said, "Remove that!" Shelby replied, "To a coward? Never." Du Preuil gasped, ordered Shelby out of his office, and demanded an apology. Shelby left but sent Thomas Reynolds back to discuss the terms of a duel. It was agreed that du Preuil and Shelby would meet at dawn. The weapons would be pistols at ten paces. As the challenged party, the Frenchman could have chosen swords, with which he was an expert. But he gave up his advantage, aware that Shelby's old wound made it impossible for him to hold a sword—a generous gesture on the part of the French colonel, who seems to have been sobered by the events he had put in motion.

A few hours later, providence in the form of Colonel Jeanningros arrived at Parras. Accompanied by four squadrons of Chasseurs, he was inspecting his northern forts. When he learned of the impending duel, he conducted a quick investigation of the argument that prompted it and arrested du Preuil for being drunk on duty. He confirmed that the Parras commander had indeed received orders from Marshal Bazaine directing him to send Shelby home or to Mexico City. But du Preuil's manner in passing along Bazaine's demand had been needlessly offensive. Jeanningros ordered du Preuil to make a "free and frank apology" to the American. To his credit, Edwards said, du Preuil did so "most cordially and frankly, regretting as much as a sober man could the disagreeable and overbearing things he did when he was drunk."

Shelby's fit of temper with du Preuil, justified though it was, suggested the strain he was under. That strain, now that he was forced to turn away from the Pacific Coast for Mexico City, was increasing. It was nearly the middle of August, and they had been on the trail in Mexico for six weeks, under the threat of constant attack. Like Shelby, the men were restive and short-tempered—the discipline and cohesion that the war had imposed on them was continuing to disintegrate. They chafed against Shelby's ban on avenging pursuits of the harassing guerrillas, and some of them violated his edict to stay clear of the local farmers and the occasional large estates—plantations occupied by wealthy hacendados who ruled like the medieval barons in Europe. Better to go hungry, Shelby said, than to raid these for food and stir up more trouble.

On a night in mid-August, about fifty miles north of the next French outpost at Matehuala, Yandell Blackwell and James Wood were on guard duty when a Mexican farmer approached them. Blackwell had already picked up a bit of Spanish and a degree of fondness for Mexicans, despite his wariness for treachery—alone of Shelby's men, he would live in Mexico until he died of old age, in 1911. He encouraged the farmer to join them by their campfire; it was a way of gathering intelligence about the country through which they were passing.

The farmer said the Americans should know about the wealthy hacienda they would pass by the following afternoon. A walled and fortified grand mansion, almost a palace, it was called La Encarnación. The ruler of this little kingdom, Luis Enrico Rodríguez, was a terrible tyrant, a thief and murderer, "the devil" in charge of the local robber bands that terrorized the countryside. He claimed to be a Spanish-born aristocrat, the farmer said, and he possessed the rapacious cruelty of the old conquistadors. The farmer was but one of many who had been turned into a virtual slave by Rodríguez.

Blackwell supposed the farmer was asking for the Americans to help him capture the bandit chief—something the redoubtable Dupin, with all his ruthless contre-guerrillas, had been unable to do—and said he was sorry but they could not help him. Not even, the farmer said, if there were an American woman being held prisoner by this villain?

Their curiosity piqued, Blackwell and Wood listened transfixed by the farmer's story, which reminded them of the old fairy tale of Bluebeard. The woman's name was Inez Walker. She was the daughter of an American prospector who had married an Indian woman in Sonora. The prospector had found enough gold to retire to Guaymas and to send his daughter to be educated in San Francisco. By the time she returned, Inez was a beautiful young woman who spoke only English. She was *muy rubia*—yellow haired, like her father, but with skin that had the shining copper hue of her mother. Her manners were refined, her accomplishments in drawing and music those of a young lady who would have been equally comfortable in the best circles of London, Paris, or New York.

Rodríguez happened to meet Inez while on a visit to Guaymas after her return from San Francisco. He was smitten. Rich and well-bred, at least by his lights, he adopted the pose of a courtly lover to humbly ask Walker for his daughter's hand in marriage. Walker turned the presumptuous bandit out of his house. Rodríguez, for his part, regarded Walker as little more than a lucky gringo peasant who had insulted him. He "determined upon abduction, a common Mexican custom," in the words of John Edwards. He kidnapped Inez and fled with her toward Encarnación. Walker pursued Rodríguez like an avenging angel, but was soon a dead man—ambushed and left unburied in the desert as carrion for the coyotes and vultures.

For the next twenty years Inez was held prisoner by Rodríguez. Powerless to escape or to resist him, she was a figure of pathos to the farmers and villagers who occasionally saw her riding in her black veil, in perpetual mourning for her father. Now she had a chance for freedom, if the Americans would help.

As Shelby's biographer Daniel O'Flaherty perceptively notes, there was no chance that Blackwell and Wood would refuse such a romantic quest: "They were not two shaggy borderers in butternut"; they were "Galahads about to rescue a lady fair, with all the splendid dash of medieval chivalry." As the brigade moved south the next day and camped within a mile of La Encarnación, the two men quietly recruited about twenty others for a rescue raid, swearing them to secrecy lest Shelby find out what they were up to.

At midnight, they gathered atop a hill overlooking the hacienda. There was no moon, but by starlight they saw that it was surrounded by a twelve-foot-high whitewashed adobe wall, perhaps a quarter of a mile in circumference. The only entrance was secured by a pair of heavy wooden doors, no doubt barred from within with a giant beam. Clustered along the inside of the wall were probably a score of squat adobe huts, where the peons lived, and several stables and corrals. Blackwell noted that a dozen horses stood outside the hacienda, saddled and ready to go, suggesting that the men inside might be vigilant in case of attack.

The main house was in the center, a sprawling, vine-covered building with deep, wide verandas and a wing that probably housed most of Rodríguez's thirty-odd men. A tower rose from the center of the house, accessible from the outside by an iron stairway. The only visible light for miles around burned faintly in the tower; this was the room in which Inez Walker spent her lonely days and nights.

John Edwards names the men who James Wood now asked if they

wanted to go ahead, reminding them that the danger was great; as they knew, Mexicans could see and fight like wolves in the dark. They included Ike Berry, who had sliced off the arm of the man who called him a horse thief in Piedras Negras; the implacable Crockett, who had won the knife fight with the offended Mexican youth in Lapazos; and Dick Collins, who had been Shelby's artillery commander, now a night raider in a foreign land. Collins must have wished he had his artillery battery at hand when Wood said the only way into the compound was to break the gate down—the high walls were embedded with shards of broken glass, and the Americans might be picked off one by one if they tried to scale them.

A gigantic timber was wrenched loose from an irrigation basin for use as a battering ram. The kinetic force of twenty strong young men dashing toward the iron hinges of a gate anchored in adobe walls was irresistible. The bottom hinge was broken at the first charge; the middle one, at an awkward height above their heads, had to be hit twice; but the top one fell away with the weight of the door. The men were quickly inside the compound, racing toward the tower room. The defenders, struck by the force and daring of the attack, were slow to respond. Assuming that Dupin's feared contre-guerrillas had tracked them down at last, they fired a few panicked shots, then retreated to the corrals to make their escape. Ike Berry led a dozen men after them as the rest pursued the attack on the main house.

Rodríguez and his men had barred the heavy front door and fired at the Americans from secure cover. Four were shot down, including a giant German from St. Louis, one of the "Dutchmen" who had gone over to the Confederacy, nicknamed "Matterhorn." Also dead was the duelist at Lampazos, the redoubtable Crockett.

The survivors brought up the battering ram and quickly broke down the door. The only illumination inside came from the flash of pistols. The Americans raced for the stairs to the roof and the outside ladder to the tower, killing whoever they encountered. A voice they assumed was that of Rodríguez screamed, "calling down God's vengeance upon the gringos." A dozen men fired in the direction of the voice, which was soon silenced.

Shelby rode into the compound with a hundred men a few minutes after the last Mexican had been shot or had escaped. He demanded to know who was responsible for the unauthorized raid, vowing to finish the job on them that the Mexicans had botched if he didn't get a good explanation. James Wood came forward, bloody and powder-burned but unabashed. When Shelby heard his story, he demanded to see the woman. Inez Walker was brought forward. Her English, unused for years, was halting, and she was no longer a beautiful young woman. Her once-glossy golden hair was gray, and her figure was stooped. Shelby took her hand gently and nodded to the men that they were free to go; there would be no recriminations. Shelby and Inez spoke at some length about her future, which had until now been full of foreboding for her.

A day later, after the dead had been buried, Inez Walker stepped into a carriage with an older woman who had been her duenna and her confidante. She would join the Shelby party for the remainder of his journey to Mexico City, where she would become a presence within the circle of the American adventuress Princess Agnes Salm-Salm.

That journey still required traversing more than three hundred miles of desert and mountains. Limited to the northernmost border regions, the Apaches were no longer a problem. And the bandits who heard how Rodríguez had been dispatched became less inclined to attack the Americans. The Juaristas remained a threat, but they were mainly occupied with Benito Juarez's important shift in tactics against the French—away from mere harassing raids toward direct assaults on French outposts such as the one at Matehuala, Shelby's immediate destination.

Matehuala was a farming center of about twenty thousand people on a mile-high plateau bordered on three sides by high mountain ranges. Its Indian name meant "place of the green water," derived from the rivers that coursed down from the snow-covered peaks. Irrigated fields of barley, wheat, and oats fanned out from the city. To the north lay alkali flats. In late summer, winds from the mountains churned up the alkali into choking clouds of white dust. Shelby was a dozen miles away from Matehaula, in the midst of one of these dust storms, when he heard a distant rumble. It sounded like thunder, but the azure sky above the white dust was cloudless. The men moved cautiously westward to a pine-covered hill above the plateau. From there they could see distant puffs of smoke, followed by the roar of cannon, but little else.

Shelby sent a scouting team ahead, four squads of fifteen men each, to approach the town from different directions. They all returned safely just before sunset. The French fort, they said, was under siege by about two thousand Juaristas. They had an artillery battery of half a dozen six-pounders and were bombarding the fort and terrorizing the town. It looked as though they were getting ready for a direct assault.

Shelby knew that the French garrison numbered about five hundred. If it fell, his own passage southward would be imperiled—and the French would in all probability be wiped out. He consulted with his men, proposing that they help themselves by helping the French. When they agreed, he marched them along the mountain ridge to within two miles of the city. After making a cold camp—no fires, not even for cooking—he sent two volunteers, Jim Cundiff and Jim Hodge, under cover of darkness into the city. They had a harrowing journey, stumbling through irrigation canals into the alleys of the city, past cantinas where Juarist soldiers drank with the locals and boasted of their coming victory over the hated French.

At midnight the two scouts persuaded the French guards at the fort not to shoot them with a few useful words provided by Thomas Reynolds: *"Nous sommes des amis, des soldats américains; venir à vous aider."* The help they offered, they were able to convey to Major Henri Pierron, the young commanding officer, was in the form of a surprise joint attack on the enemy at dawn. The grateful major agreed and sent the men back with a detachment of forty cavalrymen—*curaisseurs.*

At dawn, as the Mexicans prepared for their assault on the French fort, Shelby formed his two hundred men, plus the *curaisseurs,* into a column of fours and moved at a walk toward the attacking army.

The Americans displayed the battle guidon they had used as their banner since leaving the flag buried in the Rio Grande. A red background crossed diagonally with blue stripes and white stars, it meant nothing to the Mexicans. Puzzled at this sudden apparition, they watched as the Confederates advanced, too far away for the French soldiers dispersed among them, minus their jackets and kepis, to be recognized. They continued to watch as the horsemen went from a walk to a canter. By the time the Juaristas realized that they were being attacked, Shelby, in the lead, had sounded the charge: "Gallop, ho!" The battalion whirled through the Mexican lines, shooting and slashing as they approached the gun battery. The defenders scattered and the Americans spiked the guns.

Meanwhile, the French under Major Pierron had burst through the gates of the fort and were galloping toward the enemy. Caught between two wings of cavalry numbering more than seven hundred, the Mexican infantry panicked and fled. The siege of Matehuala was lifted. It would be the Shelby battalion's final action in the field, one of their most decisive and least costly, with only a few men wounded and none killed.

Major Pierron was properly grateful, John Edwards noted, turning Matehuala into a "paradise" for the Americans. "There were days of feasting and mirth and minstrelsy, and in the balm of fragrant nights the men dallied with the women." It was with considerable regret that they left behind "the tropical lips that for them would never sing again" for their next important destination.

This was the old silver-mining town of San Luis Potosí, 130 miles to the south. The French had captured the city in 1863 and established a major post there under General Félix-Charles Douay, an ambitious man who believed that he, not Achille-François Bazaine, should have been appointed marshal under Maximilian.

Douay was responsible for pacifying the states of San Luis Potosí, Guanajuato, and much of Jalisco, to the south. When Shelby appeared on his doorstep, fresh from saving the detachment at Matehuala, Douay received him cordially and asked what he hoped to accomplish in Mexico. Shelby, still optimistic about the chances to lure Americans to the emperor's cause, said he could have thousands of men ready for service under Maximilian within a few months. Impressed, as most men were, by his guest's obvious competence and charm, Douay sought to enlist Shelby in his own service. He sent a messenger to Bazaine to ask if the Americans might stay with him in San Luis Potosí for a time—he could employ their help in hunting down the dreaded Luis Figueroa, a bandit chief who ruled between San Luis Potosí and Tampico on the Gulf Coast.

Shelby agreed to help Douay if Bazaine had no objections to a delay in their progress toward Mexico City, though catching Figueroa would be a challenge. Edwards described him as "a Mexican past forty-five, one-eyed from the bullet of an American's revolver, tall for his race," and notorious for "deeds of desperate butchery and vengeance." Even Dupin had been unable to pursue Figueroa into the swamps and jungles of the lowland. Douay hoped Shelby could destroy this "fell spirit of the marshes" without succumbing to yellow fever—"the vómito"—though he probably was mainly concerned with sparing his own men. Fortunately, the order from Bazaine returned in time to save Shelby's men from searching the swamps for elusive bandits and probably finding only the vómito; they were directed to proceed without delay to Mexico City.

Shelby's major challenge from this point on toward Mexico City—another two hundred miles—would not be posed by lurking disease, by the French authorities, or even by the Juaristas. Rather, it would come from the continuing disintegration of discipline. Several incidents suggest how close Shelby was to losing control over his men.

The first of these occurred three days south of San Luis Potosí. The expedition now included half a dozen mule-drawn ambulances that carried those who had been seriously wounded along the way. One of these vehicles lost a wheel while crossing the pass north of the village of Sumapetla; several of the wounded were able to ride on with the brigade, but two were left behind in a shack in the village by the young captain in command of the ambulance detachment. A third man, who had been a blacksmith before the war, had stayed with them to fix the wheel. Shelby raged at the young captain. How could he "desert comrades in distress and ride up to tell me the pleasant story of your own arrival and safety?" (John Edwards, obviously embarrassed at this lapse of chivalry, omitted the names of those involved.) Shelby ordered another, more reliable officer, James Kirtley, to take twenty men to rescue those left behind: "Fight for them, get killed if need be." He would wait for their return for another day and a half.

The rescue was successful, and the expedition pressed on to Dolores Hidalgo. It was here that Miguel Hidalgo y Costilla had given birth to the Mexican Revolution in 1810 with his famous speech, "Long live our Lady of Guadalupe! Long live Independence." The men had scant interest in Mexico's revolutionary history, or in anything else, Edwards suggests; the farther south they got, and the warmer the weather and the softer the smiles of the señoritas became, the more they "began to chafe under the iron rule of the camp, and the inexorable logic of guard duty." One evening Shelby learned that ten men had refused to stand guard duty. The men were lounging by their campfire and drinking when Shelby, backed up by twenty reliable men, approached them. The recalcitrants listened sullenly to Shelby's quiet insistence that they do their duty. There would be no recriminations: "I don't seek to know the cause of this thing. I ask no reason for it, no regrets or apologies. I only want your soldierly promise to obey." The "leader of the mutineers" stepped toward Shelby, who ordered him to halt. He and the others had fifteen seconds to obey, Shelby said. If, by then, they were not "in line for duty, you shall be shot like the meanest Mexican dog in all the Empire." Cowed into submission, the leader backed down and all the mutineers became once again "faithful and honorable" soldiers.

The most perverse instance of near-fratricide among Shelby's fraying band of brothers occurred near Querétaro. The emperor's summer home, 160 miles northwest of Mexico City, Querétaro was a beautiful small city, high in the mountains, protected from attack by a sturdy permanent force of Zouaves. The battalion camped near a neighboring village where a festival was beginning the following day, Sunday, with the cockfighting that John Edwards wryly regarded as a "national blessing" because it gave the local men something to do besides robbing wayfarers like themselves. Secure at last, Shelby arranged with the mayor to let his men attend the cockfights, sealing the deal with a case of fine cognac he had received from Douay.

On the evening before the fiesta, Shelby's men lounged by their campfires and swapped stories of their adventures. One young man's escapades in particular stood out, and he was not shy about recounting them to his comrades. This was John Thrailkill, the Quantrill guerrilla.

Thrailkill was a twenty-two-year-old house painter from northwest Missouri when the war broke out. In the summer of 1863, while recruiting soldiers for Shelby in Missouri, he was approached by several men who said they wanted to become guerrillas and kill as many Yankees as they could find. Thrailkill responded that he was a Confederate officer, not a bushwhacker; he could give them no advice other than to join a recognized Confederate force. The men were federal spies; they merely arrested Thrailkill instead of shooting him on the spot, as they would have done if he had responded to their entrapment techniques. Sentenced to hard labor in an Illinois stone quarry, Thrailkill escaped in June 1864. He wrote to his sister, a Northern sympathizer, that she could not "imagine how badley I was treated whilst in the federal bastill." How could she ever think he would take "the oath of alegience" to the "abolitionis government I do so bitterly detest. No Dear sister I Should stand to be shot twenty times" before that would happen. He was "not a shaime to say that I am a rebel." He was going to "start for General Pries" that evening.

Thrailkill had saved his own life by denying that he was a guerrilla. True or not at the time, by the summer and fall of 1864 he was closely involved not only with Quantrill but with others, such as George Todd, who were even more vicious in terrorizing northern Missouri. By one account, Thrailkill was a modifying influence, preventing Todd from murdering a detachment of Federals who had surrendered. But he was included in the list of proscribed guerrillas who were told, as the war came to a close, that they would be arrested and tried as criminals if they came back to Missouri.

According to Edwards, Thrailkill's stories were usually "overgenerous" to himself in terms of "the share he took of the killing and the plunder," but he was seldom challenged by his listeners. There was a rumor that he was half-Russian by birth, and some saw a menacing Slavic cast in his flat, cold eyes and broad cheekbones. He was also said to be the regiment's best man with a pistol, capable of drilling a bottle cap on a post at thirty yards. When a soldier named Anthony West openly scoffed at one of Thrailkill's stories, Thrailkill slapped him "twice in the face with the open hand, once on either cheek." The two were separated and hustled away by the others, but later that night West's second, Captain James Gillette, delivered West's challenge to Thrailkill—with a special proviso that might neutralize Thrailkill's undoubted superiority as a marksman.

The conditions, which specified two stages, seemed to Edwards "savage enough for an Indian." The preliminary stage the following morning was carried out as planned, after Shelby, who, of course, knew nothing of the duel, had left for breakfast with the mayor. Two identical Colt revolvers were displayed to the combatants outside a tent. One was loaded with five bullets. The other was empty. The weapons were taken inside the tent and placed under a blanket with only their handles showing. A coin toss then determined which man would choose first. Thrailkill won. He stepped into the tent "whistling a tune" and reached beneath the blanket to select his revolver. He spun the cylinder, smiled when he saw that it was loaded, and stepped aside to let West pick up the empty Colt. West's jaw tightened, but he gave no other sign that he knew he was a dead man.

The second stage of the duel—which would be, in reality, an execution—was to happen at sunset. Before that, both men, along with the rest of the battalion, would attend the cockfights. Hundreds of spectators jammed the high rows of bleachers that surrounded the sand pit. Shelby was among them, seated next to the *alcalde*. On the other side of the mayor a bugler sounded joyous or plaintive refrains as one after another of the gamecocks slashed their opponents to pieces with razored spurs. The Americans, "born gamblers" all, bet the little that they had; some were on the verge of wagering their pistols and carbines until a stern look from Shelby discouraged them. Thrailkill lost everything. The only man to win steadily was the doomed West, whose pockets grew heavy with gold coins as the afternoon wore on.

As the main event was about to begin—a battle between a "magnificent cock" with "the crest of an eagle and the eye of a basilisk" and an equally formidable opponent—the betting reached a crescendo. Thousands of dollars were at stake. A priest shouted out a challenge: "A dubloon to a dubloon against the black cock!" Thrailkill searched his pockets to take the bet, found nothing, and stomped down the bleachers to leave. He was stopped at the exit by James Gillette, who asked him why he was leaving. Thrailkill glared at Gillette, who had not won his affection by acting as West's second. Because he was dead broke, Thrailkill said shortly.

Gillette offered to lend Thrailkill the money to take the priest's bet, on certain conditions. "You don't want to kill West," he said. They had been soldiers together, and the terms were "murderous." Besides,

Shelby would certainly banish Thrailkill if West died, if he didn't hang him. Gillette's deal was that if Thrailkill's black cock won he would repay Gillette from his winnings, and follow his conscience as to West. If he lost, then he would hold his fire and keep his "hands clean from innocent blood." West would be kept ignorant of the plan; his certainty that he would die should be revenge enough for Thrailkill.

Thrailkill took the money and bet it on the black cock, which soon "lay dead on the sands of the arena, slain by the sweep of one terrific blow" by his ragged antagonist. Gillette had won his wager. Would Thrailkill honor it?

That evening Thrailkill and West met beside a stream outside of the village with their seconds. The scene was as bucolic as a Constable painting of the eighteenth-century English midland: Chimney smoke rose lazily in the setting sun, cowbells tinkled as the herds were driven homeward, and in the fields sounded "the happy voices of the reapers." The handsome young West faced the semiliterate braggart and killer John Thrailkill, knowing that the man "had never been merciful," and hoped for nothing more than a speedy and painless death.

Thrailkill leveled his Colt at West's forehead, "looked once into his eyes, saw that they did not quail," and fired—into the air.

NINE

Maximilian Says "No"

O n September 3, 1865, General Jo Shelby led his ragged and restive soldiers into the City of Mexico. He followed the route of conquerors both ancient and recent—in Popotla they passed the giant cypress tree beneath whose branches Hernán Cortés mourned the death of his men during the battle with the Aztecs at Tenochtitlán in 1519, and near the Gate of Santo Tomás they removed their hats beside the American cemetery where some of General Winfield Scott's men were buried in 1848.

Shelby came not as a conqueror; he was at the end of a harrowing expedition of nearly fifteen hundred miles that had begun in western Arkansas more than three months earlier. His original band of approximately three hundred men had been whittled down, through battle deaths and attrition, to little more than half that number. The older men, including Magruder, Reynolds, and Hindman, had gone ahead to Mexico City a few weeks earlier, under the protection of a French detachment. So, too, more recently, had Shelby's virtual shadow John Edwards—dispatched by Shelby to work with the others to prepare Maximilian for his arrival.

Shelby's position was ambiguous. His sale of weapons to the Juaristas in Piedras Negras still rankled the French, who perceived that trouble and Shelby traveled together. He had also been involved in repeated clashes with the Juraristas, the Apaches, and various bandits; and though these encounters were usually defensive in nature, there were also the Inez Walker affair at La Encarnación and the narrowly averted duel with Colonel du Preuil. Shelby had learned that even his rescue of Major Pierron's garrison at Matehuala might have worked against him—Marshal Bazaine worried that when Sheridan and Grant realized that a former Confederate force was fighting in the field alongside imperial troops, they would retaliate by increasing the pressure on French positions near the border.

Ever the optimist, however, Shelby held on to his conviction that he would be well received by the French once he persuaded them he could enlist more fighting men to help Maximilian keep his empire. Even if Maximilian declined to use him as a soldier, Shelby was encouraged by reports that the emperor, and especially his wife, Carlota, were fond of the Confederates they had already met. As an American blue blood himself, Shelby was certain he could charm the Emperor and his lady into offering him a warm welcome to Mexico.

The most eminent of Shelby's fellow Confederates in Mexico City was Matthew Maury, a Virginian of French descent, now in his midsixties. Described by the historian Douglas Southall Freeman as "a keen-eyed man with a great dome of a head and pleasant composure of countenance," Maury was an internationally acclaimed scientist in the decades before the Civil War. He was called "the pathfinder of the seas" for his charting of ocean winds and currents—an intellectual and commercial triumph that shaved days and weeks off sailing times, saving uncalculated millions in shipping expenses. He had corresponded in the 1850s with the young Maximilian, at that time the commander of the Austrian navy in Trieste. Maximilian had been engaged in modernizing the fleet after the lessons of the Crimean War showed the need for steel-hulled, steam-driven warships. Maximilian, like Maury, was deeply interested in science, and had established a hydrographic institute and a naval museum. It was at his instigation that Maury was awarded the Austrian gold medal of arts and sciences.

A fervent secessionist, Maury spent much of the war in England, lobbying for support for the Confederacy. His prestige was such that it won the South more sympathy from people of influence than it might have otherwise—Maury by this time had been honored with membership in half a dozen national academies in Europe. He also had an intricate knowledge of American rivers and coastal waters and spent considerable effort devising torpedoes and mines for the defense of Southern harbors.

While in England, Maury had followed reports that Napoléon III would soon send the young Archduke Maximilian to rule over Mexico. He was pleased to hear that Maximilian had expressed an "earnest hope" that the South would win its war with the Union. Maximilian even went so far as to say the causes of the South and of Mexico "may be said to form one." This sentiment, coupled with Napoléon's plans to promote large-scale immigration to Mexico, gave Maury hope for his own future, and for those of countless other Confederates as well.

As Napoléon saw it, Mexico was a huge but underpopulated land, an independent nation in name only. It would be rejuvenated by a technical elite drawn from all of Europe, not just France: Engineers, scientists, surveyors, agronomists, mining experts, and an efficient civil service would provide the underpinnings of a sturdy new nation. Most of these experts would be Europeans, but a French newspaper, reflecting Napoléon's views, welcomed the prospect of Confederate immigration, saying that Mexico should soon be home to "thousands of planters from Louisiana, Alabama and Texas, whose energies and intelligence will open for their adopted country incalculable riches" and whose hatred for the Yankees would help secure Mexico's northern border.

As the Civil War was ending, Maury learned that he would be among those ineligible for the general amnesty proposed by Washington because of his great contributions to the Confederacy abroad. He contacted Maximilian, who invited him to Mexico in the spring of 1865. Maury soon became a member of the emperor's inner circle. Well before Shelby and the other Confederates began to converge on Mexico City, Maury was promising Maximilian that he could draw tens of thousands of industrious Americans from his home state to found a "New Virginia" in Mexico. Once Shelby and the first waves of Confederates started arriving in the summer of 1865, Maury found it easy to persuade the impressionable Maximilian that many more would soon follow. All Maximilian had to do was to announce his formal support of Southern immigration into Mexico. Fortunately for Shelby, he arrived just as Maximilian was putting the finishing touches on the immigration policy that Maury had suggested to him.

Shelby was aware of Maury's presence and his influence. He had good cause to believe that the emperor would receive him warmly and would at least consider Shelby's offer to raise soldiers for him— men who would first fight to secure the empire, then settle down as farmers and tradesmen. Edwards reports him asking one of his fa- vorite officers, Maurice Langhorne, while they were still well north of the capital, if Langhorne agreed that he could draw thousands of "young men for war" from the South. Shelby thought the sky was the limit. The more skeptical Langhorne replied shortly that the French "want no soldiers from among us."

But Shelby's optimism seemed to be confirmed by the enthusiastic reception given to him and his men upon their arrival in Mexico City. A contingent of Chasseurs d'Afrique greeted them with a flourish and led the men to their lodgings in an old stone fortress called the Ciu- dadela. Shelby himself was taken to the Hotel San Carlos, where he learned from John Edwards that Maury had arranged for him to meet the emperor in two days.

The meeting took place in a modest reception room at the Palacio Nacional. In addition to the emperor, Marshal Bazaine, Commodore Maury, and Edwards were present. So, too, was John Magruder, who had made himself indispensable to both the emperor and to Maury. Although Maximilian had a more than adequate command of English—as well as German, French, Hungarian, Italian, and Spanish—the meeting was conducted in French through his chief of staff, Count de Noue. (It is one of the oddities of historical circum- stance that de Noue's wife was the daughter of William S. Harney, the Union general who commanded the Department of the West in 1861—and that it was Harney, a Mississippi native, who had opposed the actions of General Nathaniel Lyon and Frank Blair that led to the incendiary "Camp Jackson" incident witnessed five years earlier by fu- ture generals Shelby, Sherman, Grant, and Price.)

Shelby and Edwards agreed afterward that Maximilian was noble in appearance and gracious in manner. At thirty-three, Maximilian was two years younger than Shelby. He was over six feet tall, blond and blue-eyed, with a high forehead. John Edwards, his belief in phrenology typical of the time, noted that Maximilian's mouth was large and sensuous, with "the Hapsburg lip, that thick, protruding, semi-cleft underlip, too heavy for beauty, too immobile for features that, under the iron destiny that ruled the hour, should have suggested Caesar or Napoleon." Particularly striking for Edwards was Maximilian's "great yellow beard" as it "fell in a wave to his waste . . . silkier, glossier, heavier than" those of any of the Huns or Hungarians who had "followed him from the Rhine and the Danube."

In his customary direct fashion, Shelby described his plan to the emperor. He proposed to recruit as many as forty thousand Americans. These men would take precedence over the Mexicans in the emperor's army, who, he said, were demonstrably incompetent. The Americans would, as well, take the place of the French, who were clearly eager to pull out. Shelby said he would also encourage civilian immigration, as he knew the emperor desired, and help to develop the natural and mineral resources of the country, which were vast.

Maximilian looked with some bemusement at this confident and aggressive American. He asked why Shelby thought the French were about to leave. Shelby noted Bazaine's raised eyebrows but forged ahead, drawing on his knowledge of American politics from his own experience and from Frank Blair. (He said nothing, of course, about his original intention, following Blair's suggestion, to volunteer his services to Juárez rather than Maximilian.) The United States was troubled by the presence of France in Mexico, Shelby said, regarding it as "a perpetual menace." Because France did not want to go to war with the United States, it was clear that it would have to withdraw from Mexico. But once the French were gone, Maximilian should have no difficulty "in establishing friendly relations with the United States. In order to put yourself in a position to do this," Shelby said, it was essential that Maximilian "should have a corps of foreign soldiers devoted to you personally, and reliable in any emergency." Shelby and his men would be pleased to serve as the heart of such an army if the emperor were so inclined.

As Edwards recounts this scene, Shelby's unusual willingness to subordinate himself to Maximilian seems out of character, a rare departure from his usual prickly independence. But it is consistent with his practice that, once committed to a course of action, he would give it everything he had. It may well have been that intensity that gave Maximilian pause. That, and the unlikely notion that the United States would be friendly to a neighboring empire defended by Confederate soldiers. "It appeared as if Shelby was an enigma he was trying to make out," Edwards observed. Accustomed to relying on Commodore Maury, Maximilian "would look first at Shelby and then at Maury, as if appealing from the blunt frankness of the one to the polished sincerity and known sound judgment of the other." As for Bazaine, he seemed to acknowledge the truth of Shelby's assertion that the French must soon leave, though it pained him to hear it put so directly. Edwards believed that Bazaine "was strongly in favor of the employment of the Americans, and had the bargain been left to him," it would have been sealed immediately: "He was a soldier, and reasoned from a soldier's viewpoint."

After a few moments, Maximilian rose and called de Noue aside for a whispered conference. He then politely took his leave of the Americans and withdrew, accompanied by Marshal Bazaine. De Noue said to Shelby, "It is no use, General; the Emperor will not give you employment."

Maximilian's reasoning should have been obvious to Shelby from the first, because it followed the same line of thought that had led to Senator Gwin's earlier being refused the virtual rule of Sonora: Maximilian feared a Trojan horse in the form of thousands of armed foreigners under the command of men who had nearly succeeded in destroying their own country. Moreover, the emperor was trying to establish friendly relations with the United States by means of diplomacy, rather than through force of arms. He believed that once Secretary of State Seward saw the virtue of his good intentions regarding Mexico, American hostility to the empire would cease. He would not need the French or anyone else to protect him.

Shelby thanked de Noue and asked if he might speak frankly. His comments suggest that he now regarded his offer of military service to Maximilian as a mistake and that he was relieved that it had been refused—and that he could resume his customary attitude of principled independence. He said he was not surprised at the emperor's decision. Maximilian was clearly a man who had "faith but no enthusiasm, and what a man in his position needs is not only enthusiasm but audacity." The emperor was doomed to fail in his diplomatic efforts, Shelby explained, not just because he lacked time; he also lacked the support of his "subjects," who were hardly subjects at all. In his long travels from Piedras Negras, Shelby told de Noue, he had seen that "you have not one foot of Mexican territory in sympathy with you." By the time Maximilian managed to get Seward to recognize the empire as legitimate, there would be no empire.

Toward the end of that eventful afternoon, Shelby ordered his men to gather outside in the square of the Ciudadela and then gave them the news: "We are not wanted." There was no place for them as soldiers in Maximilian's empire. This day—September 5, 1865—would therefore be their last together as a military unit.

As Shelby explained the emperor's decision, he understood that many of his men were undoubtedly relieved, after their initial dismay. For the first time in four years or more, they were no longer in danger of losing their lives because they belonged to a unit that drew trouble to itself as a magnet draws iron filings. They had no duties, no obligations, no claims on their bodies or minds or souls. In a word, they were free.

He had other news for them that would be welcome, Shelby said. That very afternoon, Maximilian had issued an imperial invitation to all foreigners, but especially Americans, to become farmers—"land colonists" was the term used—in Mexico. Shelby and his men had the great advantage of already being on the scene. It was an offer that Shelby himself intended to take.

Shelby explained that much of the nation's land previously taken from the Catholic Church by Benito Juárez would now be open to colonization by European and American immigrants. Those who had little money would be offered free passage by ship to Mexico, plus a travel allowance. Single men were eligible for 120 acres of uncultivated land in the public domain, at no charge; a family could receive as much as an American section, or 640 acres. The land would be free from taxes for five years. Newcomers could bring whatever they liked, duty-free, in the way of farm animals and machinery. Slavery was illegal under Maximilian, as it had been under Juárez, but any former slaves who chose to join their onetime masters could do so if they wished. (None did.)

Shelby joked with the men that they could learn some Spanish, marry the señoritas, and grow breadfruit, tobacco, and corn: "We cannot starve, boys."

Shelby saved what some would consider the best news for last. Each man was to receive enough money from Marshal Bazaine to get himself home, if he wished, or to serve as a grubstake here in Mexico. They had Thomas Reynolds to thank for that, Shelby said briefly, leaving out the complicated reasoning behind Bazaine's generosity. Reynolds, the widely traveled, multilingual former diplomat and governor, had reminded Bazaine that Shelby's men were now broke and homeless because of his orders. Bazaine had prevented them from going on to Mazatlán from Parras earlier that summer, as Ben Elliott had been permitted to do. Elliott was already prospering in Mazatlán as a farmer, Reynolds had learned, and some of his men had easily made their way back home by way of California and Arizona. Shelby and his men, had they also been allowed to go to Mazatlán, could have done the same, and would have done so if they had known that Maximilian had no use for them as soldiers.

Bazaine revealed to Reynolds that he had ordered Shelby to come to Mexico City because he was impressed by what he had heard about him, and that he believed he could persuade Maximilian to use Shelby in a military capacity. He had been wrong, Bazaine admitted. To make up for his error, he would give each man fifty dollars in gold—worth at least five hundred dollars in today's currency.

The final mustering of the Iron Brigade at sunset is affectingly described in Edwin Adams Davis's book about Shelby, *The Fallen Guidon.* According to information Davis learned through his research in Mexico and from his grandfather, who had fought with Shelby, the event was attended by the Southern exiles then living in Mexico City, meaning that Price, Reynolds, Magruder, Maury, and dozens of others were present. The French officers and men were also there, as were some of the officials from Maximilian's court. They heard, as did the men, Martin Kritzer's bugle call the men to attention, and they watched as Shelby moved down the line to say good-bye to each man.

He "patted them on the shoulder, calling them by their first names or nicknames," recalling shared adventures, and occasionally "straightening a collar or buttoning a button with hands that trembled."

There were tears in the men's eyes as they mounted their horses and passed in review before their commander, "first at the walk, then at the canter, and finally at the gallop, a gallop which became a wild battle charge with the Rebel yell echoing from the time-softened old buildings which had witnessed the parading of the Conquistadores."

John Edwards, usually so emotive, says of this event only that "soldiers never repine." They were still young men, ambitious and restless and full of energy. In the weeks that followed, more than a few followed Shelby's suggestion and accepted land grants. Others struck out for Mazatlán, where they found passage to California, the Sandwich Islands, and even Japan and China. A few, according to Edwards, went chasing after a treasure buried somewhere in the Pacific by the Scottish pirate Captain William Kidd.

About fifty men did end up serving with the French army. They made their choice of regiments carefully: They would become Zouaves. A Zouave officer who served in Mexico described the Zouave ethos in a way that explains why Shelby's men were attracted by it: "When bugles echo, a feverish trembling flows in our veins. We are exalted by the thunder of the cannon. The odor of powder awakens in us those warlike instincts which sleep in our breasts. We fill our lungs with the hot breath of battle and throw ourselves with fury—indescribable fury—into the combat."

That was reason enough, but the Zouaves offered something else to the new recruits as well. It was not in the nature of an American soldier to follow the French custom, which required an enlisted man to remove his cap when addressing an officer and stand humbly before him, like a supplicant. Only the turbaned Zouaves—who looked to Edwards like "great, bearded, medaled fellows, bronzed by African suns and swarthy" as any Arab—were exempt from this requirement. The Zouave would salute, but his turban stayed in place.

Major Pierron, the legionnaire whose command Shelby had rescued at Matehuala, had been temporarily reassigned to Mexico City. He now supervised "the metamorphosis" of Missouri farmers and mechanics into Zouaves. "When the toilette was complete even Shelby himself" could hardly recognize his men. They traded in their faded butternut shirts and trousers for white blouses, billowing crimson trousers, white gaiters, and green turbans with scarlet tassels. They were last seen one morning shortly after sunrise, "marching away to Monterrey at the double quick."

By the end of that busy first week of September 1865, Shelby was awarded a sizable land grant in the Córdoba Valley, 150 miles southeast of the capital—several days by stage. The area was tropical, inland from Veracruz about fifty-five miles, but high enough so that the yellow fever that made the coast so dangerous was not a problem. Shelby sent a letter to Betty in Lexington, asking her to go to New Orleans with the boys as soon as possible and book passage for Veracruz. He hoped to meet her there no later than mid-October.

The wheels of Maximilian's bureaucracy spun more efficiently than Shelby might have expected, but it still was not until late September that he was able to move to Córdoba. During the intervening weeks, he was compelled to relax and simply enjoy himself, for the first time in years. He became a tourist in Mexico City. He had time to wander, usually with John Edwards, through the ancient city of the Aztecs— in Edwards's words, "the city of the swart cavaliers of Cortez and the naked warriors of Montezuma, who rushed with bare bosom on lance and sword blade."

Their frequent guide was an acquaintance from the last days of the war, the former Louisiana governor Henry Allen. Allen was an appealing figure to both Shelby and Edwards—a war hero, talented writer, and ladies' man. And, like them, he was an entrepreneurial spirit, preparing to launch an English-language newspaper called *The Mexican Times*. In the months to come, he would replace Shelby as John Edwards's mentor and guide, in part because he was so like Shelby in his daring and imaginative response to the challenges of war and, later, of peace.

Born in Virginia in 1820, Allen earned a law degree in 1841. In 1844, he eloped with a wealthy heiress, alluringly named Salome Crane. Four days after their wedding he nearly left Salome a widow: He was shot through both thighs in a duel, ending his dancing days and perhaps more—the wound was "high up," a friend noted, detailing the injury tastefully in Latin, which read, in part, *"ictu transcidente et lacerante prorsus membra vitalia."* A greater blow was Salome's death a few years later, in January 1851. Allen recovered in true Victorian fashion by taking to travel, writing a series of amusing articles for national newspapers as the cynical and foppish "Guy Mannering," after the Waverley novel by the favorite writer of all Confederates, Sir Walter Scott.

In an account written by a female admirer when he was in his thirties, Allen sounds like a Scott hero: tall and slender, graceful but muscular, and remarkably handsome, with "high cheek-bones, denoting his Scotch extraction, bright gray eyes, fair hair and moustache," and a square chin. He was "like an antique knight" in his courtesy toward women, whom he admired for their delicacy of taste and manners, and he positively "worshipped intellect."

By the end of the war, Allen was a retired brigadier general. He had been seriously wounded in two battles before becoming governor of Confederate Louisiana. In May 1865, he was among those participating in the conference of governors and generals in Marshall, Texas, attended by Shelby and Kirby Smith, and he had strongly seconded Shelby's announcement that surrender was not a word in his or his soldiers' vocabulary.

Unlike some of his Confederate brethren—Sterling Price, most notably—Allen had a sense of humor. He had crossed the Rio Grande with Kirby Smith and enjoyed the hospitality of Jeanningros at Monterrey—a sixteen-course breakfast, "everything in elegant style." Riding alone one morning while staying in Saltillo, he had been approached by a non-English-speaking French soldier who had ordered him to dismount and walk back to the fort. The former general protested vigorously, he later wrote to a friend: "You damned frog-eating, red breeches devil, I'll make you smoke for this. You shall be punished, sirrah, for your conduct. I'll have satisfaction from your commandant!" The soldier simply responded, *"Oui, Monsieur: Marchez!"*

Allen was able to point out to Shelby and Edwards some of the anomalies of life in Mexico City, judging from his written comments. A typically nondemonstrative Protestant, he was surprised by the religious fervor, both past and present, that he saw around him—from the "huge sacrificial stone, covered with hieroglyphics" in the museum to a military mass with Bazaine and his staff. "The old church was crowded, a full band of music played, and during the ceremony, soldiers who were around the altar, with their muskets in hand, knelt and saluted, a la militaire." One day he noted that "the carriage containing the Host is just passing my windows. All are on their knees. Even the Emperor, in passing, has stopped his carriage, and has gotten out, and is on his knees." The French officers and men did not kneel, but simply raised their caps.

At the Imperial Opera, Allen was usually more impressed by the elegant French ladies in their Eugénie hats, wearing elaborate gowns with daring décolletage, set off by displays of "rare and costly jewels," than he was by the performance—though he was moved to tears by a production of *Il Trovatore*. Those who could speak a language other than English could visit a theater at the Iturbide showing the French comedy *The Mysteries of Summer* or at another, the Principal, featuring a drama called *Pobres y Ricos*. Allen also enjoyed the Hotel San Agustin, with its "choice liquors and ices," its fine billiard tables, and bracing baths, "cold or warm." A particular draw for the Americans was the "New Saloon" at the Hotel Nacional; the proprietor, whose former establishment had been the St. Louis Hotel in New Orleans, could satisfy what Allen called "the most fastidious taste in the art of mixing liquors, and preparing elegant drinks."

Through Allen, Shelby and Edwards were introduced to the Yorke family, whose comfortable home was the heart of Confederate society in Mexico City. There they met, and were charmed by, a remarkably intelligent and observant teenager named Sara Yorke. Sara's father was a prosperous cotton broker from Louisiana, where her mother's family owned a large plantation. They had been living in Paris when Sara was born, in 1847. When she was ten, her parents returned to Louisiana, leaving Sara to attend a boarding school in Paris. In 1861, as Juárez was canceling his country's debts, Sara's father took his wife and two sons with him to Mexico City to look after his business interests there. He sent for Sara in 1862, after her older brother was killed by Mexican bandits while carrying a message to the American diplomat Thomas Corwin, who was then in Veracruz.

Sara's diary of her years in Mexico was published as a book in 1899,

by which time she was Sara Yorke Stevenson, a prominent cultural anthropologist living in Philadelphia. Its value as a window onto the
time by a keen observer of French, Mexican, and American character
and customs, enhanced by her later education, is profound. At various
times skeptical, shocked, amused, and touched, Sara recorded observations that were very astute from the beginning—even assuming the
advantage of hindsight.

On the evening her ship left Saint-Nazaire, Sara overheard two
young men talking about their coming trip to Mexico. They were sur-
geons, she learned, being sent to the French military hospital at Veracruz. She realized then that the speeches she had heard about the
Mexicans greeting French soldiers with flowers might not be true: "It
was my first serious disillusion."

Before her ship had docked at Veracruz, Sara Yorke had taken the
measure of the French merchants and bureaucrats who were her fellow
passengers. It was, she said, as though they had found Aladdin's lamp:

> Mining companies, colonization companies, railroad companies,
> telegraph companies, etc.—all the activities that go to constitute the
> nineteenth-century civilization—were in a few short years to de-
> velop the mining and agricultural resources of the country. A new
> outlet would open to French industry, and the glory of French arms
> would check the greed of the Anglo-Saxon, that arrogant merchant
> race who would monopolize the trade of the world. The thought
> was brilliant, grand, generous, noble, worthy of a Napoleonic mind.
> There were millions in it!

By the time the Confederates began arriving in Mexico City, Sara
was a poised and sometimes saucy nineteen-year-old, unimpressed by
splendid uniforms and august titles. For example, she was amused
by the results of Maximilian and Maury's misguided efforts to create
a Department of the Navy. "As the Mexican government did not own
a canoe, and as there was at that time no serious likelihood of its ever
owning a battle-ship," the appointment of a young officer as Admiral
of the Navy "caused no little merriment among us, and many were the
practical jokes of which the hapless cabinet officer was the victim."
The officer lived on a street that was prone to flooding in the rainy

season. During the first big storm, "his comrades, bent upon fun, purchased a toy flotilla, which they floated, flying the Mexican flag, down the street. In mock dignity the tiny ships came to an anchor before his door, much to every one's merriment, excepting, it was whispered, to that of the powers that were, who found a sting in the harmless levity."

But Shelby's benefactor, Marshal Bazaine, was a particular favorite of Sara's. The gruff old legionnaire—as he seemed to Sara, though he was then only in his midfifties—had seen service in North Africa, Spain, Italy, and the Crimea. He was short and stocky, with "a certain coarseness of thought and expression too common among Frenchmen," but Sara was entranced by the story of the little girl he had rescued from poverty when he was serving in Spain: "He picked up the little wild rose as it grew on the roadside," and transplanted it into the "good, rich soil" of a convent. Some years later—not long before he left for Mexico in 1863—he had married the young woman, "breaking through all rules of French matrimonial usage." After he was posted to Mexico, Bazaine learned of his wife's sudden death and was heartbroken; though he soon returned to his duties, "no one ever knew what had passed in his innermost soul."

A year later, Sara saw the marshal at a ball staring openmouthed at a beautiful young Mexican girl and murmuring how extraordinarily close in appearance she was to his lost wife. Within months the marshal had a new wife, Doña Josefa de la Peña, whom the empress herself described as "a very pretty girl, with great grace and simplicity, beautiful blue-black hair and an expressive Spanish type of face." Maximilian's wedding gift to the happy couple was a palace valued at more than $100,000.

Sara wrote that her mother, "being a Southern woman, and knowing" the Confederate leaders, opened her doors to Shelby, Price, Maury, and the others. Her house, at the corner of the Calle de San Francisco, opposite the Iglesia de la Profesa,

> soon became a center where they gathered in the evening and freely discussed their hopes. Thus was added a new element to the already motley assemblage which collected about us at that time. Truly a most heterogeneous set! Confederate officers, members of the

diplomatic corps, newly fledged chamberlains and officials of the palace, the marshal's officers,—Frenchmen, Austrians, Belgians, and a few Mexicans,—would drop in, each group bringing its own interests, and, alas! its animosities.

These "animosities" were complicated by the combative personalities of most of the Confederates—men who were, by definition, rebellious. All of them were opinionated, and most were competing for appointments or commercial franchises from Maximilian. Even in wartime, when their very existence was at stake, they had found it difficult to work together. Now they were charged with putting into place a vaguely defined set of plans for making Mexico a modern, functioning state.

Among these contentious Confederates were three of Shelby's former associates—Thomas Reynolds, Sterling Price, and John Magruder—who were about to receive special recognition by Maximilian. Magruder, in particular, had won the affection of the young emperor by becoming his fashion consultant. According to Alexander Terrell, the Texas judge and general, Magruder showed up one day for an audience with Maximilian wearing a smart new dove-colored top hat, a salt-and-pepper cutaway, and patent leather boots. The next time the two met, Maximilian wore a dove-colored top hat, a salt-and-pepper cutaway, and patent leather boots.

Magruder was appointed chief of the Colonization Land Office, at a yearly salary of $3,000—worth about $35,000 in today's purchasing power; he reported to Commodore Maury, who made $5,000. Though close in age and political sympathies, the two found it difficult to work together. "Prince John" was at base a practical man of action, accustomed to commanding and inspiring large numbers of men to do his bidding. Maury was, by contrast, a scholar, at home in his laboratory or study, but he was also an inspirational dreamer on whom Maximilian showered money: extra funds for furnishing his office and for hiring a clerk; a position for his son, Richard, at nearly the same salary as Magruder's; and a section of land in Carlota, the major new land colony then in the planning stages.

The problem was that Maury's "New Virginia" scheme, which now envisioned bringing in two hundred thousand settlers from old Virginia's finest families, was accurately regarded as a pipe dream even by his family and friends at home. (Indeed, it would turn out that all of the grand projections by Shelby, Gwin, Maury, and others were castles in the air; the number of Americans who came to Mexico during the 1865–67 period was fewer than five thousand in all, and only a handful of them remained for more than a few months.) Magruder, unsympathetic to Maury's plan and affronted by the increasing influence of his son, tried to mitigate Maury's influence on the emperor, without much success. Thomas Reynolds was his untitled assistant and ally for a time—until Reynolds got tired, as he said, of being a mere "amanuensis in Maury's absurd colonization bureau," and found more satisfying work as superintendent of two short-line railroads in Mexico City.

But during that hopeful autumn and early winter of 1865 there were grounds for the emperor's enthusiasm for Maury's efforts. Confederate immigration agents were spotted throughout the Old South, from Virginia through the Carolinas to Louisiana and Alabama, as well as in Missouri and California. They circulated a sixteen-page pamphlet describing Mexico as a paradise, a new Eden for those who had been expelled from their own gardens in the South. Garish circulars headlined "Ho for Mexico!" also generated great interest—John Edwards reported that seven hundred inquiries arrived in a single mail delivery that fall.

More important, the new colony at Carlota was about to be launched. The centerpiece of Maximilian's plan for colonization, named after the empress, Carlota would be situated at the heart of half a million acres of fertile land in the Córdoba Valley. Sterling Price, whose imposing presence had favorably impressed Maximilian, was to be the colony's leader. Jo Shelby's land was not far from Price's, near the town of Córdoba, ensuring a close and continuing association with the man he still thought had been incompetent during the last critical year of the Civil War. Toward the end of September, after finally securing the necessary approvals, Shelby and Price traveled together to the sites of their new homes—their permanent homes, or so they hoped.

———

John Edwards stayed behind in Mexico City. It would be the first time in years that he was apart from Shelby for more than a few weeks, but it was time to resume their separate lives as civilians in what they hoped would be a more peaceful society. Just as Shelby was about to return to his prewar roots as a farmer, businessman, and family man, Edwards now had the opportunity to return to his earlier career as a newspaperman.

The newspaper was Henry Allen's weekly, *The Mexican Times*, subsidized by Maximilian as a boon to the American colonists and as a recruiting tool to draw in more of them. His eighteen-month tenure at the *Times*, the first part of it under Allen, would give Edwards the same kind of privileged insight into his and Shelby's Mexican adventure as had his role as Shelby's adjutant into the events of the Civil War.

Edwards considered himself fortunate to be working under Allen, whose zeal for the Lost Cause burned as pure and holy as his own. Praised by one historian as the only "great administrator produced by the Confederacy," Allen provides a useful touchstone for the American experience in Mexico, marked as that adventure is by frustrated energy and the pathos of the unwilling expatriate.

Allen's first four-page issue of *The Mexican Times* came out in mid-September 1865. He was soon overwhelmed. He was in constant physical pain from his war injuries, and he feared that he might have to have one leg amputated. Nevertheless, he wrote to a friend, "I labor twelve hours every day, for I have to write all the editorials," set the type, crank out the two or three hundred copies, sell the advertisements, and do the bookkeeping. "I can't afford to employ an assistant." By the end of the month, though, he was able to hire John Edwards, first to set type and then to contribute articles—some of these, including a long description of Shelby's capture of a Union riverboat, would eventually make their way into his book *Shelby and His Men*.

The *Times* had only a relative handful of paying subscribers, never more than a few hundred. But its local audience was influential and copies were circulated in the United States. Much of the paper's content was designed, as Allen's first editorial, on September 16, 1865, announced, to encourage "immigration and progress in their fullest meaning and extent. . . . We shall urge with all our influence, emigrants from the United States and Europe who wish rich, productive, and cheap lands, to come to this country without delay." Those who did so would be able to "grow sugar-cane, coffee, indigo, cotton, cacao, and tobacco." They would enjoy a climate of "eternal spring, where, strange to say, there are no fevers, except in the tierra caliente of the coast."

The remaining pages of the *Times* were given over to what Allen called "the arts and sciences, to polite literature, and to the general news of the day, foreign and domestic." Potted Mexican history, chapters from *Oliver Twist* and other popular fiction, and statistics relating to commerce and industry were enlivened by speculations that General Sterling Price might soon lead an army of Confederates against Sheridan's men on the Rio Grande and diatribes against Horace Greeley for his attacks on the Mexican colonies. Keeping in mind their local audience of homesick Southerners, Allen sometimes printed poems such as "The Harp that Once Through Tara's Halls," which he introduced with this comment: "Some years ago when we were younger than we are now—when we were full of romance and poetry—and money—we visited the 'halls of Tara,'" which still exerted their mystic hold on his imagination.

In private letters and in the pages of the *Times*, Allen wrote that he found much to like about his new home, especially the warm climate. He asked an editor in Boston, "How many overcoats does it take now to keep a body from freezing?" How many "flabby-lunged asthmatics and consumptives" were there who could save their lives by coming to the balmy, refreshing air of Mexico? The vitality of the place was itself enlivening, he said elsewhere. "Bullfights, masques, and music, and the giddy dances have been all the rage. The entire population of this great city seems to have turned out en masse for frolic, and fun, and general enjoyment." He was reminded of "those good old times" in New Orleans during the carnival, though thinking of these also brought to his soul "sweet but melancholy reflections."

Allen and Edwards frequently met their fellow Confederates on the daily walks both tried to take for their health. As Allen's biographers Vincent H. Cassidy and Amos E. Simpson explain, they were all exiles together, "chastened by adversity and saddened by the recollections of the past," and lonely for their families. Men who had been rich and powerful now worked, like the two editors, for pennies. But they put on a brave face: the bread they earned was by their own sweat, and "in an atmosphere congenial to the lungs of exiles."

After a time, though, the newspaper began to show a profit, thanks largely to its editors' political connections. By virtue of their roles as publicity agents for the empire, as well as their intimacy with Maury, Magruder, and Hindman, Allen and Edwards were privileged observers of the political and social scene in Mexico City. Allen's experience in government and his sophistication in the arts and sciences led him to appreciate what the emperor had already done to make Mexico City into a modern metropolis. Maximilian's engineers had swarmed through the sprawling capital, constructing museums, office buildings, dams, irrigation canals, sewers, and even macadamized highways; they also repaired the ancient aqueduct constructed by the conquistadores and the crumbling fortified walls of Chapultepec.

Edwards grew increasingly fascinated with Maximilian, even as he saw his failings. It was important that the emperor was a master builder; it was vital that he was impetuous, brave, honorable, observant, and an unusually good writer—in another time he would have made a first-rate foreign correspondent or travel writer. His attitude toward riding, his favorite pastime, was an aspect of his character that John Edwards, journalist turned cavalryman, particularly applauded. A daring, even reckless rider from his youth, Maximilian always took every jump and hazard, going all out to win a race. He said, in a memoir published after his death, that "to walk one's horse is death. To trot is life. To Gallop is bliss. It is not given to me to ride slowly."

Maximilian's admiring biographer Count Egon Caesar Corti noted that his "pride in his Habsburg descent had developed his sense of honour to the highest degree," and he was "full of ardent ambition." At the same time, the Archduke Max, as he was known when a young man—"Maxl" to his wife—was a "typical Viennese," easygoing, lighthearted, with "a merry wit which won him success in the salons." He also had a tendency to be superficial and flighty in his enthusiasms and erratic in his judgment of people's hearts and their intentions. Kind and gentle by nature, he assumed "that everybody was like himself, and could only think, feel, and act like a thorough gentleman." He carried with him a card that summarized his code of conduct, among them these injunctions: Always tell the truth; avoid vanity; be kind to all; seek justice always; think before speaking; moderation in all things; "two hours' exercise daily"; do not scoff at religion or authority. And, in English, "Take it coolly."

Edwards also admired Maximilian's earnest efforts to immerse himself in the culture of his adopted country. He took pains to speak Spanish as much as possible, he dressed in the fashion of a Spanish grandee, and he devoured Mexican and Spanish literature.

But Edwards, at heart a Midwestern democrat, drew the line at Maximilian's ridiculous handbook of courtly etiquette, the *Reglamento de la Corte*. A sumptuously bound volume stamped with the gold imperial crown, this six-hundred-page guide to royal protocol included elaborate diagrams indicating where everyone should stand in the throne room when receiving visiting dignitaries, as well as three classifications of banquets, with instructions as to which guests were to receive handwritten invitations and which were downgraded to mere printed invitations. Everything was regulated, regimented, and anticipated—even procedures for mourning the emperor in the event that he was assassinated or felled by yellow fever.

The problem with the emperor's manual—one of many—was, according to a later biographer, that "there was not the slightest hint of Mexico anywhere in its crowded pages; and though careful charts told everyone where to stand on all occasions with meticulous distinctions between their respective magnitudes that strained the typographical resources of a local printer, there was no provision in their majestic fairyland for a French general"—a telling omission that would lead to trouble with the man who held Maximilian's future in his hand, Marshal Bazaine.

It was the queen of this "majestic fairyland," the empress Carlota, who was responsible for Bazaine's continued exclusion from court—she saw the marshal as a peasant upstart, competing with her for influence over her husband. In the end, it would be Carlota more than anyone else who would share responsibility for her husband's death, not least because she estranged Maximilian from Bazaine.

Carlota was a tall, slender young woman, only twenty-five in 1865 (a year older than Betty Shelby). Her blood was as blue as her husband's, and her pride in it even more deeply felt. Their marriage in 1857, when she was seventeen and Maximilian was twenty-five, had been an old-fashioned union between dynasties, not a love match. Her father was King Leopold I of Belgium, a German from the House of Saxe-Coburg-Gotha. Her mother was the daughter of King Louis-Philippe, of the Orléans dynasty in France that had been driven into exile by the first Bonaparte. Related by marriage or blood to virtually all of the royal houses of Europe—Queen Victoria of England was a cousin to whom she wrote frequently—she had changed her name from Charlotte to Carlota long before arriving in Mexico, when she and Maximilian were in residence as rulers in Italy and living at Miramar, near Trieste.

Carlota gave a weekly ball at Chapultepec that followed an unvaried routine. First, she and Maximilian mounted the throne, which was topped by a crimson canopy and an imperial crown. Two palace guards dressed in parade uniforms and helmets and carrying halberds stood beside the throne. The guests were then presented in their turn to their majesties, after which a quadrille opened the ceremonies—"always a great success and very animated," Maximilian wrote to his brother Karl, during which "a bevy of the loveliest women join in the dance."

Sara Yorke attended one such ball and came away feeling that Carlota was the stronger monarch of the two. Maximilian was a good-looking man with a fine figure, but "the whole expression of his face revealed weakness and indecision. He looked, and was, a gentleman. His dignity was without hauteur. . . . He had the faculty of making you feel at ease; and he possessed far more personal magnetism than did the Empress." But she seemed to be "the better equipped of the two to cope intelligently with the difficulties of practical life. . . . Hers was a strong, intelligent face, the lines of which were somewhat hard at times." She was "reserved, somewhat lacking in tact and adaptability," and she showed "a certain haughtiness of manner, a dignity too conscious of itself," which put people off.

Carlota did try, like her husband, to become one with "her people."

Writing to her cousin Eugénie, the wife of Napoléon III, she said, "As for our costumes, we dress in the Mexican fashion, I go out riding in a sombrero, our meals are in the Mexican style, we have a carriage drawn by mules with quantities of bells, we never use any wraps but serapes, I go to Mass in a mantilla." But she betrayed her true attitude by adding, "And so in all that is external and puerile we conform to all that is most Mexican, to such an extent as to amaze the very Mexicans themselves."

Carlota's ineffectual attempt to reconcile her natural diffidence and unacknowledged contempt for the Mexicans with her sense of obligation to the local culture led her to frequent revealing gaffes, such as one recalled by Sara Yorke. In that instance, the young empress was warmly embraced by the elderly wife of a Mexican official—a custom in Mexico as common as a handshake in Europe. Carlota recoiled in disgust at this infringement on her royal dignity. The "poor señora dissolved in tears," and a pall of embarrassment descended upon the room.

John Edwards saw a different side of Carlota—that of a romantic girl who was thrilled and intrigued by the gallant Confederates, perhaps unconsciously recognizing in them fellow adherents of a lost cause. Like Maximilian, she was charmed by the bashful writer—a friend of Edwards said he was always "shy as a fawn"—and invited him to tea at Chapultepec several times to tell her and Maximilian stories of the war in Missouri and Arkansas and of Shelby's adventures in Mexico. Five years later, when he mistakenly believed she had died, Edwards wrote a loving obituary for *The Kansas City Times* entitled "Poor Carlotta," and enshrined her as "a queen of all hearts where honor dwelt."

Poor Carlota indeed—and even poorer Maximilian. It would later be clear that the Confederates had arrived at the high-water mark of the empire, which lasted from midsummer through December 1865. The French tide was already ebbing, and that of Juárez was beginning to surge. But many new arrivals, like Shelby and Price, were sufficiently confident of a future in Mexico to send for their families, and new immigrants were flocking to Carlota, Córdoba, and the other colonies. Henry Allen, who was privy to the inner workings of the government, assured a friend at home in November 1865 that he considered "this empire perfectly secure. France, and Spain, and Austria can't back out. Their honor is at stake."

As for the United States, Allen saw little reason to fear that it would invade Mexico, where it would have to contend not only with the French but with intransigent old soldiers like himself and Edwards—"for the South, although overwhelmed, is not conquered."

TEN

"A Fortune Awaits"

Jo Shelby was ready to settle down at last, he told the readers of *The Mexican Times* in mid-October 1865, right there in Córdoba: "I was raised in the best part of Kentucky—lived in the best part of Missouri, and I tell you honestly, it is the best country I have ever seen. You will agree with me when you see it. Sugar, Tobacco, Coffee, Corn, Cotton and Rice grow as finely upon it as in any country in the world." There was room to spare and money to be made: "A fortune awaits any man who owns a farm in this Valley, and who will exercise energy and economy for a few years."

Privately, Shelby was still bitter about giving up what he had lost at home, and he resented those who, unlike him, had saved their properties by surrendering. Writing to a friend in Missouri on November 1, 1865, he said, "I am here as an exile; defeated by the acts of the southern people themselves" who loved their lands "more than principle. . . . Let them reap what their deserved, *eternal disgrace*. D——n 'em, they were foolish enough to think by laying down their arms they would enjoy all the rights they once had." His "heart [was] heavy at the thought of being separated from you all forever; but I am not one of those to ask forgiveness for that which I believe *to day* is right. The party in power has manifested no leniency."

Nevertheless, Shelby had reason to feel good about his prospects. Just a few days earlier he had greeted Betty and the boys, Joe and Orville, at the dock in Veracruz. He thought Betty looked worn from the long journey; she marveled that, for all his travails, he still had not a white hair to show in his lustrous beard and hair. That evening, as they settled into their hotel room for the night before the return trip to Córdoba, Betty removed a money belt filled with five hundred dollars in gold coins that Anna and Benjamin Gratz had given her when she left Lexington. For the first time since their home in Waverly had been burned in 1862, they were together again as a family, with money and, they hoped, security.

Betty and Jo Shelby's new home was set in the midst of twelve acres of century-old pineapple fields and groves of fruit trees: mango, papaya, lemon, orange, figs, and bananas. It was more than a house; it was a magnificent hacienda that Maximilian had generously bestowed upon Shelby for a nominal rent. It had red tile roofs and stone walls crawling with jasmine and bougainvillea. There were half a dozen bedrooms, set back under deep covered porches; an oak-beamed library with leather chairs and reading lamps; a game room with a billiard table; a kitchen and dining room capable of feeding dozens—and eight or nine quietly reliable Indian servants to look after the house and grounds. The new tenants must have derived considerable satisfaction from the confident assertion in *The Mexican Times* that the property had previously belonged to the now-disgraced and exiled former president Antonio López de Santa Anna, best known to the paper's American readers as the villain of the Alamo in 1836—though this charming irony may have been an invention of the always ingenious John Edwards.

Córdoba itself elicited different reactions from foreign visitors. Ernst Pitner, the young Austrian infantry officer, had been housed there the previous year in a deconsecrated church; he described a town of three thousand people set in the midst of a tropical jungle dotted with plantations of coffee, sugar, and maize. The region abounded with wildlife, including tapirs, monkeys, pumas, eagles, vultures, and innumerable screeching parrots that raced about like chickens in the passageways and courtyards of the town. What most struck the lieutenant were the scattered heaps of bronze bells ripped from the churches and monasteries by would-be entrepreneurs hoping to sell them after Juárez expropriated church property. The sales had been rescinded after Juárez fled, and the bells lay unclaimed and abandoned along the roads, next to overturned cannons.

The heavy bells and cannons were safe, though, because the roads in and out of the town were terrible. To the west lay the town of Orizaba, five thousand feet above sea level; above it towered the eighteen-thousand-foot, snow-covered peak of the same name. Orizaba and its nearby sister, Popocatépetl, were no longer active volcanoes, but the earth still shook repeatedly with quakes, including a major one, in 1864, that tore fissures in the mountain trails and loosened the rocks that loomed over them. There were deep ravines over which flimsy bridges had been flung. Steep, eroded hillsides erupted spontaneously with cascading boulders and mud slides that tore away the bridges and sent carriages and wagons tumbling to their doom. The twenty-five-mile road between Córdoba and Orizaba had been a nightmare for the French and American armies in the past on their approach to Mexico City, and it remained one afterward for the colonists.

The first twenty-mile section of the eastward approach toward Veracruz, to the railhead at Paso del Macho, was much easier, at least in the dry season, when Betty Shelby arrived. But there was no proper roadbed for the enormous freight wagons that sometimes weighed up to five tons and required twenty mules to pull. Lighter carriages toppled and lost wheels in the deep ruts left by the wagons. When the monsoons hit with deluges of ten inches and more in a few hours, the soft loam and clay turned into quicksand-like bogs that sucked down mules, horses, carriages, and freight wagons, one of which vanished entirely with all of its mules.

For Betty Shelby, though, Córdoba was a pleasant relief after the dirt, squalor, and omnipresent vultures of Veracruz—cleanup crews for carrion that were protected by law as municipal necessities. Córdoba impressed her more favorably than it did Pitner. An old colonial city, a way station on the 260-mile journey from Mexico City to Veracruz. At a thousand feet above sea level, it was still tropical but above the lowlands fever zone. It was flanked by *barrancas*, or ravines, to the north and south, which allowed the heavy rains to drain instead of flooding the cobblestoned streets. There was a gracious square in the middle of town, surrounded by *portales,* a series of "splendid arched streets laid out in a grid," according to *The Mexican Times.* A church was under construction, and two others were being planned; there was also a convent of St. Anthony of Padua, built in 1714; a hospital, founded in 1730; a poor house; and a "college for educating girls," not yet finished. Visitors lodged in a combined municipal building and hotel that was fronted by a hundred-yard-long arched gallery that provided much-needed shade.

The social center for the colonists in Córdoba and the adjoining Carlota was the Confederate Hotel. A shabby two-story brick building, under the management of a Texan named W. D. Johnson, the Confederate featured Saturday night cotillions, a bar stocked with expensive Kentucky bourbon, and newspapers brought in from New Orleans, full of stories about Reconstruction and carpetbaggers destroying what was left of the Old South.

Many of Shelby's former associates spent much of their time in the Confederate, among them Sterling Price and his son, Herbert, a former captain now running a sawmill in Orizaba with ex-general James Slaughter; Thomas Hindman, who had learned enough Spanish in three months to set up a law practice in town; and several men from the Iron Brigade who had acquired farming land in the area: Jim Cundiff, Jim Hodge, and the veterinarian and surgeon, John Tisdale, who had gone in with the absent John Edwards to buy about six hundred acres.

Shelby met others after his arrival in Córdoba: William Oldham, formerly chief justice of Texas, who had set up shop as a photographer; a Kentucky clergyman, T. E. Holeman, who had left home after refusing to perform a marriage ceremony for "a Yankee man and a Secesh gal"; and an enterprising young Missourian, a Major McMurtry, who was trying to talk Shelby into joining him in a freight-hauling business for the French army. All told, there were about three hundred Southerners living in the two colonies by the end of 1865.

Shelby's closest neighbor, Isham Harris, was the mayor of Carlota. His last post, rather more significant, had been as wartime governor of Tennessee. He was an unwilling émigré; at war's end the Reconstruction governor of Tennessee, who called himself the "fighting parson," William Brownlow, had issued a warrant for Harris's arrest. Together with a Kentucky general, B. H. Lyon, and two of his former slaves, now paid servants, Harris trekked through Arkansas into the swamps and bayous of Louisiana. The last part of their journey to Shreveport, through federal lines, was by means of a small boat. Missing the connection with Shelby at San Antonio, Harris sent his former slaves home with his blessing; he then made his own way to Monterrey, where, like Terrell and Allen, he enjoyed the hospitality of Colonel Jeanningros. The grandiloquent Magruder was there as well, Harris recalled, offering a banquet toast to "the Lost Cause, to Lee, Jackson, and to the Sovereignty of the States."

In Monterrey, Harris traded his valuable saddle horse for a broken-down wagon drawn by mules. Two Mexicans drove the wagon while he studied a Spanish grammar. After a trip of twenty-five miles a day for two weeks that he called "one of the longest, most laborious, and hazardous of my life," Harris reached the capital. He found temporary employment with Maury's Colonization Land Office, and the inspiration there to join the new colony of Carlota.

Although John Edwards admiringly calls Harris a veritable Cromwell in his zealous devotion to the Southern cause, Harris was a sociable sort, fond of euchre and dancing. He threw himself into his duties as mayor of Carlota, sending for his wife and children to join him in the spring of 1866. He could not go home to get them, even if he wanted to; there was a five-thousand-dollar price on his head set by the Reconstruction legislature of Tennessee, which had declared him guilty of treason. Governor Brownlow's widely circulated description of the mild-mannered Harris conveys the tone of the times and does much to explain why Harris, Shelby, and the others were disinclined to return to the States:

> This culprit Harris is about five feet ten inches high, weighs about one hundred and forty-five pounds and is about fifty-five years of Age. His complexion is sallow—his eyes are dark and penetrating—a perfect index to the heart of a traitor—with the scowl and frown of a demon resting upon his brow. The study of mischief, and the practice of crime, have brought upon him premature baldness and a grey beard. With brazen-faced impudence he talks loudly and boastingly about the over throw of the Yankee Army, and entertains

no doubt but the South will achieve her independence. He chews tobacco rapidly, and is inordinately fond of liquor. In his moral structure he is an unscrupulous man—steeped to the chin in personal and political profligacy—now about lost to all sense of honor and shame—with a heart reckless of social duty, and fatally bent on mischief.

Shelby was also doubtless encouraged in his decision to stay in Mexico by Betty's news of the fate of one of his key aides, Charles Brownlee. Captured in the spring of 1863 near Boonville, Missouri, while on a recruiting mission for Shelby, Lieutenant Brownlee was sentenced to death by a military tribunal as a bushwhacker and spy. He escaped and rejoined the Iron Brigade until the end of the war, when he returned home to surrender; under the generous peace terms offered by the Union, he anticipated that the wartime sentence would be set aside. It was not: Brownlee was executed on May 10, 1865. Dozens of other men who had been with Shelby died after the war in federal confinement from illnesses—smallpox, measles, diarrhea, pneumonia—brought on and exacerbated by overcrowding and neglect.

Though returning home was dangerous, staying in Mexico presented the Confederate colonists with myriad challenges as well—the tropical climate, homesickness, resolving old grudges, finding the money to stay alive, coping with the fact that they had no say in the political future of the country. But their most immediate problem was how to deal with the natives. The greatest insight into these conflicts was provided by William Marshall Anderson, who decided they were too profound to overcome and returned home, ill with yellow fever, in early 1866. Anderson, one of the first Confederates to arrive in Mexico, had been commissioned in the spring of 1865 by Maximilian to look into the potential for a colony in Coahuila—the northern state through which Shelby had traveled.

Born in 1807 in Louisville, Kentucky, Anderson was a lawyer and an amateur anthropologist with a sharp eye for both landscapes and their inhabitants. As a young man, he had explored the Rocky Mountains in the 1830s with the trader William Sublette; he later managed two farms in Ohio and worked as a surveyor in Virginia. Like the other Confederates who went to Mexico, he thought the land offered opportunity for development—but not in the barren deserts of Coahuila, he told Maximilian after an inspection tour in April. Córdoba, which he then visited, was far better suited to agriculture, with its "long rains, rich soil and warm sun."

But Anderson warned Maximilian that he saw formidable cultural obstacles to any enterprise requiring Americans and Mexicans to work together. The Mexicans had given their "submission and allegiance" to the "Grand court & council of General Mañana," Anderson said; American and northern European notions of punctuality were beyond them. (Maximilian could only agree; shortly after his arrival he and his royal entourage had shown up for an opera at the stated performance time and had to wait in the dark and empty hall for an hour until the audience, singers, and musicians drifted in.)

Anderson also thought the social and cultural gap between Mexicans and North Americans, the "difference between Catholic conviction and Protestant impression," was unbridgeable. As an example, he described witnessing a poor woman, a "bare-legged, shoeless supplicant kneeling before the statue of St. Anthony of Padua" on "the cold, hard pavement of a local church. . . . She begs, she implores him [St. Anthony] to give vigor and vitality to her sick infant. She says, 'You see how he suffers, why don't you cure him? Why don't you go to God and ask him to help me?' She knows that God is everywhere. She knows that God is there on the altar." But when God does not respond, she is helpless in a way that a Baptist woman in Tennessee or Missouri would never be able to understand, and would never tolerate.

Initially, Shelby and the other colonists were able to elicit enough cooperation from their less-than-enthusiastic labor force to survive economically, thanks to the richness of the lands they occupied. But there was another, more serious problem with the local population: active resistance in the form of Juárez-supporting guerrillas and bandit chiefs who joined the guerrillas when it pleased them, or simply stole what they could from the colonists. The problem became more serious just as Shelby was settling in at Córdoba; on October 3, 1865, Marshal Bazaine persuaded the emperor to sign the infamous Black Decree, requiring the death sentence for any Mexican actively opposing the emperor's rule with arms or oratory. That decision would greatly increase the opposition to government-sponsored land colonies such as those in Córdoba and Carlota. It would also become Maximilian's own death warrant less than two years later.

Marshal Bazaine had bullied Maximilian into signing the decree because he was a hard man to say no to. He had a record of success, and he had the support of his real boss, the emperor Napoléon. He also had a distinctively Gallic panache, often leading men into battle brandishing no weapon except a small white cane, and had already thwarted a guerrilla insurgency in Algeria.

Promoted to lieutenant in the newly formed French foreign legion in 1832, Bazaine had found himself facing a nomadic enemy, desert Arabs who attacked when and where they chose, then disappeared into the sandy wastes. Though fierce and unyielding as individual warriors, the Arabs were no match for a modern European army and thus avoided direct engagements with the legion. Bazaine stymied Arab resistance with a ruthless program called the *razzia:* punishment of the villages that harbored the fighters by means of sudden, overwhelming attacks on their homes and livestock. This selective scorched-earth policy was designed to turn the population against the insurgents and to deny them safe havens and supplies.

Bazaine headed up a branch of the Bureau Arabe, an intelligence and governmental arm of the legion. As such, he "became the channel through which the French authorities imposed their will upon the population," according to one of his biographers. The Arabs were crushed, or at least subdued—until they rose against France in the twentieth century and forced the French to withdraw under Charles de Gaulle.

For his bravery in the assault on Sebastopol during the Crimean War in 1854, he had been decorated and promoted to general. Thus when it fell to the French army to attack and secure Mexico, the Spanish-speaking general with experience in putting down guerrilla insurgencies as well as in traditional warfare was the natural choice for a leading role.

In Mexico, Bazaine had been successful initially with massive search-and-destroy operations against the Juaristas, both the regular army and the guerrillas. By the early summer of 1864, when Maximilian arrived, the capital was securely held within a huge arc to the north and east. The southern and southwest regions were not secure, and the opposition forces there were capably led by General Porfirio Díaz, but they were not sufficiently strong to pose a serious threat to the occupation. By the spring of 1865, Bazaine thought the military situation in Mexico was sufficiently in hand to allow him to consider sending General Douay's division in San Luis Potosí back to France.

But Bazaine's triumph was short-lived. The mountains and deserts of Mexico and its stubborn, long-suffering inhabitants made it impervious to any form of secular civil administration. Only the Catholic Church, now crippled, had been able to impose its will on the country. The technique of the *razzia* that Bazaine brought with him from North Africa, designed to curb guerrilla terrorism, only generated more resistance by Juárez's Liberals, including outright atrocities. In April 1865, almost two hundred Belgian soldiers were lined up against a wall and shot after surrendering at Tacámbaro. More recently, and uncomfortably closer to the Confederates in Córdoba, about four hundred guerrillas had stopped a train near Veracruz by pulling up the rails. They then shot the engineer and crew, robbed all the passengers, and murdered seventeen Frenchmen, some of them civilians. Bazaine's soldiers' morale was plunging; despite the certainty of the death penalty for desertion of the legion, many men had not only run away but, in some cases, sought safety by joining the Liberals. Eventually, Juárez authorized his own "foreign legion," made up of those French, Belgian, and Austrian soldiers, and more than a few Americans, including members of Shelby's former brigade.

By October 1865, the French posts in Monterrey, Saltillo, and Parras that had harbored Shelby just months earlier were either abandoned or about to be. One town had changed hands fourteen times before Bazaine finally gave up on it altogether. French forces were constantly lured into pursuits of the enemy that drew them out just far enough to be isolated and threatened with disaster. Bazaine became convinced that what he called Maximilian's "dreamy" vision of earning Mexican loyalty by means of good works and benevolent liberalism was failing. His "misplaced clemency" in repeatedly pardoning those whom military tribunals had condemned to death was undercutting the army's efforts. Citing a false rumor that Juárez had fled to the

United States, Bazaine argued that he had given up, meaning that those left behind were not rebels but "bandits."

The Black Decree was an even harsher measure than the one Maximilian had issued a year earlier, which required the execution of "all persons who are members of armed bands or societies not authorized by law." The reason for the decree, Maximilian wrote, was that the cause "which Don Benito Juárez upheld with such constancy and valor has succumbed both to the national will and to those very laws invoked by the rebel chieftain in support of its titles." The "indulgence and clemency" previously shown had been abused by "a few brigands misled by unpatriotic passions and supported by a demoralized rabble, as well as that unbridled soldiery constituting the sad dregs in all civil strife." From this point on, the government would be "inflexible in punishment, for such are the demands made by the precepts of civilization, for the rights of humanity, and every moral canon."

An immediate consequence of the Black Decree followed shortly after the capture, in a surprise attack by the French, of about thirty Juarist officers, including two generals. All were tried, convicted, and shot within twenty-hour hours. One of the condemned generals, Salazar, left behind a touching, soon-to-be-famous letter to his mother, later reprinted on clandestine presses and circulated throughout the country. "I have just been condemned to death," it read. "I go down to the grave at the age of thirty-three, without a blot on my military career or my name. Do not weep, have courage; for the crime of your son is that he has defended the sacred cause of the independence of his country. For this I am going to be shot. I leave no money," Salazar concluded, no possessions other than a silver watch and four suits. "But God will aid you and my children who will be proud to bear my name. Bring them and my brothers up in the path of honor. The scaffold does not stain the name of a patriot."

Bazaine had sworn to protect the colonists at Carlota and elsewhere. The Black Decree was intended to prevent raids such as those in the Córdoba region by a local bandit called Don Miguel Rodríguez. Shelby respected Bazaine as a brave and unyielding officer but had doubts about his judgment. In a casual conversation over brandy and cigars before Shelby had left for Córdoba, Bazaine had wondered about the chances of the Union army crossing the border to attack the French. He said he didn't think very much of General Grant, who he assumed would lead any such attack. He conceded that his legionnaires exaggerated when they boasted that one of them could whip any ten Yankees, but Bazaine was certain that his army could easily handle Ulysses S. Grant. Shelby smiled and said he begged to differ.

If he had been asked his opinion of the Black Decree before it was issued, Shelby would have told the marshal that the Confederates had had their own experience with draconian measures, one in particular that was a good deal milder than Bazaine's. Thomas Ewing's Order No. 11 in 1863 had been issued for the same reason as the Black Decree: to force locals to declare their fealty to the government and to deny insurgents the support of civilians in their homeland. Ewing's decree had done nothing but light the fuse for two more years of bloody insurrection in Missouri. There was no reason to suppose the Mexicans would react any differently from the Americans in this instance, and with a justifiably even greater sense of outrage.

But he had not been asked, so Shelby took it upon himself to seek out Rodríguez, the local bandit chieftain. There was a time to fight, he said, and there was a time to deal, and to separate himself from the repressive policies of Maximilian and Bazaine. "Just how the negotiations were commenced and consummated," John Edwards wrote, nobody knew. "But true it is that in the cool of the evenings, and when the French drums had beaten tattoo at the fort only half a mile away, Rodriguez would come down from his fastnesses as a peaceful visitor, and sit for hours among the Americans, asking of the Yankee country, and the ups and downs of the Yankee war, for, to a Mexican, everything is Yankee which is American."

The *préstamo*, or protection money, Shelby and the others paid the guerrillas allowed the colonies to survive the winter intact. In late January 1866, an old comrade, Alonzo Slayback, found him flourishing:

> I stopped to see how my American friends were prospering and remained at the house of Gen. Shelby, where I felt very much at home. Mrs. S. and the children are here, and the General seems

contented: is opening a farm, preparing to plant coffee and sugar, cotton and rice. The plantain and banana, with their broad tropical leaves and delicious clusters of fruit—the oranges and lemons, the mango and lime, pine-apple and palm—fill the air with delicious odors, and offer to the sight a constant variety of romantic and interesting scenery.

Shelby was glad to see Slayback again—it was the first time since the poet/warrior had fallen ill on the trail and been left behind to recover. The soldier charged with looking after Slayback had robbed him and disappeared, leaving him only his horse, saddle, and pistols. It was October before he was able to make his way to Mexico City, where Edwards and the other Confederates were able to look after him. He had met the emperor, Slayback said, who in return for a few English lessons had given him a medal and dubbed him "The Knight of Oaxaca." But it was time to go home. His mother was so anxious for his safety that she had gone to Havana and was waiting for him there.

A more surprising departure, about a month later, was that of Matthew Maury, who passed through Córdoba on his way to Veracruz to board a ship for England. There were problems at the Colonization Land Office, Maury told Shelby and Price over dinner at the Confederate Hotel. Maximilian was an absentee emperor, spending most of his time at his new estate in Cuernavaca chasing butterflies—his companion and instructor was a portly, bearded man named Otto Bilimek, the former director of collections at a museum Maximilian had established in an old monastery on the Adriatic. Maury had warned the emperor in October that in his absence the conservative clerics and incompetent bureaucrats were arousing public resentment; his ministries were riddled with graft, the postal system was a joke, and the streets were becoming too dangerous to walk at night or even during the day. Maximilian needed to put down the *insurrectos:* to be present, in uniform, and surrounded by a "brilliant general staff." In November, Maury wrote again to Maximilian, praising the clear-sighted Empress Carlota, who saw the empire drifting rudderless and knew that something had to be done.

Shelby knew that it was Carlota more than Maximilian who had hoped the Confederates would succeed in Mexico—it was largely due to Carlota that Magruder and Reynolds had been appointed to Maury's staff the previous summer while Maximilian was away from the capital on one of his inspection tours of the countryside. It now appeared that pressure from the United States to expel the Confederates was beginning to get to Maximilian. The historians Alfred and Kathryn Hanna sardonically assert that "Maximilian's decision to double-cross Southerners was one of the few he seems actually to have carried out." That is, while he told Washington he could not fire the Confederate appointees, he would, as the Hannas put it, "render their positions so illusory that they would ask to resign." Support for this interpretation is suggested by the letter that Maury received in April 1866, after arriving in England, in which Maximilian coolly thanked him for his services and informed him that for "reasons of economy" he had abolished the Imperial Commission on Colonization.

In New Orleans, General Phillip Sheridan learned of Maury's dismissal but continued to fret about the Confederates. Months earlier, he had boasted to Grant that he had "caught" the immigration commissioner appointed by Maury in Louisiana, meaning that all communications about the colonies sent to him "will be received by me." But now he was more cautious. He said he saw it "reported in the public press that the emigration scheme of Maury, Price, Louis-Napoléon and company is a failure. I have no good reason to believe this to be the case; on the contrary, a large number of emigrants, or adventurers, are going to the Valley of Mexico. Some few have gone from this post by evading the surveillance which I have established here." Sheridan said that a steamship agent had informed him that about three thousand men were seeking passage.

"These adventurers are mostly young men, not of industrious habits, and it is certain that if they cannot earn their living by honest labor here, it is a certainty that they will not be able to do so in Mexico, so that it may be considered a certainty that they will enter into the army of the so-called Emperor. I enclose communications addressed by me to the British Consul . . . from which you can judge of the systems adopted to break up this indirect violation of neutrality." He ended by complaining that he could prevent many emigrants from boarding in New Orleans, but they could still "sail with perfect liberty from New York or other ports, for Vera Cruz."

Although he exaggerated the numbers of potential emigrants, Sheridan was right to be cautious—five hundred arrived in Córdoba in March 1866, even as Maximilian was pulling the welcome mat out from under them. These new arrivals, wrote Henry Allen in *The Mexican Times,* were men and women with "brave hearts and strong arms," and there might be thousands like them on the way. He had bought land in Córdoba himself, Allen said, and planned to stay, living out his "declining years amidst our own fruits and flowers—free from all envy—all hate—but with good will toward all men." Privately, Allen was less hopeful; he wrote to a friend that there was plenty of land for the wave of newcomers, but too many were merely adventurers and ne'er-do-wells without skills, energy, or money, especially the latter: "I fear there will be much misery among the colonists who come here without money. *They had better stay at home.*"

ELEVEN

The Collapse of the
Confederate Colonies

Readers of the major newspapers in the United States were fascinated by the Confederate exodus to Mexico that Sheridan so deplored. Correspondents for *The New York Herald* and *The New York Times,* based in Mexico City, sent frequent dispatches describing the progress and travails of the colonists. The *Herald* correspondent who visited Córdoba and Carlota in April seems to have taken his cue from Henry Allen. "This is no country for drones," he said; any man without energy "had better go hang himself." Of those who were successful, "General Shelby is the most energetic and enterprising, and consequently his prospects are more flattering than any American's in the country. Besides working in his hacienda, he runs large wagon trains"—Shelby having recently been persuaded by McMurtry's earlier proposition to begin a freight-hauling business—"from the railroad terminus at Paso del Macho to the City [of Mexico]. His wagons are all of Yankee manufacture, are drawn by ten mules each, and every wagon carries a load of six to seven thousand pounds, the freight of which is 300 to 350 dollars."

The reporter also spent time with Sterling Price, who seems to have had more of it to spare than did the busy Shelby. According to another visitor, his lodgings also suffered by comparison with Shelby's hacienda; he was said to be living next to the railroad tracks in a shack surrounded by an adobe wall encrusted on the top with broken glass. The *Herald* reporter's description was more appealing—the house was made of bamboo, and was set

> mid a grove of mango trees near the *casa* which afford a cool and inviting retreat for the old soldier, and here he may be found at all hours, seated upon a chair of his own manufacture, cracking jokes with old companions in arms, or giving orders respecting the cultivation of his plantation. Everything is of the most primitive description, the tables and chairs being the General's own handiwork. General Price is not a little of a Yankee, and is about as ingenious and handy as any New Englander. Governor Isham Harris and the General are inseparable companions, living together until the Governor's house shall be completed.

"I have six hundred and forty acres here," Price told the reporter, "which I would not exchange for twelve hundred anywhere in the United States." He also claimed to have exported $25,000 worth of coffee, as well as tobacco, sweet potatoes, fruits, and even cattle and horses—though whose coffee he was selling is unclear, given that it took three years for a crop to mature. Expansive as always, Price advised the reporter to give up journalism and "settle down in this magnificent country, and turn farmer."

Henry Allen continued to boost Price and Shelby in his *Mexican Times* after his return to the capital in March, but not for long; he died abruptly on April 11, 1866. As romantic a soul as John Edwards, Allen had always been given to speculations about death; once, he recalled the medieval monks who met one another with the greeting "Brother, thou shalt die," and said, "If all of us would think oftener of this warning, it would make us wiser and better, and prepare us for that long and dark journey across 'Jordan's swelling flood.'" He had also written with particular horror about yellow fever—the *vómito:* "Cold chills and burning fevers, black vomit and convulsions! Save me from such a death, rather a thousand times the cold steel or 'swift winged lead.'"

Allen's most recent biographers think it was yellow fever that killed him, at just forty-six years old. In his consoling letter to a friend of the editor's, John Edwards, who, along with Marshal Bazaine's personal physician, attended Allen during his illness, substituted poetry in place of the grisly details that Allen had foreseen and undergone: "One bright, mild, tropical Sunday morning, with the soft whisperings of the breeze, and the chiming of the cathedral bells coming in through the half-opened window, he breathed his last. One short, sharp struggle, and all was over."

But all was not quite over. The American chargé d'affaires authorized Allen's burial in the American cemetery but objected when he learned that Allen's body would be dressed in his uniform and covered by a Confederate flag. A more politically discreet burial ensued, with Allen wearing his "fatigue uniform coat" instead of his full uniform.

John Edwards took on the editing of *The Mexican Times* after Allen's death. Both he and Allen had finally earned enough from the enterprise, which was generously subsidized by Maximilian, to invest in Córdoba land—and, in Allen's case, $3,500 dollars in a traveling circus, soon lost: "It was a total failure," Edwards wrote to a sister in Missouri. "The actors were imported Yankees who broke up in a row, and the stockholders lost every dollar."

Edwards was no businessman, and the *Times* would soon founder, but in April 1866, he was still enthusiastic about the land he and John Tisdale, the brigade surgeon, had bought in the Córdoba Valley. Coffee and sugarcane thrived on it, he told his sisters, and he was excited by the prospects of raising hogs: "Bacon is worth 75 cents a pound, and cured hams sell readily at $1 per pound and scarce at that. Hogs thrive excellently, and are fattened on bananas, oranges, and pineapples, which grow so plentifully as persimmons in old Loudoun." But he added a dark note: "You say this is all very fine, but the Empire will not last—Maximilian will be forced out—anarchy and revolution will usurp the present order of stability."

Edwards was prescient. Only a month later, on May 15, 1866, the first serious raid on the Confederate colonies occurred at Omealco. Situated about fifteen miles southeast of Córdoba, on a navigable river that led to the coast near Veracruz, Omealco had been settled by about twenty immigrants from half a dozen Southern states, including Missouri and Tennessee. It had been a plantation of ten thousand acres owned by the church before it was taken by Juárez. The surrounding forests were thick with mahogany and rosewood. Maximilian had authorized Thomas Hindman and several others to build a sawmill there, using the expertise gained by General Slaughter's operation at Orizaba, but construction had not yet begun. The colony's main source of income was the immensely profitable acreage devoted to coffee beans; each acre held six hundred trees, each tree yielded as much as two pounds of beans per season, and the costs of cultivation and harvesting, thanks to the plentiful supply of Indians, were minimal.

These laborers had been living as squatters on the plantation after the church had lost it. They resented the new landlords, who treated them as they had treated black slaves at home and who, unlike Shelby, had refused to pay protection money to the local guerrillas. Stoking their resentment was none other than the elusive Luis Figueroa after whom General Douay had earlier planned to send Shelby. In his comprehensive study of Confederates in Mexico, *The Lost Cause,* Andrew Rolle describes Figueroa as the leader of a gang of "cut-throats and robbers who fought with Juárez mainly for the purpose of stealing." He now led the Omealco Indians against the Confederate settlers, drove them from their houses, and marched them off to Veracruz, where they could board ships back to the United States. The Americans were given almost nothing to eat on their forced march; according to Rolle they were "insulted and spat upon" and were "fortunate not to have been shot." A few chose not to go home but to Carlota.

Carlota was supposed to be safe because of its special provenance in the eyes of the emperor and the large French presence of several thousand soldiers nearby. But on June 9, 1866, *The Mexican Times* featured a story by John Edwards describing a nighttime raid eight days earlier by guerrillas—again led by Figueroa. This was a far more serious affair than Omealco; there were as many as a thousand men involved in the attack on several hundred terrified colonists. Stores and houses were looted and burned as their owners huddled in the streets. Several men were shot, and dozens were taken into the hills as captives—including, according to Edwards, "some in their sick beds." The prisoners were held without food for several days and "beaten with sabres and pricked with lances." Eventually they were released, but the structures of the colony of Carlota were burned to the ground.

Among those who lost their homesteads was Sterling Price. He traveled to Mexico City afterward and persuaded Marshal Bazaine to send Dupin, "the tiger of the tropics," and his contre-guerillas to hunt down Figueroa. They succeeded, Price noted with satisfaction in an early July 1866 letter to his son: "The Imperial troops went in search of the robbers a few days since, came upon them in camp and scourged them terribly, killing their commander and about twenty others; six thousand dollars were found upon the person of the commander." In the meantime, Price had moved with his wife to neighboring Córdoba—two miles away and as yet untouched.

Mrs. Price wrote to relatives at home that she was distressed at the state of Price's health and of their finances: "We must economize at every point. We have been living in Córdoba, and it is very expensive. Rent high; provisions enormous." By early January 1867, Price had returned to St. Louis, "his once powerful frame," according to a local newspaper, "a mere wreck of its former self." Local supporters organized a campaign to raise fifty thousand dollars to buy and maintain a house for the general—according to a biographer, Price "remained the personification of their cause and struggle" to most Missourians.

But not to Jo Shelby, who conspicuously declined to offer the hospitality of his large house when Price and his wife were penniless in Córdoba. One reason may have been Price's behavior when Carlota was under attack. If the account in a South Carolina newspaper shortly afterward is to be believed, Price fled to Córdoba to ask for help; "he begged the Americans there to arm themselves and go to Carlota, excusing himself from going on the ground that if the Liberals caught him they would send him to hell or the United States, and he would as soon go one place as the other." But the deeper reason lay in the past, as Shelby's reaction to the fund-raising campaign for his old commander suggests: Better to spend the money not on Price but on the "widows and orphans" created by his "dam'd blunders" during the war, Shelby wrote to a friend in Missouri. The wounds of that war still rankled, in various ways.

Shelby's mood was darkened by the knowledge that Córdoba, too, was doomed. The French were pulling out, leaving only a series of fortified positions between Mexico City and Veracruz, and several in the San Luis Potosí region, to enable a months-long evacuation. Pressured by Secretary of State Seward to announce a phased withdrawal in three stages, concluding in February 1867, Napoléon had conceded defeat of his own imperial ambitions in the New World. He dropped the hammer on Maximilian in a letter dated January 15, 1866. The reason for the withdrawal was financial, Napoléon said—France could contribute no more money, and Maximilian showed no signs of paying back more than a part of what had already been spent, as the Treaty of Miramar had stipulated. But at least the Americans now would have no cause for interfering in Mexico, Napoléon added consolingly; Maximilian should be able to keep his throne. He could always return with the French army if he feared otherwise.

Maximilian's support for the Confederate colonists had steadily diminished, largely because he feared that the American army would cross the border in force. In July 1866, the Confederates' most sympathetic advocate, the empress Carlota, left Mexico for Europe, where she hoped to persuade Napoléon, the pope, and the Austrian emperor Franz Josef to send aid to Maximilian, despite Napoléon's earlier refusal to do so.

After Carlota's departure, John Edwards wrote to his brother at home that the Córdoba colony was virtually "dead beyond resuscitation." Its demise was caused less by the guerillas or by lack of imperial support, than by the human failings of the immigrants. Edwards, heretofore the champion of ancient Scottish chivalry, now rued "the infernal greed and avarice of the Anglo-Saxon race. They wanted more land than they could cultivate, they wanted doubloons to grow on trees and coffee to be sacked ready for shipment, and because all these things were not found most of the emigrants went back cursing the world, the flesh, and the devil."

As for himself, Edwards said later, "I obtained from the Emperor about 500 acres of magnificent land—a river rising in it, wild coffee bearing upon it, and its bottoms beyond comparison. I hired hands, furnished $780 to cultivate it, cleared about 40 acres and had elegant prospects. When the French Army left, murders, robberies, and anarchy came, and we were all forced to abandon the half-tilled land, the half-matured crops." Mexico's land and climate were such that no man could fail, if it were only peaceful. But "the profits arising from my paper in the City of Mexico I expended upon the farm, and lost every dollar thus invested. I tried hard, I was economical, sober, and determined—I worked eighteen hours a day—I failed."

Jo and Betty Shelby now felt especially vulnerable; their third son, Benjamin Gratz Shelby, was born in July 1866, only weeks after the attack on Carlota. Jo sent Betty and the children to Mexico City with Edwards for safety and gave up active management of the farm in favor of his more lucrative freight business. He hauled settlers' provisions and salable commodities over the rugged road from Veracruz to Mexico City, and north to San Louis Potosí. He had a profitable monopoly, but for good reason—hazardous enough at the best of times, due to weather and road conditions, the unglamorous occupation of hauling freight was now as dangerous as any wartime campaign. Not content to let the vanquished enemy simply withdraw, Juárez's generals hoped to destroy Napoléon's army and to mortally wound the French emperor. Civilians such as Shelby who supplied the French were special targets.

In late July 1866, Shelby delivered eighty wagons to General Douay in San Luis Potosí. Douay asked him to take ten of those wagons, with an escort of twenty men, about forty miles north to the outpost at Cesnola. Several of the men were old comrades from the Iron Brigade, including the reliable James Kirtley, accustomed to scouting ahead for trouble. Shortly before noon, about five hours out of San Luis Potosí, Kirtley reported back to Shelby that a large Mexican force numbering in the hundreds was hard upon them. Encumbered by the wagons, Shelby sent Kirtley with two others back to San Luis Potosí to bring help and retreated to the crumbling walls of an abandoned hacienda. He circled the wagons within the walls, reinforced the walls with bags of corn meal and sand, hastily shoveled dirt embankments, and waited for the Mexican attack.

The Juarist commander, a Colonel Gutierrez, sent a messenger under a flag of truce. He said he had five hundred men. He promised that if the Americans surrendered, no harm would come to them. Shelby's force now numbered only seventeen—he was in approximately the same dire situation that had faced the one-handed Captain Danjou during the battle for Puebla. He could not hope to hold off such a large force for long. But he also knew, according to Edwards, that the colonel had a reputation as a renegade priest with an abiding hatred of foreigners and an appetite for torture. Stalling for time—it would take five or six hours at least for Douay's relief force to arrive, assuming Kirtley got through—Shelby replied that his honor as an officer required proof that he was faced with insurmountable odds.

Gutierrez observed the strong defensive position facing him—dozens of rifles perched ready to fire atop heaped bags of sand and two ominous black cylinders peeking from holes in the hacienda walls. He could not know that there were many fewer bodies than there were rifles to fire them, or that the cannons were blackened logs, a reprise of Shelby's trick years earlier when he bluffed the Union steamer into surrendering at Waverly. The Mexican colonel obligingly marched his men up and down on a dusty field before the Americans, exhausting them in the blistering sun and consuming several hours in the process. At the end of the long afternoon, the colonel formed his muttering soldiers into ranks and sent the messenger back to Shelby. Now, the colonel asked, would the Americans surrender? He needed time to think about it, Shelby said. Another hour went by. His patience exhausted, the colonel insisted on an answer. No, Shelby said at last, as dusk approached, he regretted to say to the colonel that he would have to come and get him.

John Edwards was, for once, not on hand personally to observe Shelby's adventure, but he described it with his usual élan.

With a shrill, short yell, the Mexicans dashed forward to the attack. Had the wave held on its course, it would have inundated the earthwork. It broke, however, before it reached halfway across the open space behind which it had gathered for the onset. Those in front began to fire too soon, and those in the rear, not seeing from the smoke what was really in front, fired too, and without aim and object. With unloaded guns they dared not go on—the fire of the

Americans was distressing beyond endurance—the wave broke itself into fragments—and the sun sank lower and lower.

At that moment two squadrons of Chasseurs d'Afrique, guided by
Kirtley, arrived and charged the demoralized Juaristas. Those who survived disappeared into the cacti. The Chasseurs were under the command of a young Captain Mesillon. He told Shelby that General
Douay's spies had just informed him that the battalion manning the
French outpost ten miles to the east was in great danger. Unbe-
knownst to its commander, Colonel du Preuil, a Mexican force had
nearly encircled it; within a day or two it would have its artillery in
place and the battalion would be doomed. Douay asked Shelby to take
command of the Chasseurs and rescue the man who had so grievously
insulted him the year before at Parras. Douay had learned about the
incident from General Jeanningros, according to John Edwards, and it
pleased him to allow Shelby to exact his "revenge" in this manner.

Shelby left the wagons behind and rode through the night toward
the outpost. It cost the lives of a dozen French soldiers, shot from their
saddles by Juaristas lying in ambush, but the rescue party arrived well
before dawn and quickly explained the situation to a properly grateful
du Preuil. The French officer asked if Shelby agreed that he should
leave his artillery behind in order to beat a hasty retreat. Shelby said
that he had made a practice of never surrendering his artillery during
the late war in Arkansas and Missouri, but that it was du Preuil's decision to make. The artillery was not abandoned.

Shelby then, at du Preuil's request, led the French force southward
to safety at San Luis Potosí. When they arrived on the morning of the
fourth day, General Douay turned out the garrison to welcome his
nearly lost battalion and its rescuers with "sloping standards, presented
arms, and the long exultant role of triumphant music."

That evening Douay pressed Shelby to take money for his services—above and beyond the contract amount. Shelby declined. Then
take it as compensation for the freight business, which was now surely
ruined, Douay begged; it would be impossible for him to continue in
that line after helping the French as he had done. Shelby agreed, but
only on the condition that payment wait until they could both meet

again in Mexico City—knowing that Douay was already well on his way to Veracruz for departure to France.

The colony at Córdoba and the hauling business both now defunct, Shelby briefly considered returning to Missouri but rejected the idea: The fact that Jefferson Davis was still in prison signaled that the Radical Republicans leading the Reconstruction would not welcome his return. In early October 1866, Shelby was summoned to Mexico City by Maximilian, who introduced him to a French financier, Baron Enrique Sauvage. The emperor had bestowed upon Sauvage a land grant near the Gulf Coast along the Tuxpan River, about seventy miles south of Tampico and a hundred miles north of Veracruz. As big as the state of Delaware, Tuxpan was cut off from the more troubled parts of the northeast by virtue of the surrounding impenetrable tropical jungles that ended only when they met the miasmatic swamps near the coast. The only inhabitants were a primitive and impoverished but reportedly friendly band of Toluca Indians, Sauvage told Shelby. They could be paid to harvest the rubber and mahogany trees that abounded in the area, which would then be sent as rafts to Tampico for shipment to the United States and Europe.

Sauvage wanted Shelby, based on the emperor's recommendation, to be his partner and managing director; he himself would remain in Mexico City to handle the international business end of the deal. Maximilian advanced earnest money in the amount of twenty thousand dollars toward the building of a railroad from Tampico to Veracruz, which would further enhance the viability of the new colony.

The Mexican Times, in a story written by John Edwards, announced Shelby's new venture on October 8, 1866. Two hundred shares of the Tuxpan colony would be sold at five hundred dollars per share in order to raise capital; colonists would be allowed to buy up to 320 acres of land at one dollar per acre. Two ships were ordered up to carry immigrants from New Orleans to Tampico. In mid-November, Edwards wrote in *The Mexican Times* that he had received "gratifying intelligence that General Shelby has gone to work with his accustomed hardihood in this really important enterprise." If Shelby had been entrusted with the direction of Córdoba, said Edwards, it would have succeeded as gloriously as Tuxpan certainly would. "With him there is no such word as fail, and the man who went up from captain to major general" would no doubt "find it easier to destroy the obstacles of nature alone than to overcome the barriers of man and nature combined, as he always did."

In late November, Shelby went to Havana and, with Sauvage's money, purchased enough plows and other farming equipment for the colonists he hoped to bring to Tuxpan. Returning by way of Veracruz, he encountered Marshal Bazaine. The harbor teemed with French transport vessels ready to take the second contingent of French troops home. Shelby said he needed weapons with which to defend Tuxpan. Could the marshal see his way clear to letting him have some of the muskets he would no longer need? With those, he said, "I promise you that we can build a colony as prosperous as the colony of the Emperor Napoléon in North Africa."

Considering the pressures that Bazaine was under, it is remarkable that he made time for Shelby. The emperor Maximilian, even as he had been persuading Sauvage to take on Shelby as a partner in yet another enterprise, was already contemplating leaving the country himself. Now he was dithering at Orizaba, trying to decide whether to descend to Veracruz where a transport waited to take him to Miramar. The French, including Bazaine, did their best to persuade him to leave. But Maximilian, convinced that the marshal was complicit in Napoléon's plot to deprive him of the means for defending his empire, distrusted Bazaine. The Mexican Conservatives, led by the Catholic bishop Antonio de Labastida and the mysterious German-American adventurer known as Father Fischer, played on Maximilian's sense of responsibility for their lives and pleaded with him to stay.

Most of all, Maximilian was influenced by his wife, who, in a long letter, had tried to stiffen his spine before she left for Europe. In it Carlota rehearsed the arguments she would use with the powers in Europe who had placed Maximilian in his intolerable position, and who were honor-bound to rescue him. Even if they did not do so, Maximilian had to keep his throne; she recalled other abdications and noted how they were regarded unfavorably in the light of history: Charles X of France resigned after the July Revolution of 1830 and thereby "made the future of his dynasty impossible," and her grand-father Louis-Philippe in 1848 had, by abdicating, "condemned his family to a lasting exile." They had at least the excuse of being old men by comparison with Maximilian, who was now just thirty-four, "full of life and hope in the future." He was no coward, she knew: "I say that emperors do not give themselves up. So long as there is an emperor here, there will be an empire, even if no more than six feet of earth be-long to him. The Empire is nothing but the Emperor."

Carlota's low opinion of Benito Juárez as an Indian peasant made abdication especially intolerable. "One does not give up one's place to such an opponent as that." What about Maximilian's sense of duty, "loyalty, patriotism, and honor"? "One does not abandon one's post before the enemy; why should one abandon a crown?" Finally, she said, Maximilian had presented himself as "the introducer of civiliza-tion, as a saviour and regenerator." How could he "retire on the plea that there is nothing to civilize, to save, or to regenerate"? To do so would concede that the whole enterprise "has been the greatest absur-dity under the sun."

Carlota's eloquence and political intelligence exceeded Maximil-ian's, but she was less stable emotionally. Once in Europe, she begged Napoléon to save Maximilian by sending him more troops and money. Napoléon ignored her, as did Maximilian's brother, the emperor Franz Josef. Both said the Mexican empire was finished, and Maximilian should come home directly.

Carlota's anxiety became hysteria, and finally madness. In October 1866, she was taken in a straitjacket to an asylum in Belgium, where she would die at age eighty-seven in 1927, sixty years after her ill-fated husband. She never understood that she had inadvertently put her fin-ger on the critical error in the whole French-Austrian enterprise—imposing Western civilization on a distant, supposedly benighted people by force will almost always fail. Given that presumably wiser individuals and nations today still persist in this belief, perhaps Maxi-milian and Carlota can be forgiven for finding it persuasive.

But in late November 1866, Maximilian had still not made up his mind to stay or to go home. Weeks earlier, London newspapers erro-neously reported that Maximilian had abdicated his throne, prompt-ing an American diplomatic mission led by none other than General

William T. Sherman to set sail for Havana. Sherman was accompanied by Lewis Campbell, an undistinguished Ohio politician selected by President Johnson to be his new minister to Mexico. The two, with their delegation, were en route to Veracruz, where they would wait on board their ships until Maximilian had departed. They were then to find Juárez and present Campbell's credentials to the reinstated president of Mexico.

Around November 20, 1866, just after Shelby had returned to Tuxpan, his old comrade "Prince John" Magruder passed through Veracruz en route to Havana. He carried with him a message from Bazaine for Sherman and Campbell, which Bazaine hoped would reach President Johnson as soon as possible. The message was blunt: "The moral influence of the United States has destroyed the Empire, and thus the obligation rests upon the United States to keep Mexico from anarchy and protect the thousands of foreigners there. Ten or fifteen thousand American troops properly distributed through northern Mexico and a similar number of French soldiers, all working together, would do the trick."

After all of Grant and Sheridan's fulminations and threats against the French, it would be interesting to know what Sherman thought of Marshal Bazaine's invitation to do exactly what his fellow generals had itched to do for the past two years—occupy Mexico. But Sherman made no comment on this message in his *Memoirs,* or on Bazaine's remarks on American "obligation," other than to note the marshal's cordial invitation to visit Mexico City while his ship was anchored a week later at Veracruz.

General Sherman, as it happened, had been out of sorts from the start of the mission, only taking it on as a favor to his friend General Grant, who had refused it three times himself. Grant rightly suspected it was a plot by Secretary of War Edwin Stanton, an old enemy, to get him out of Washington, and he had apparently lost his lust to conquer Mexico. Sherman complained in a letter to his brother, Senator John Sherman of Ohio, that it was all a waste of time. He particularly resented his implied duty to find Juárez, wherever he might be, after Maximilian announced his firm decision to stay on as emperor on December 1, 1866. He refused to do it, Sherman said: Juárez was reported to be in far-distant Chihuahua, "for no possible purpose other than to be where the Devil himself cannot get at him." He said he had "not the remotest idea of riding on mule back 1,000 miles" to find anyone. He was going home. (Philip Sheridan agreed with Sherman, for his own reasons. Ever distrustful of the French and scornful of Seward's policy of letting them down gently, he assured Grant that Sherman had been saddled with a "ridiculous mission," the only purpose of which seemed to be to get the Liberals "to hold off and let the French get out so that [Seward's] diplomacy will not appear to the world as ridiculous.")

Magruder, too, was going home; he never returned from Havana to Mexico. Sterling Price was also on his way, and the instigator of the colonies plan, Commodore Maury, was already long gone. Only Shelby and Edwards, with Reynolds, Hindman, and a handful of others, were left in Mexico. Of these, only Shelby remained in harm's way. But at least he had his weapons, five hundred muskets that Bazaine had given him in Veracruz; Shelby's biographer Daniel O'Flaherty says that while John Magruder could charm the birds from the trees, "Shelby could charm thousands of dollars out of a Frenchman without even promising to pay it back." For the next three months he worked hard to make Tuxpan a going concern. He hired two hundred Indians as laborers and tried to outwit Sheridan's efforts in New Orleans to prevent settlers from joining the colony.

It was not easy. Sheridan was still obsessed with Shelby and the other Confederates. He told Grant in November 1866, that "the appearance of our troops, and the knowledge that friends were on the border, went like electricity to the hearts and homes of the Mexican people. The Rebels who had escaped from our country had received no sympathy." He continued to believe the French had been in league with the Confederates during the war—"that the occupation of Mexico was a part of the rebellion, and knowing that the contest in our country was for the vindication of Republicanism, I did not think that vindication would be complete until Maximilian was forced to leave." The "Cordova emigration scheme" had not been an innocent effort to begin anew in a foreign land; it had "had for its object the formation of a Maximilian-American party, composed of Confederates harboring antipathy towards our government. Many of these, having no means, would have drifted into the army of Maximilian. I had to take strong grounds against this emigration, and finally broke it up, by refusing to permit emigrants to embark from the seaports within the limit of my command."

About twenty men did manage to slip through Sheridan's net to join Shelby. They were too few to make the colony viable, though Shelby did his best—"the work of a giant," according to John Edwards: "He was alcalde, magistrate, patriarch, surveyor, physician, interpreter, soldier . . . everything." But the climate decimated the colonists: "The rank forests, the tropical sun, the hardships and exposures of the new and laboriously life told heavily against the men, and many whom the bullet spared, the fever flushed."

As Shelby struggled to keep Tuxpan alive, events in Mexico City were sealing his fate—and Maximilian's. The final breach between the emperor and Marshal Bazaine occurred in early January 1867, when Bazaine complained to Maximilian that a Mexican general, Leonardo Márquez, was undermining the war effort by impressing civilians as soldiers. A curt note to Bazaine from the Conservative president of the Council of State reprimanded the marshal for interfering. Bazaine responded, saying, "The wording of your letter betrays a feeling of mistrust undoubtedly based upon calumnies which affect our honor" and declining to have "any further communications with your ministry." Maximilian then had an aide write to Bazaine, saying that "for the future His Majesty can hold no direct communications with you."

The way was thus cleared not only for Bazaine to expedite his departure, but to deprive Maximilian of useful weapons and ammunition, according to an English army officer then living in Mexico City: "I cannot but condemn the conduct of Marshal Bazaine during the latter portion of his sojourn in the country," Captain J. J. Kendall wrote in the *Times* of London. "Several pieces of cannon that he could not take with him were spiked at the gates of Mexico City; an immense quantity of surplus small arms and ammunition were thrown into the Vega Canal."

On February 5, 1867, Marshal Achille-François Bazaine led the last regiments of the French expeditionary force out of Mexico City, to the stirring sound of snare drums and the ripple of unfurling banners. Captain Paul Laurent, one of the Chasseurs d'Afrique, thought they carried with them the affections of the Mexicans because "our careless gaiety" was "in tune with the Mexican character." The Prussian officer Felix Salm-Salm, who had fought on the side of the Union during the Civil War and would stay with Maximilian until the end, thought otherwise:

> The departure of the French was a happy event for everybody, for they had made themselves hated by all parties. . . . They despised the Mexicans with a French arrogance and insulted the inhabitants of the city every day. Gentlemen on the sidewalks who did not get out of the way fast enough were kicked from it in the street. . . . When the troops passed our hotel the French ladies waved their handkerchiefs and went into ecstasies. "What a brilliant army! Let them only return to la belle France and they will march against Berlin and take it a la bayonet!" I did not regard their talk, but only wished to be in Berlin to meet them there."*

Most of the remaining colonists from Carlota and Córdoba—no more than a few score of the hundreds from the previous year—left Veracruz with the third and final detachments of the French forces. The exodus, which took place between February 18 and March 11, 1867, was a marvel of efficiency, conducted under constant threat of attack by the republicans and requiring thirty army transports and seven chartered steamers. Onto these were loaded almost all of the troops remaining of the original thirty thousand in Mexico, including three thousand Austrians and Belgians. Maximilian was left to confront an estimated sixty thousand republican soldiers with a few thou-

---

* Salm-Salm died three years later, in August 1870, fighting for Prussia in the Franco-Prussian War that would topple Napoléon III and send him, disgraced and humiliated, into exile. Marshal Bazaine, too, would end his career in exile, after being condemned to death for surrendering his army to the Prussians and escaping from prison with the aid of his young Mexican bride. Historians have since argued persuasively that Louis Napoléon's imperial adventure in Mexico was among the chief causes of his ultimate fall from power, weakening France as it did—that it was indeed his Waterloo.

sand Austrian volunteers and a Mexican imperial army whose loyalty and competence were dubious at best.

In mid-February, as the French were leaving, Shelby moved Betty and the children from the capital back to Córdoba. He was busy with arrangements for sending his family back to New Orleans—he would remain behind for a time to manage the colony at Tuxpan, which he still believed could succeed—when he received a summons from Maximilian to visit him at Chapultepec. Despite the danger of the trip and the unfinished details for Betty's journey, Shelby left immediately for the capital.

He arrived to learn that Maximilian was planning to leave for the mountain town of Querétaro. He was wan and haggard but calm. He asked Shelby, according to Edwards's account of the meeting, how many Americans remained in Mexico who would come to his defense. "Not enough for a corporal's guard," Shelby replied. "I don't know of two hundred effective men among my countrymen who could be got together before the evacuation is complete." Maximilian shook his head and said he needed twenty thousand men at least. Shelby was forced to tell Maximilian about the reports he had heard of rampant desertion by imperial Mexican troops in regions near and far.

Shelby also said he was aware that his old comrade Thomas Reynolds had been among those urging Maximilian not to abdicate, to fight on. Shelby, who had learned something about when to fight on and when not to, thought Bazaine was right—Maximilian should leave with him for France. But he did not presume to advise the emperor beyond suggesting that he keep his Austrian soldiers close by him and not waste them in useless battles. There was little else he could say. It would have been cruel to remind Maximilian of his offer eighteen months prior to raise the number of Americans who could have saved his life now. "The Emperor mused some little time in silence," then said, "It is so refreshing to hear the truth" from someone "who neither fears nor flatters." The interview was concluded when Maximilian took from his neck the Order of Guadalupe, a golden cross, and pressed it into Shelby's hands. He murmured his thanks once again for Shelby's service, said that death in the service of a great principle was never wrong, and left the room without look-ing back.

Shelby's clear-sighted perception of Maximilian's precarious situation had not extended to his own position in Tuxpan. His belief that his new colony was secure from aggression by virtue of its remoteness was shattered in early March 1867: An overwhelming attack by guerrillas and native Indians destroyed the structures of the colony in an hour. Fortunately, no American lives were lost; forewarned, Shelby had evacuated the Tuxpan colonists to Tampico. But there he found that his two schooners had been attacked, their crews murdered and tossed into the bay for the sharks. Once again, the hard work of months lay in ruins.

A week later, Shelby put Betty and the children on the train to Veracruz at Paso del Macho. With them was John Edwards; loyal to the last, he would see Shelby's family safely home. Among their few possessions, after nearly a year and a half in Mexico, was a small dog, a present for the boys from Bishop Labastida. When their ship docked at New Orleans, Edwards told a reporter that Shelby had remained in Mexico to salvage what he could from his various enterprises, but that he would soon return. "With the evacuation of Mexico by the French, the rest of the foreigners think it best to leave the country; and those of all nationalities are leaving as fast as steamers will bear them from Veracruz. The great idea in the Mexican mind is to get rid of foreign-ers, *nolens volens* [willing or unwilling]; and whether it is the French this year or the people of the United States the next, it makes but lit-tle difference to them."

Shelby stayed in Mexico long enough to confirm his sense that Maximilian was a man both reckless and indecisive, and that he would continue to make the wrong moves every chance he got. The choice of Querétaro as a refuge had been based on the region's reputation as a bastion of Catholic conservatism and of the empire. It was a charm-ingly picturesque city of thirty thousand inhabitants, nestled in a green river valley; there was plenty of food and water for Maximilian's seven thousand men. But the surrounding hills, which the republican army of General Mariano Escobedo soon occupied with three times that number, provided easy sites for launching artillery shells and mortars into the city. When one of Maximilian's more competent generals begged him to break through the enemy lines and escape to a more defensible position, he hesitated, heeding instead the bad advice of another general to stay put. When he finally did try to escape, on the night of May 14, 1867, he was betrayed by one of his own officers, Colonel Miguel Lopez, a man whose capacity for treachery had long been obvious to everyone but Maximilian.

On the morning in early June when Shelby boarded the American gunship *Tacony* in Veracruz, Maximilian's fate had not yet been decided. He was being held as a prisoner in a Mexico City convent, awaiting court-martial and a certain sentence of death; that sentence, ratified by Benito Juárez despite appeals for clemency from Washington, London, Paris, and Vienna, was duly carried out on June 19, 1867.

In yet another curious historical coincidence, Shelby almost crossed paths on the *Tacony* with the notorious General Antonio López de Santa Anna. The old schemer—he was now seventy-three and minus a leg from a long-ago battle but still ambitious for power—hoped to resume his position in Mexico after years of exile. He still had legions of admirers in the state of Veracruz who would support him against Benito Juárez. On June 7, 1867, after he arrived in Veracruz harbor on board the American commercial ship *Virginia*, Santa Anna was taken into custody by the aggressive commander of the *Tacony*, F. A. Roe. Washington wanted no part of Santa Anna's power play, Roe told the general. It was committed to supporting Benito Juárez as the president of Mexico. Santa Anna spent the night on the *Tacony* and was released the following day, on condition that he not try to enter the country via his old stronghold, Veracruz.

Jo Shelby took Santa Anna's place on the *Tacony* on June 9, 1867, as a more willing guest, as eager to leave Mexico as the general was to enter it. John Edwards, unfortunately, was not on hand to interpret Shelby's thoughts for us as he waited for the *Tacony* to cast off. Shelby may have simply watched the vultures peeling off the flat, red-tiled roofs of Veracruz in the morning haze and thanked God he was getting out with his skin intact. But it's reasonable to assume that this highly intelligent and idiosyncratic adventurer was indulging in a moment of thoughtful reflection. He was by now a man of considerable experience in the world of politics and revolution, of hopes raised and shattered. He had participated in one revolution, as he understood the Civil War to have been, and had stubbornly refused to acknowledge his defeat. He had then volunteered to uphold an imperial dynasty foisted upon a neighboring country, and he had lost again.

The defeat this time, however, was easier to bear—in part because he had never really believed in the empire as he had in the Confederacy, but most of all because of recent good news from home: Jefferson Davis, who had been in prison, sometimes in chains, the entire duration of Shelby's stay in Mexico, had finally been released. In the words of the historian David Blight, "On May 11, an emaciated, gray-bearded, and feeble Davis rode aboard the steamer *Sylvester* up the James River from the place of his two years' imprisonment, Fortress Monroe, to Richmond." If Jefferson Davis could go home—more to the point, if the political climate at home had changed sufficiently to allow him to go home a free man—so could Jo Shelby.

Some support for this speculation is provided by the diary of Seaton Schroeder, at the time an eighteen-year-old Annapolis cadet serving as an ensign on the *Tacony*. Given Captain Roe's actions in preventing Santa Anna from landing and opposing Juárez, it might be expected that the Mexican warships in the harbor would not hinder the departure of the *Tacony*, but Schroeder was not so sure. He thought that, as chaotic as the political and military situation was, they might have to fight their way out to sea.

In that context, Schroeder noted the impressive presence of "the celebrated cavalry leader in the Confederate army, of whom it has been said, that had he remained loyal to his country, he would have been Sheridan's stoutest rival." It was a curious "caprice of fate" that Shelby was leaving Mexico, the country that he had tried to "adopt in place of his own," under the protection of the American flag. But Schroeder also noted that, when the Missouri rebel saw that there might be trouble, he told Captain Roe to count him in "if there is going to be a row." The threat came to nothing, as it turned out, but the offer "was thankfully accepted, and revolvers were prepared for use" in defense of the Stars and Stripes.

The last holdout of the Confederacy was finally ready to accept his place as an American citizen and patriot.

PART THREE

FROM RESENTMENT TO RECONCILIATION

1867–97

TWELVE

Shelby Saves Frank James
from Hanging

In August 1877, ten years after his return to western Missouri, Jo
Shelby was asked by an enterprising reporter for the *St. Louis
Times* what he thought of the current state of affairs in Mexico. There
had been a number of cross-border raids by Mexican bandits into
Texas and the Mexican government seemed unable or unwilling to
stop them. Rumors abounded that Shelby, because of his adventures
south of the border a decade earlier, would be approached to lead a
punitive expedition into Mexico. What was Shelby's response to that
idea?

The general, who entertained the reporter on the front porch of his
rambling farmhouse in Aullville, near Waverly, was described as genial
and candid. He remembered the current Mexican president, Porfirio
Díaz, as a pretty good general himself during the days of Maximilian,
and he laughed off the notion of Americans, including any named
Shelby, trying to tell the Mexicans how to run their country. He also
explained, for the first time in public, how Frank Blair's letter back in
1865 had persuaded him that President Lincoln would look favorably
on any moves by Confederate forces to go to Mexico, if they resulted

in the expulsion of Maximilian, and how disappointed he had been when his men chose not to fight for Benito Juárez but for the emperor.

The reporter that summer day was John Edwards. During the years since his return to Missouri, his abilities as a newspaperman in Kansas City, St. Louis, and Sedalia had won him increasing renown. So, too, had his two lively, fact- and legend-stuffed books, *Shelby and His Men* in 1867 and *Shelby's Expedition to Mexico* in 1872.

Shelby's later accomplishments also drew Edwards's praise. In 1869, Edwards wrote a florid account of Shelby's attempt to build a railroad from Lexington to St. Louis ("From a raid to a railroad, Jo Shelby is invincible. He works like he fought—that is to say, 24 hours out of the 24"). The following May, when Shelby's house in Aullville burned down, Edwards said Shelby cared nothing about such ill strokes of fortune; he accurately predicted that the general would have another built in a couple of months—"the welcoming lamps will be hung again in the window" by the famously hospitable Shelbys, "and the guest chambers will be arrayed as of old." When Edwards married Jennie Plattenburg of nearby Dover the next year, in March 1871, it would be in the Shelbys' parlor.

In the years to come, however, Shelby and Edwards would grow apart. Shelby and Betty's burgeoning family alone would have kept him busy; there would be a total of seven boys and finally, in 1883, a girl, Anna, all of whom lived to maturity. He also tried to recoup his lost fortune with various business ventures—the railroad, a coal mine, a store—all of which failed, either because of bad times, such as the Panic of 1873, or because Shelby was simply not a good businessman. And he involved himself in state and national politics, most notably in 1876 with the disputed Hayes-Tilden contest to succeed President Ulysses S. Grant. Samuel Tilden, a New York Democrat, was favored by the South because he advocated states' rights at a time when that meant curbing or diluting the gains won by blacks during Reconstruction. Tilden won the popular vote, but Rutherford Hayes won the electoral college vote and became president as a result. Before that happened, however, some Southerners muttered about a new civil war (the editor of the *Louisville Courier* promised to send a hundred thousand armed Kentuckians to Washington to make sure "the right man"—Tilden—was chosen). Shelby ridiculed such talk and promised to support President Grant in whatever action he chose to take, "whether that action be favorable to Tilden or Hayes."

Shelby remained a Democrat. But his support of the Republican government in Washington, and even on occasion of Missouri Republicans he admired, dismayed some of his old friends, including Edwards. Others, like Alonzo Slayback, now an influential attorney and businessman in St. Louis, often joined with Shelby. Once famous as a bitter-ender, Shelby was now regarded by large numbers of Republicans and Democrats alike as a moderating force for reason in Missouri politics. In 1882, while on a visit to Washington, Shelby even enjoyed a cordial evening of dinner and drinks with his old nemesis, Philip Sheridan.

It was the only time the two ever met, and it must have been for each like seeing a doppelgänger. Like Shelby, Sheridan was hot-tempered (he almost failed to graduate from West Point for threatening to gut a classmate with his bayonet), opinionated, occasionally insubordinate, and a gifted leader of cavalry. Several inches shorter than Shelby, and, like him, growing stout in his later years, he had been described by Abraham Lincoln as "a brown, chunky little chap, with a long body, short legs, not enough neck to hang him, and such long arms that if his ankles itch he can scratch them without stooping."

Sheridan's apex during the war had been the destruction of the great Jeb Stuart. After the war he had striking success as an Indian fighter in the west, and at the time of his meeting with Shelby was on the verge of being named commanding general of the army. Sheridan had triumphed in almost everything he attempted, with one notable exception. In 1865, he had believed that Shelby's "Córdoba emigration scheme" had been not just an innocent effort to begin anew in a foreign land; it had "had for its object the formation of a Maximilian-American party, composed of Confederates harboring antipathy towards our government."

The *New York Herald* reporter who listened in on their conversation did not indicate whether Shelby told Sheridan now that he had been mistaken in this notion, or of Blair and Lincoln's role in his going south, but it would probably not have mattered. "I was very anxious to go over into Mexico after you," Sheridan told Shelby. In fact, he had begged for permission to stop Shelby instead of just following him—

which explained why the young federal officer had declined Shelby's invitation to battle north of Eagle Pass. If Sheridan had had his way, he told Shelby, "You would not have gone to Mexico. While I was waiting for orders, you slipped in. The orders to go after you never came, and it was one of my bitterest disappointments."

Shelby smiled, touched his glass to Sheridan's and said, "I wish you had got them, for we found it mighty lonesome over there for two years."

"Shelby," replied Sheridan, "I believe that every man who went through our war felt lonesome for two or three years after it was over."

Privately, Shelby was less sanguine in his acceptance of defeat. In a revealing 1885 letter to his old comrade George Lankford, he voiced the central doctrine of what had come to be known as the Lost Cause: "We were overcome by the hirelings of the World, who were avaricious, Mercenary, ignorant of our people, devoid of honor and patriotic duty." Nevertheless, he added, "It is over, and as we all surrendered it behooves us all to abide by the terms imposed. As to the institution of slavery, nobody cares that it is obliterated. All the World is opposed to it, and in due time the South would have abolished it. So it was not the loss of it we so much objected to, but the manner in which it was taken from us. The War has demonstrated that so far as the Constitution is concerned, it amounts to naught. It is force that frames Constitutions."

Shelby's willingness to say in public, as he did, that "we of the South are glad that slavery is dead for all time" was one thing—that issue at least was in the past. It was quite another for him to agree with the Republicans that Missouri needed to encourage immigration, both from Europe and from the North, for its economic well-being in a growing industrial economy. He mocked as "mossbacks" those who wanted to hold on to antebellum notions of Missouri as a transplanted medieval Scotland; they were "Bourbon Democrats," so called not for the whiskey but for the French aristocrats who famously learned nothing and forgot nothing.

John Edwards was the archetypal Bourbon Democrat, and proudly so; he was saddened to see Shelby taking up the position of certain "glib" Republicans who used the term in reptilian fashion, "as the forked tongue in the mouth of the snake." The Bourbon Democrat had been an admirable "pastoral American" who "hunted, fished, plowed, loved the woods, laughed and sang at his work, indulged in much reverie, which is the parent of sadness, did not know how to lie"—a man, Edwards might have been recalling, such as Shelby and he had both been before the war. But now, Edwards complained, Bourbon Democracy had come to signify not just resistance to change and progress; it was misunderstood as the celebration of mindless violence and lawlessness, of "guerrillas out in the underbrush," and of train and bank robbers on the prowl.

Edwards was a proud mossback, moored in the past; Shelby had become, almost in spite of himself, a commonsense progressive looking to the future. And yet the link suggested by Edwards between the Civil War guerrillas and the modern phenomenon of banditry in Missouri would be critical in the unfolding of one of the stranger stories of their long association—one that suggests just how torn Shelby was between his loyalty to the rule of law and his fidelity to his old comrades in arms.

That story harked back to Civil War when men like Quantrill, Bloody Bill Anderson, and Frank and Jesse James enlisted themselves under Shelby's command—and, in particular, to the day in 1863 when Frank James was among those who saved Shelby from capture and probable execution for allowing such criminals and bushwhackers to fight for him. Several of those men, most notably John Thrailkill, had gone to Mexico with Shelby. But most preferred to return to their homes and resume their normal lives at war's end.

This would have been hard in the best of circumstances; it became impossible for many because of the punishment to which former rebels were subject in Missouri as the result of Reconstruction polices run amok. Contrary to Lincoln's intention, the Radicals had revised the state's constitution, stipulating that every man had to swear that he had not committed any one of some eighty-six possible acts of disloyalty during the war. These included everything from taking up arms to oppose the Union to participating in guerrilla warfare, and even to expressing sympathy with the Confederate cause. Thousands of Missourians like Shelby who had fought on the losing side, and who could not in good conscience swear to a falsehood, became, in effect, noncitizens. They were not allowed to vote; they were also precluded from holding elected or appointed offices, from working as teachers, ministers, or lawyers, and from holding corporate positions, including board memberships.

Frank Blair and Shelby's stepcousin B. Gratz Brown were among those strongly opposed to the Radicals. One measure of the intense emotions of the time is indicated by Blair's experience during a speech he made in the fall of 1866 opposing the loyalty oath. A farmer called him a liar and moved toward the stage. When the farmer was restrained, his son attacked Blair with a knife. The young man was himself stabbed by a Blair supporter and hauled away to die. Blair, unruffled but fingering a derringer he carried in his vest pocket, went on to finish his speech. (Blair's vigor did not endure, nor did his once almost limitless political power. He was the Democratic Party's vice-presidential candidate in 1868, when Ulysses S. Grant crushed Horatio Seymour, but in 1872, while serving as a U.S. senator, he suffered a severe stroke. Shelby was with his old friend in January 1873, when the Missouri Democratic caucus declined to renominate him for another term as senator. Blair died in 1875, only fifty-four years old.)

The worst of the Radical excesses were set aside with the election of B. Gratz Brown as governor in 1870—as were, unhappily, many of the new benefits rightly bestowed on the black population that had long suffered from the same deprivations visited upon the Confederates, and that would continue in varying degrees for generations yet to come.

In the meantime, the James brothers and others like them had turned to crime. Targeting mostly railroads and banks—themselves predators in the eyes of most Missourians and thus considered fair game—the brothers survived for nearly sixteen years, thanks to a network of sympathizers who turned a blind eye to their depredations. Shelby himself allowed former Confederates turned highwaymen to stay at his farm—at one point, in 1872, harboring Frank James, who was recovering from a gunshot wound, for several months.

The continuing fascination in popular culture with Jesse James as an American Robin Hood derives largely from John Edwards, who would become the foremost apologist and propagandist for put-upon killers with his third book, *Noted Guerrillas,* published in 1877. As the historian and Edwards biographer Conger Beasley has said, Edwards portrayed the James brothers, among many others, as "ordinary farm boys, stirred to action by unprovoked outrages from Yankee demons who rode over from Kansas to burn, loot, and kill."

To be sure, Jesse James was a more attractive character by far than Quantrill, Anderson, and their ilk—handsome, smart, and not without charm, he easily won the public support for his marauding that was essential for his continued freedom. But he was still a killer, and that support was threatened when he shot down a bank cashier in cold blood in 1869. He asked John Edwards for advice on cleaning up his image. Edwards responded by ghostwriting for Jesse a persuasive denial of his crime in the form of an open letter to the then-governor of Missouri, Joseph McClurg, and advanced the same argument as he would later in *Noted Guerrillas* and after Jesse's death: "We called him outlaw, and he was, but Fate made him so. . . . Proscribed, hunted, shot at, driven away from among his own people, a price put upon his head, what else could a man do?" In gratitude, Jesse named his firstborn child Jesse Edwards James and gave Edwards a gold watch.

In April 1882, shortly before Jesse's death, a newspaper reporter asked Jo Shelby if there was "any truth in the rumor circulating around to the effect that you are a friend of the James boys." Shelby chose to answer the question by recalling the incident during the war when he was rescued by Frank James. He said, "I do not feel it incumbent on me to betray a set or class of men who offered to sacrifice their lives in defense of mine." He added that if he could be persuaded by "responsible witnesses" of the James brothers' guilt, he would not hesitate "to place them in the hands and fangs of the law." But until then, it was not his "purpose, when everybody is turned against them, to betray or give evidence against them."

When Jesse was shot in the back by his friend Robert Ford—surely the most famous American murder of the nineteenth century after Lincoln's—Edwards was editor of the *Sedalia Daily Democrat.* He wrote an impassioned editorial denouncing the then-governor of Missouri, Thomas Crittenden, for having put a $10,000 reward on Jesse's head—equivalent to more than $1 million today by one calculation. His ire increased when Crittenden pardoned Ford, an act of courage or folly that meant the end of his political career. But when Jesse's brother Frank decided the following September that he had better surrender before he, too, was killed, it was John Edwards, with Shelby's help, who persuaded Crittenden to personally accept his surrender.

The precise details of Edwards's dealings with Crittenden as Frank's intermediary were never made public, but their general outline is clear. For all his publicly proclaimed fury at the governor, Edwards fell back on his and Shelby's long-ago association with Crittenden—in one of those extraordinary links of people and events that run throughout the Shelby story, the governor had been part of the wedding party (including Edwards) that went by steamboat with Jo and Betty Shelby to St. Louis in 1858.

Frank James's surrender six months after Jesse's death was a triumph of stagecraft, carefully choreographed by John Edwards. It was initiated with a long letter from Frank to the governor, again probably ghostwritten by Edwards, in which the aging bandit rued his wrongdoings and said he wanted to give himself up. On the afternoon of October 5, 1882, Edwards walked into the governor's office in Jefferson City with a tall, hollow-cheeked man who dramatically whipped off his gun belt. "Governor, I am Frank James," the man said. "I surrender my arms to you. They have not been out of my possession" since the war. He added, helpfully, "I have taken out the cartridges."

Conger Beasley suggests that it was at this moment that the Civil War in Missouri, which had begun in 1854 with the cross-border raids into Kansas, "came to a peaceful, dignified close." But the result of the Frank James murder trial that followed—part of the deal that Edwards and James had worked out with Crittenden—was widely regarded as a miscarriage of justice, and its dignity was sorely tested by one of the state's most revered citizens, General Jo Shelby.

As had been the case with Jesse's shooting of the bank cashier in 1869, there was nothing remotely romantic or redeeming in the charge of murder against Frank James. That charge was as follows: On the evening of July 15, 1881, Frank and his brother Jesse, along with Dick Liddil and the brothers Wood and Clarence Hite, boarded the

Rock Island Line railroad train in Winston, Missouri. Within minutes of leaving the station two men on the train had been shot and killed, one by Jesse James and one by Frank. By the time of Frank's trial more than two years later, only he and Liddil of the five robbers were still alive. It was Liddil on whom the state's case rested—he swore, in return for immunity from prosecution, that Frank was guilty of murder and had admitted as much to him at the time: "Frank said a man peeped in and he shot at the man and he fell off the train."

The prosecution had abundant supporting evidence. The robbery carried the familiar stamp of the James gang, and dozens of witnesses swore they had seen Frank James in the Winston vicinity the night of the robbery, along with several other bearded men in white linen dusters—though Frank swore he was in Texas at the time. The witnesses' memories were aided by Frank's distinctive appearance. He had a huge, bony nose, deeply hollowed temples, a sloping forehead, a small head, and a thick neck. Though he had just turned forty, he looked older—and, even seated quietly in court, still dangerous.

The robbery and its attendant murders had prompted Governor Crittenden, who had been in office for just a few months, to end once and for all the activities of the James gang. Once Jesse was dead, Frank was a marked man, even in distant Baltimore, where he had since been living in quiet obscurity. His surrender for trial was a calculated risk—a bet that the Robin Hood halo around Jesse's head, plus the influential General Shelby's testimony as a witness to Frank's admirable character, would persuade a jury to find him innocent.

The trial was held in the small town of Gallatin, near the scene of the crime. Though it was only sixty miles due north of Lexington, this was a part of Missouri that had been hostile to slavery and secession, and the prosecution hoped jurors would reject appeals to Confederate solidarity.

The prosecutor was an ambitious young Kansas City man, William Hockaday Wallace. Born in 1848, he had been a boy during the war and did not participate in the camaraderie of the older men involved in the trial. In a hard-drinking time and place, he was a square-jawed and upright teetotaler who supported closing saloons and pool halls. Wallace had billed himself as a "law enforcement Democrat" in his recent successful campaign for election as the public prosecutor of Jackson County. A major plank in his platform had been his vow to have the bandits of Missouri swinging at the end of a rope or breaking rocks at hard labor for twenty-five years.

The defense counsel was John Philips, an old acquaintance of Crittenden and Shelby's, also from Kansas City. As a Union officer during the war, Philips crossed paths with Shelby twice on battlefields, most notably at Westport. They were then "mortal enemies but at a respectful distance," Philips said later, but he came to feel the "utmost esteem for the wily, lion-hearted rebel cavalry leader." Crittenden's own role in the trial, as it was in the surrender, remains puzzling; he may have been trying to recoup his political fortunes by seeing to it that Frank James went free. At the very least, suggests Gerard Petrone, who wrote a good account of the trial, "It is not too far-fetched to imagine Crittenden doing everything in his power to help Frank James as a personal favor to his old friend John Philips, who was acting on behalf of Edwards and Shelby. Perhaps this was one of the many secrets surrounding the Frank and Jesse James affairs that the governor once admitted were so sensitive and politically damaging that he could never divulge them to the public."

The prosecution's case against Frank depended in large part on the testimony of Dick Liddil, one of the mainstays of the James gang who sought to save himself from hanging by incriminating Frank James. Philips did his best to impugn Liddil's character as a killer and a turncoat, which he certainly was. The problem was, as a Kansas newspaper correspondent wrote, that Liddil had turned out to be an extremely good witness, with a steel-trap memory and amazing composure under the most intensely hostile questioning imaginable: "If Liddil is not telling the truth, he is certainly a very expert liar."

Given Liddil's powerful testimony to Frank's guilt, Shelby's defense of his character assumed added importance. On the day he was to testify, the tenth of the sixteen-day trial, Shelby had lunch with John Edwards. Edwards had been struggling for years with alcohol, periodically sending himself off to asylums to dry out, and Shelby, a man of his time, would not have let his best friend drink alone. They must have stoked each other's indignation with the prosecution's dependence on traitorous testimony from the likes of Dick Liddil, for when Shelby arrived in court he was clearly drunk. The *St. Louis Republic*'s reporter vividly described his entrance:

"The afternoon session opened with the testimony of Gen. J. O. Shelby, a confident, slender man of 52, his brown beard streaked with grey, who came into court with the stride of a dragoon, and with a savage glare in his eyes which promised trouble." After being sworn in and asked by Philips to state his name and residence, "the general maintained a silence, turned his fierce glare to the various attorneys' tables," and said that he wished to be introduced first to the judge. He then turned toward Judge Charles H. Goodman, "smiled blandly on him and assured his honor that while he had not had the pleasure of meeting him, he was glad to know him now, and entertained the most kindly feeling toward him. All this was in a loud, bluff, genial voice, and it was apparent that the general was disposed to shake hands with the court if he could just get at him."

The judge "fidgeted rather perceptibly as a titter ran through the court" and suggested that the witness answer the question posed by the defense regarding his identity. Shelby agreed, after asking for the jury to be pointed out to him—the trial was being held not at the courthouse but at the opera house, the only building in town large enough to contain the large audience that had come for the entertainment, so perhaps the request was not as strange as it seemed.

When it was time for Wallace, the prosecutor, to cross-examine him, Shelby was asked what his association with Frank James had been. He had last seen him in 1872, Shelby said, adding, "I believe he sits there right now. With the permission of the court, can I be tolerated to shake hands with an old soldier?" The judge, irritated, said, "No, sir, not now." Wallace pressed Shelby on the details of his association with Frank and Jesse James, suggesting by his manner that Shelby had been coached.

Shelby said, "Do you, sir, accuse me of lying?" The judge rebuked Shelby, bringing a smile to Wallace's face. Provoked, Shelby said, "Mr. Wallace, if you want to make this a personal matter, you can do so." Wallace ignored Shelby's implied challenge, simply replying that the general had to answer questions like everyone else. Shelby calmed down and the proceedings continued more sedately. He repeated that he had not seen Frank James after 1872. He added that he had seen Jesse James and Dick Liddil in the fall of 1881, two or three months after the Winston train robbery. At that time, according to Shelby, Jesse said Frank had been in the South for some years and that Liddil said he had not seen Frank for two years.

With this statement Shelby attempted to undermine Liddil's identification of Frank as a fellow participant in the train robbery. He also corroborated Frank's assertion that he had been in Texas during the summer of 1881. Upon being excused from the witness stand, he asked Judge Goodman once again if he could shake hands with the defendant. "You can call on him some other time," the judge brusquely replied. "God bless you, old fellow," Shelby said to Frank James as he stepped down from the witness stand.

The next day Shelby returned to the court, apparently sober. Approaching the bench, he said to the judge, "If anything that I may have said or done yesterday offended the dignity of the court, I regret it exceedingly." He paused and glared at the team of prosecutors, adding, "As to other parties, I have no regrets."

Judge Goodman, exasperated, said, "General Shelby, I must say your conduct yesterday in appearing before the court in an unfit condition and showing an insubordinate spirit was reprehensible in the extreme, as it was not only defiance of the dignity of the court, but calculated to prejudice the interest of the defendant. You are a man of national reputation and enjoy the respect and confidence of a large number of people of Missouri. I can only say that I was much astonished at your very reprehensible actions. It is in testimony that you have drawn a pistol right in the verge of the court which is in itself a contempt of court."

The judge was referring to an incident two nights earlier in Lexington when Shelby mistook a traveling salesman for Dick Liddil and threatened him with a revolver—again, drunk. "That, sir, is false!" Shelby shouted.

"The marshal of Lexington testified to it under oath," Goodman replied.

"Then he lied!" Shelby said.

Goodman said, sighing, "The court is amply satisfied with your apology to it, but your attitude towards the attorneys for the state yesterday in answering in a threatening and offensive manner and talk of calling them to personal account cannot be overlooked." He declared Shelby in contempt of court and fined him ten dollars. Apparently relieved at having gotten off so lightly, Shelby paid his fine and left the courtroom.

The following afternoon Frank's attorney admitted that General Shelby had been guilty of improper behavior in the court, but "he spoke truth. His high character needs no defense and no eulogy by me. His name is a household word in Missouri. As splendid in courage as he is big in heart, his home is a model of hospitality. No man, however poor and outcast, was ever turned from it hungry. Truth and chivalry are to him as modesty to the true woman, azure to the sky."

The jury deliberations were over quickly: Frank James was found not guilty. Apparently the jurors were persuaded that Liddil was the "viper curled in a chair" that Shelby termed him during his testimony and an unreliable witness for the prosecution. They also proved more sympathetic to Shelby's appeals to personal loyalty above the law than William Wallace had anticipated.

Later that afternoon, Wallace and Shelby met on the street, at opposite ends of a plank that lay across a mud puddle. Their final exchanges had been so contentious that Wallace could be excused for believing rumors that Shelby had threatened to shoot him if they met. The two antagonists gazed silently at each other across the puddle, each waiting for the other to make a move. Finally, Shelby smiled slightly, bowed courteously, and said, "After you, Mr. Wallace."

Unmollified, Wallace later complained that the James acquittal had been a travesty of justice. "The defense had used the trial as a public forum to reenact the war and stir up old feelings. General Shelby was the most flagrant example, swaggering into court and unfurling the faded colors of the Confederacy, and treating the ex-Quantrill raider like a hero." A Kansas newspaper editorial agreed: Frank James, it said, was "a murderer and robber of the lowest and most fiendish type" who has been "feted, petted, worshipped as if he were a public benefactor instead of a scourge and pest among men." He was acquitted "because there is in Missouri a feeling that to have been a rebel bush-whacker in the war was commendable, that to have participated in the hellish atrocities committed by Quantrill, Pool, and others was heroic and praiseworthy."

THIRTEEN

U.S. Marshal

B ecause Shelby was seen to be motivated by the warrior virtues of courage and loyalty, his willful defense of the villainous Frank James did him no lasting harm (except, perhaps, with his family back in Kentucky, who were disgusted by his association with criminals). It was barely mentioned ten years later when he was nominated by President Grover Cleveland to be U.S. marshal for western Missouri. But in a larger context, Shelby's actions must be seen as part of the ongoing postwar trauma of adjustment that he and the other men all went through, some more successfully than others.

It is true that some of those men survived, even thrived. Matthew Maury, the prime mover behind Maximilian's land colonies, taught at the Virginia Military Institute until his death in 1873, and was memorialized for a time by having a state holiday in his honor. Edmund Kirby Smith lived comfortably until his death in 1893, teaching mathematics at the University of the South in Sewanee, Tennessee, raising eleven children, and assiduously avoiding the continuing controversies concerning his role during the war. Of those who served under Shelby and did well later, Dick Collins was elected twice to the state legislature; Maurice Langhorne started a newspaper in Independence; and Jim Cundiff became a prominent Democratic politician and circuit court clerk in Buchanan County, Missouri. Ben Elliott, who had parted from Shelby in Monterrey and gone to Mazatlán, ended up raising cotton for ten years in Mexico; he served two terms as sheriff of Lafayette County, Missouri, when he returned, and died at the age of eighty-one in 1911.

But many of Shelby's associates lived lives of disappointment and met untimely deaths. Sterling Price died impoverished in 1867 at the age of fifty-eight, and "Prince John" Magruder was just sixty-three when he died in 1871, alone and broke in Houston. The feisty Thomas Hindman, who had preceded Kirby Smith as the commander of the Trans-Mississippi Department and later lived in Córdoba, became involved in heated political disputes when he returned to Helena, Arkansas. In 1867, as he sat reading in his living room, a rifle shot fired through the window struck him in the throat and mortally wounded him—though Hindman still managed to sit for a while on his front porch before a small crowd, according to a friend, for whom he "reviewed his career in a speech of rare eloquence."

Thomas Reynolds, the gifted linguist who sometimes served as Shelby's interpreter, met an even sadder fate. He could "never quite forget past scenes of horror in Mexico," according to Andrew Rolle in *The Lost Cause:* "the rawhide whippings of deserters, brutal executions in the name of national loyalty, maimings and killings," including the execution of a sixteen-year-old boy by a dozen stone-faced soldiers. "But, above all, he never forgot the Emperor whose death his advice had helped bring about." Back in Missouri, his path to political recuperation was blocked by the gubernatorial election of the man he had once wounded in a duel, B. Gratz Brown. By one account, he came to feel that he was losing the mental acuity on which he had always prided himself. In March 1887, he climbed the stairs to the top floor of the tallest building in St. Louis and leaped to his death in an elevator shaft. He was sixty-five years old.

The men most associated with Shelby's Mexican adventure, Alonzo Slayback and John Edwards, seemed for a time to have adjusted more readily to the pressures of postwar life. In 1882, happily married and the father of six children, Slayback was forty-eight years old. The impetuous chevalier who had ridden out to do single combat with the enemy, the poet who celebrated the burial of the flag in the

Rio Grande, the expatriate who tutored the emperor Maximilian in English, was now a prosperous St. Louis attorney. Much in demand as a public speaker, he was also a civic booster who helped to found a yearly event called "the Veiled Prophet's Ball"—a festival modeled after Mardi Gras in New Orleans. Local leaders said Slayback was a man to watch: "Where he fails to convince, he captivates. Should he live out the allotted span of man, it requires no prophet's pen to predict for him an exalted and enduring place in the history of his city, State, and Republic."

Though he sided with Shelby against political positions of the Bourbon Democrats, Slayback shared their propensity to take offense. In the fall of 1882, John Cockerill, the managing editor of Joseph Pulitzer's crusading new newspaper, the *St. Louis Post-Dispatch,* questioned the probity of Slayback's law partner, James Broadhead, in a matter concerning the use of city funds. Slayback thought his own honor, as well as his partner's, had been called into question. Cockerill was warned by a friend, Sam Williams, that he should carry a gun because the famous "fire-eater" Alonzo Slayback was looking for him. When Cockerill tried to laugh off the warning, Williams said he had to understand that Slayback was a bully. "He will meet you in a public place some time. He will taunt you, threaten you, humiliate you and he won't hesitate to kill you."

Cockerill bought a revolver and carried it with him for a time until he left it parked in his office desk. Slayback continued his attacks on the editor in public speeches and in conversations with friends and acquaintances. Among the latter was the most prominent citizen of St. Louis, the retired general William T. Sherman. Sherman told Slayback that Cockerill's father had served ably under him as a colonel and that his son had also performed well in battle as an enlisted man: "Have no doubt—John Cockerill will fight, if he must."

Cockerill tried to defuse the tension by meeting Slayback for a private conversation at the Elks Club. Slayback seemed to calm down. But before the evening was out Cockerill overheard him abusing his city editor, saying that "the *Post-Dispatch* is a lying, blackmailing sheet and everything connected with it is a liar and a blackmailer—and you can tell Colonel Cockerill I said so."

"Colonel" Cockerill (the title was honorary) was so furious at this charge—the worst that could be brought against a reform crusader—that he dug out an old attack on Slayback and reprinted it on his editorial page on October 13, 1882. The attack was in the form of a paid advertisement, a "card," commissioned the year before by John Glover, a local politician whom Slayback had called "an insolent puppy." Glover responded that "so far from being a brave man, the Colonel, notwithstanding his military title, is a coward. He dare not be brave except in a courtroom or a church and he will beg or cringe out of any difficulty into which his vaporing humor may have gotten him." Glover's most incendiary remark maligned not just Slayback but the Confederate cause: With Slayback, "the title 'Colonel' is never applied except in derision and originated in the gallant manner in which the 'Colonel' once marshaled a female sewing society."

Slayback had never seen Glover's insult because Pulitzer, sensing trouble with libel suits, had stopped the presses in order to expunge it from the edition in which it was originally to appear. Glover had, in the meantime, withdrawn from the scene. Now Cockerill dug the ad from his files and splashed it across the editorial page; Pulitzer, who might have vetoed it again, was out of town. Cockerill explained to his readers that they had a right to know what kind of man it was who had strung together "so many vile and virulent epithets" against him and the *Post-Dispatch*, "making charges which he knew to be false."

Late that afternoon, Slayback and another attorney, William Clopton, entered Cockerill's office at the *Post-Dispatch*. According to his family and friends, Slayback did so with "the intention of slapping the editor and demanding an apology." Clopton said that Slayback was not armed, and that as he was pulling off his coat to thrash the editor, Cockerill grabbed a revolver and shot him dead. Police later found a gun on Slayback's body, which the dead man's family said must have been planted there by a *Post-Dispatch* employee. The grand jury did not accept this explanation. It did accept Cockerill's argument that he had killed in self-defense and declined to recommend an indictment against him for murder.

Cockerill was a sufficiently important figure in nineteenth-century American newspaper history to warrant a substantial biography in 1965. The author, Homer King, provides a detailed account of the circumstances of Slayback's death. According to the testimony of two of

Cockerill's editors who were on the scene, both Slayback and Clopton entered the office with weapons in their hands. Cockerill had anticipated that Slayback and his chosen second would come to issue a challenge for a duel, but now saw that his life was in danger. He opened his desk drawer and pulled out his revolver. Slayback said, "Is that for me?"

"No!" Cockerill shouted, which Homer King interpreted as hoping he would not have to use it.

"At this point both visitors had crowded in on Cockerill," King writes. "Slayback leveled his revolver at Cockerill, who was by now against the wall. Slayback's finger was on the trigger." One of the assistant editors reached out to disarm Clopton, who also appeared ready to shoot. Cockerill fired a single shot into Slayback's heart, killing him instantly.

King's defense of Cockerill is persuasive. But even if Slayback was in the right, his impetuous aggression, which had carried him successfully through so many earlier scrapes, certainly contributed to his death.

Alonzo Slayback, the poet-warrior of the Iron Brigade, was killed just a week after John Edwards engineered Frank James's October 5, 1882, surrender to the governor 130 miles to the west, in Jefferson City.

Edwards's own demise seven years later would be less dramatic than Slayback's, though he, too, had been involved, in the summer of 1875, in a shoot-out—a semi-comic duel that turned around a perceived insult to Jefferson Davis. Edwards had complained about objections raised in neighboring Illinois to a speaking engagement featuring the former president of the Confederacy. A rival journalist in St. Louis, yet another "colonel" named Emory Foster, objected to Edwards's defense of Davis. Edwards took offense, Foster responded in kind, Edwards issued a challenge, and the two men met at dawn. The setting was a field near Rockford, Illinois, "in a beautifully shaded valley in which horses and cattle were grazing," according to a reminiscence by Edwards's father-in-law, the Reverend George Plattenburg.

As the preparations by their seconds were arranged, both men "displayed marvelous nerve, Foster smoking his cigar in an unconcerned way." The weapons were Colt .38-caliber navy revolvers, the distance between the antagonists twenty paces. Each man fired, each missed. Foster exclaimed that he had shot "a little high," though whether this was accidental or on purpose was not clear. In any event, honor had been satisfied for him; he was the offended party, and he had done all that was necessary. Edwards excitedly responded that he was willing to carry on with the duel "if it takes a thousand fires" and promptly "sat down on the grass," saying he had not received satisfaction. But "after the interchange of a few words, Edwards concluded to make the thing up. He approached Foster and shook hands. There was mutual congratulation all round, and it was interesting to see the brotherly love displayed by the men, who two minutes before, had faced each other with death in their eyes. The genial Bourbon was produced, and the agreeable termination to the affair toasted. A short time was spent on the grass in mutual explanation, and everything was forgotten and forgiven."

Edwards's problem during the postwar decades, as noted earlier, was that the "genial Bourbon" flowed too generously. He tried various cures and remedies. Sometimes they seemed to work—once he wrote to his publisher that he had "no more desire to drink than if whiskey were prussic acid"—and when they didn't, he kept on fighting his demon. In a December 3, 1885, letter to Shelby he wrote, "I have quit liquor, General, forever. It came very near killing me, and I have been powerful sick the past summer; but I am done forever." But he was not done. That letter, almost an illegible scrawl, is remarkable evidence of Edwards's deterioration when placed beside the chatty reports he had sent his family from Mexico twenty years earlier—those earlier letters are marvels of penmanship, almost like calligraphy in their graceful, effortless flow, line after line, page after page. The controlled intelligence that they reflect had given way to the sad, sometimes frantic desperation of a man who knew that he had lost his bearings.

But Edwards kept working, or trying to. He was on the job when he died on May 4, 1889, in a hotel room in Jefferson City, at the age of fifty. Both houses of the Missouri legislature, whose proceedings he was in town to report, passed resolutions praising Edwards for his work and regretting his untimely death, then adjourned for the day out of respect for his memory. The Missouri Pacific Railroad sent his body home to Dover in a special car, and tributes appeared in newspapers from New York to Denver.

Many of these tributes included the response of Jo Shelby to a Kansas City reporter who informed him of his old friend's passing: "The news of Major Edwards's death is a great shock to me. I have known and loved him since he was a boy. It is hardly within the power of language to portray or describe Major Edwards as his noble character merits. God never created a more noble, magnanimous and truer man than John N. Edwards." A few days later, passing by the open casket in Dover, Shelby said to a friend, with tears in his eyes, "He was the bravest man in war and the gentlest man in peace I ever saw."

In 1892, Shelby's name was put forward to be marshal for western Missouri by President Grover Cleveland. Though subject to confirmation by the Senate, the appointment was presumably a routine matter. It was based largely on the recommendation of Thomas Clement Fletcher, a former Union officer and Missouri governor from 1865 to 1869, who told Cleveland that although Shelby "was the most dangerous man we had to deal with during the war, no man was so widely instrumental in helping us bring order out of chaos when the war was over. His influence with the people of Missouri was inestimable and he worked night and day to restore peace by appealing to them to accept the new order of things in a spirit of resignation."

Given that Shelby was not even in the state until two years after the war was over, this encomium drew scornful responses from his political opponents. The New York press questioned the wisdom of appointing a leading rebel as the chief law enforcement officer for the region—to which the *St. Louis Republic* replied that the bandits and road agents in Missouri would have no chance against the old general, who "knows all the short cuts. He has used them when their use counted."

Shelby was more vulnerable to charges of vanity and military braggadocio, thanks to John Edwards. His wartime after-battle reports were mocked for their effusively romantic and inflated descriptions of his own heroism. "If 'Jo' Shelby's sword had been as mighty as his pen," a *New York Tribune* story began, supposedly quoting an ex-

Confederate detractor, "there wouldn't have been a grease spot left of the Federal forces in Missouri after his raid in the fall of 1863. . . . If you want to read some of the finest descriptive writings ever published—writings that are steeped in all the glories of the wildest and most poetic imagination that was ever given to man—you should read 'Jo' Shelby's official reports of 1863 and 1864. Why, Baron Munchausen was tame, flat and insipid compared with Shelby."

For example: His victories, Shelby had said, were "a beacon light of hope and help reared in the dark night of despotism"; his opponents were "mongrel soldiers, Negroes and Yankee schoolmasters imported to teach the young" how to shoot; and a typical military engagement, the capture of a Union steamboat, was described in this fashion: "It was a beautiful moonlit night" with "white fleecy clouds hover[ing] over the sleeping river, over the doomed craft with all her gala lights in bloom." Then, "as the white hand of morning put away the sable clouds of night four pieces of artillery sent their terrible messengers crashing through the boat."

The charges of vanity against Shelby based on his supposed writings did not stick. Senator George Vest, a Shelby friend and fellow officer during the war, explained that Shelby's reports were written by a young newspaperman with "a vivid imagination and remarkable descriptive powers" and "were not to be taken seriously." If the style is the man, there should be no confusion between Edwards and Shelby, who was articulate but never flowery—though Daniel O'Flaherty surely goes too far in claiming that "not only had Shelby not written" the reports, "he had not read them."

The more important point, however, is that both Shelby and Edwards represented a tradition of military valor—one chiefly concerned with celebrating courage and honor and comradeship—that many viewed as quaint in the 1890s. Younger Americans who had grown up in peacetime, during the period of political and economic corruption inaugurated by the Grant administration, were now inclined to cynicism. Their literary touchstones were Stephen Crane's *The Red Badge of Courage*—that badge ironically won by a man injured while fleeing from battle; Ambrose Bierce's grotesque, hyperrealistic accounts of battle in stories like "Chickamauga"; and Mark Twain's satiric account of his desertion from a Confederate unit in the early days of the war, "The Private History of a Campaign That Failed." These were descriptions of war that fitted the ironic, skeptical temperament of the 1890s, and that continue to do so today. From Ernest Hemingway to Norman Mailer to Tim O'Brien, American writers who describe war have been diametrically opposed to the kind of romantic effusion that frequently characterized the writing of John Edwards—paradoxically, a man who saw far more of it than any of them ever did, and whose writing at its best sometimes approaches theirs.

Another attack on Shelby's fitness to serve as marshal was led by Joseph Pulitzer's *New York World*—which was now edited by none other than John Cockerill, who had killed Alonzo Slayback. Shelby blunted the attack by telling a Kansas City reporter that Slayback's "assassination was of such a character that it behooved every man that had opposed such methods to denounce the act," including himself. "Through the St. Louis *Republic* I denounced the assassin [Cockerill] as a man tattooed in spirit and all over with the brand of Cain, who escaped from the country with a conscience gnawing on his putrid soul, that gave him neither rest of body nor peace of mind." Cockerill's attack on him now was merely payback, Shelby said.

As it happened, there was no shortage of Shelby supporters to offset the opposition to his candidacy. Prominent among these was a former postwar Kansas governor, Samuel Crawford, who wrote that he had led the Second Kansas Cavalry into battle against Shelby many times; while Shelby "would fight and sometimes exhibit staying qualities that were absolutely provoking," nobody "ever questioned for a moment his honesty and integrity of purpose of what he did." A reporter in St. Louis noted that his "name has been a household word" for four decades in Missouri, that "his career during the war as Brigadier General and finally as Major General gave him a national reputation, and yet he has never before been a candidate for any office. While beginning to border on the shady side of life, Gen. Shelby is as active as a boy, his energy never flags, and if the reception accorded him in St. Louis is any criterion, he has not been forgotten by any of his old friends and is making hosts of new ones."

What would strike many today as the greatest objection to appoint-

ing Shelby to a position of law enforcement—his long and close involvement with the James brothers well after the war was over—seems
never to have been an issue in the press or with the public.

By early February 1893, all the obstacles had been cleared away, and
Shelby's nomination was confirmed by the Senate. The *St. Louis Republic* reported Shelby's return from Washington that month. He was
in good spirits, noting with satisfaction that "I am in the sixty-third
year of my age, and this is the first time I ever made application for an
office, and this is the first public position that has ever been given me.
I hope to make a record that will satisfy everybody and prove that no
mistake was made in my selection."

The *Republic*'s correspondent observed that "General Shelby has
the appearance of a gallant cavalier of bygone times as he walks across
the corridors of the Laclede [Hotel] under the shimmering rays of the
electric lights, a broad-rimmed, black slouch hat casting a shadow over
a florid face and an iron-gray mustache and imperial. The General,
notwithstanding his years, walks with erect, military bearing, and
shows the same spirit as in the days when he led the famous expedition into Old Mexico."

The next four years, from his appointment as marshal in 1893 until his
death in 1897, would be deeply satisfying to Jo Shelby. His job was no
sinecure—western Missouri was still a violent territory, and there were
new threats to civil order, such as the Pullman strike of 1894, which he
handled with aplomb and dispatch, plus the armed muscle of seven
hundred special deputies.

But Shelby had a team of six full-time deputies to handle the more
dangerous cases that he once would have tackled himself—among
them his son Sam, who captured a murderer in the southern part of
the state and brought him safely to trial—and much of his time was
spent in his offices in the grand old federal courthouse in Kansas City.

The once hard-bitten soldier who had seen so much death and misery during the war and in Mexico was surprised and touched by the
mundane miseries of those whom he met in the course of his duties.
He had been a soft touch for bank robbers such as Frank James; he

now became famous for his sympathetic treatment even of those he had to escort to prison, such as a teenager convicted of petty theft. Instead of brusquely handcuffing the prisoner, he wrapped his arm around his shoulder and whispered comforting words into his ear—prompting the boy to burst into tears.

He was equally generous to those who were not guilty but simply unfortunate. *The Kansas City Star* noted that among Shelby's bailiffs were two boys so short that they barely reached the height of the chief clerk's desk. It was true, Shelby admitted to the judge, that the lads did not quite meet "the ancient standards for bailiffs." But their mother was poor and "dependent upon them for support and he would like to give them a better job."

Appropriately for a Southern gentlemen, Shelby showed particular solicitude for the gentler sex. A *Star* reporter said that he never failed to address her in a "knightly and courtly fashion." She said that if a man should pass by her wearing a hat, the general would snatch it, saying, "Do you know no better, sir, than to remain covered in the presence of a lady, sir?"

And to the old soldiers, both blue and gray, many of them now ailing and down on their luck, he was a friendly, gregarious host as they passed their idle hours telling war stories. Always sociable, Shelby was now avuncular. He had made his reputation after the fashion of Shakespeare's hero in "The Seven Ages of Man"—as a soldier, "bearded like the pard, / Jealous in honour, sudden, and quick in quarrel, / Seeking the bubble reputation / Even in the cannon's mouth." Now he was "the justice / In fair round belly, with good capon lin'd, / With eyes severe, and beard of formal cut, / Full of wise saws, and modern instances, / And so he plays his part."

Marshal Shelby actively participated in Confederate veterans' affairs. He was the commander of the Missouri Division of the United Confederate Veterans, and one of his last public acts was to honor Jefferson Davis at a huge UCV reunion in Richmond in January 1897. "Like many from Missouri, I have come here to mingle with you for the love and affection I entertain for you," he said. "We are here, as ex-Confederates, to watch the laying of the cornerstone for a monument to the memory of Jefferson Davis, whom we all love and revere, and I

stand here as a representative of the Confederate cause west of the
Mississippi, and I speak for the Missourians when I say that this for all
time shall be our Mecca."

At the same time, Shelby was lauded for his moderation in public
affairs by a Kansas City newspaper, which considered him a likely
choice to be the state's next Democratic governor. "He is a man, popular with all parties. He is a nineteenth century man, full of the progressive spirit of the times, with no futile clinging to the buried issues"
of the past.

For someone whose reputation rested in part on leading hundreds
of bitter-enders like himself out of the country rather than submit at
the end of the Civil War, Shelby's transformation into a model of
nineteenth-century progressivism was little short of astounding and
accounts for his appeal at the time to the more liberal northern parts
of Missouri. It seems even more important today in that it identifies
him as a truly independent and generous-hearted man, capable of
growth, and not merely a fine soldier and adventurous spirit.

But being in tune with the "progressive spirit" of the times got
Shelby into hot water with some old Confederates for whom those
"buried issues" remained very much alive.

The most obvious of these issues was the racial enmity many whites
still felt for blacks. One of Shelby's first acts after taking office as marshal was to name a black man as one of his deputies. Exasperated by
the complaints that subsequently flooded his office, Shelby finally
published a statement, saying the "young Negro" was efficient and capable, and that was all that counted. As for himself, he had "no patience with that sentiment that gropes always among the tombstones
instead of coming out into the bright light of existing life and conditions." It would be "unmanly" to deny this young fellow "the right to
do for himself everything that will improve and better his condition. I
trust that this is the last I shall have to say in defense of my official action. I am right in what I have done, and by the right I propose to
stand."

Shelby also stepped into the middle of a controversy concerning the
display of the Confederate flag during a Fourth of July parade in
Kansas City—he opposed it as "waving the bloody shirt," or needlessly inflammatory, and was harshly criticized as a result. But more

upsetting still to many lost-cause devotees was Shelby's repeated assertion that slavery had been wrong and that he regretted his partici-
pation in the border raids into Kansas before the war, which had been
undertaken to spread slavery beyond its former boundaries. His fullest
statement was recorded in an interview by the historian William Elsey
Connelley shortly before Shelby's death, in which he praised the very
embodiment of Northern abolitionist fervor, the martyred John
Brown—startling words indeed from a former Confederate officer.

"I was in Kansas at the head of an armed force" in the 1850s, Shelby
said. "I was there to kill Free-State men. I did kill them. I am now
ashamed of myself for having done so," he continued. "I had no business there. No Missourian had any business there with arms in his
hands. The policy that sent us there was damnable, and the trouble we
started on the border bore fruit for ten years. I ought to have been shot
there, and John Brown was the only man who knew it and would have
done it. I say John Brown was right."

Shelby said little in public about his other famous cross-border
incursion—the one into Mexico—beyond passing comments in newspaper interviews. He certainly did not apologize for it. But like most
of the Confederates who had left the country at the end of the Civil
War, he regretted what he felt was the necessity to do so and had been
happy to return home when he could.

Much of Shelby's popularity as a military man had been due to his insistence on being in the thick of every battle. As marshal, he could no
longer go far afield in search of action, and his local duties were hardly
dramatic. But some, such as serving summons papers, could be oner-
ous, and Shelby insisted on performing this task himself. During the
unusually bitter, damp chill of early February 1897, Shelby delivered a
summons in spite of suffering from a severe cold. He soon came down
with pneumonia. After lingering for ten days, most of the time in a
coma, he died on February 13. He had revived briefly, according to
one account, to utter his last words as his wife conferred with his
physicians near his bed: "Betsy, don't let the doctors go without their
supper."

Shelby's death was widely seen as the end of an era in Missouri, if not the nation—a national magazine article at the end of 1897 included him among other notables who had died that year, including Johannes Brahms, George Pullman, the economist Henry George, and the journalist Charles A. Dana.

Unlike those luminaries, Shelby was important not so much for what he had done—though that was considerable—as for what he represented: Shelby was the model of the gifted, principled man who had fought bravely for a doomed cause, and who ultimately reconciled himself not only to defeat but to the fact that his cause had been fatally flawed by the greatest evil in American life, chattel slavery. He could easily have become a pathetic Bourbon Democrat like his friend John Edwards. Instead, in classic American fashion, he reinvented himself and showed the way for others to do the same.

Two thousand people attended Shelby's funeral in Kansas City, and four thousand joined the procession to the cemetery, said to be the largest number to turn out for any Confederate leader other than Jefferson Davis. The funeral had to be held in the National Guard Armory because the Presbyterian church was not large enough. It was, said *The Kansas City Star* on February 18, 1897, "one of the greatest demonstrations of public esteem" the city had ever seen. "Indeed, where was there ever, in any civilization, witnessed such a scene as we beheld . . . as his body lay in state in the federal building? Literally buried in flowers, contributed by all classes, baptized with the tears of affection from men, women, and children, white and black, covered with the flag of the stars and stripes."

The newspapers noted that among the black mourners were two men who had known Shelby since he was a child. The first identified himself as "Pap" Singleton. Nearly blind and hobbling with a cane, he said that he had been twenty years old and the property of Orville Shelby, Jo's father, when Shelby was born. Now he stood over the coffin of the man he had once looked after as a baby and said, "with tears running down his face, 'Dar's a friend, dar's a man.' And then, in a softer voice, broken and trembling as he leaned over again and brushed the dead face with his fingers: 'Poor old Marstah Shelby.' "

Also present was Billy Hunter, who proudly told a reporter that Shelby's mother had paid the huge sum of two thousand dollars for him and given him to young Master Jo so many years earlier. Not long before Shelby's illness, a reporter visiting his farm was invited to stay for dinner, a "sumptuous repast prepared and cooked by 'Bill,' the General's former favorite colored servant, who also has a history well worth repeating one of these days." The story attached to Billy was that he had gone his own way after the war and had not been seen or heard of for decades. Shortly after becoming marshal, Shelby had learned that Billy was working in a saloon in Indianapolis. He sent one of his deputies to ask Billy to come home and work for him again.

Now, on the day of the funeral, Billy Hunter performed his last duty for Jo Shelby, leading his riderless bay horse with its empty saddle, boots, and spurs, to the burial site at Forest Hill Cemetery; Shelby had asked to be buried near the graves of his comrades who were killed at the battle of Westport.

Since the end of the war, Shelby had maintained a friendly correspondence with many former enemies, some of whom wired the Shelby family upon learning that he was ill and after his death. Among these consoling messages was one by the notorious Dan Sickles, who as a congressman before the war had shot and killed his wife's lover, won acquittal on the then-novel grounds of temporary insanity, and gone on to lose a leg in battle during his controversial career as a Union general.

Shelby admired Sickles as a "stayer," if eccentric. He would have been even more pleased with the note Betty received from the noted cavalry general Alfred Pleasonton. It was Pleasonton who had defeated Sterling Price at Westport in 1864, and from whose clutches Shelby had rescued the hapless Price. On his deathbed himself, one of Pleasonton's last recorded thoughts was that "Shelby was the best cavalry general of the South. Under other conditions, he would have been one of the best in the world."

One of the more touching responses to Shelby's death was that of his former artillery colonel and companion in Mexico, Dick Collins, who wrote to a mutual friend from a St. Louis hospital. Collins said he was confronted "with the most sorrowful feeling I have had during my whole life" upon learning of Shelby's death. Only his illness prevented him from joining those who would surely shed "thousands of tears" for "the greatest soldier of this department."

The eulogy was delivered by the minister of the Central Presbyterian Church, who took as his text "War the Good Warfare." It was followed by remarks by Judge John Philips, the former Union officer who had once crossed swords with Shelby and later worked with him to defend Frank James, who was also among the mourners present. Philips had come to know Shelby well during the course of that controversial episode in his life and afterward. Now he rehearsed the major events of Shelby's life, paying particular attention to defining the aspects of his character. Philips's summation deserves to be the last word on Jo Shelby; it is the best explanation of his appeal for his contemporaries—and for modern audiences who might regard him not simply as a Confederate soldier but as the embodiment of certain enduring American characteristics and values:

> He was not what might be termed a round man, uniform and regular in his mental and moral composition. On the contrary, he was angular to acuteness. It was the sharp angles, the abrupt curvatures in his character that created the constant surprises in his career and lent to his life its singular attractiveness and picturesqueness. There were no dead planes, no monotonous levels in his journey through life, and it ran along rugged mountains, cataracts and varying scenery, much of it exciting, and much of it beautiful.

ACKNOWLEDGMENTS

I am grateful to my agent, Deborah Grosvenor, for her encouragement and assistance in presenting the Shelby idea; to my editor, Bob Loomis, for his demanding close reading of the manuscript and for his understanding of the special problems it represented for me; and to Conger Beasley, Jr., Deryl Sellmeyer, and Anne Shelby Jersig for reading all or parts of the manuscript and for their valuable suggestions. Finally, to John Hinz, Waverly historian and Shelby expert, my thanks for sharing his voluminous files and for his guided tour of Waverly.

NOTES AND DOCUMENTATION

The major readily available primary sources for information about Jo Shelby's life and times are the two books by John Newman Edwards. The first of these, *Shelby and His Men,* was originally published in 1867; it was reissued in 1993 by the General Joseph Shelby Memorial Fund in Waverly, Missouri. It is available through Google books. The second is *Shelby's Expedition to Mexico: An Unwritten Leaf of the War* (Kansas City, 1872), reissued in 2002 by the University of Arkansas Press with an introduction by Conger Beasley, Jr. *Shelby's Expedition to Mexico* was also reprinted in a book published in Kansas City by Edwards's widow after his death in 1889, entitled *John N. Edwards: Biography, Memoirs, Reminiscences and Recollections,* available through Google books.

All subsequent work on Shelby's journey to Mexico has depended heavily on Edwards, as virtually all of Shelby's personal papers were destroyed in two house fires. The Western Historical Manuscripts Collection (WHMC) at the University of Missouri in Columbia, Kansas City, and St. Louis, Missouri, contain letters, newspaper clippings, and information regarding Shelby and his family, friends, and associates, which have aided me in my research.

I have benefited from the good work of two Shelby authors: Daniel O'Flaherty's *General Jo Shelby: Undefeated Rebel* (Chapel Hill: University of North Carolina Press, 1954), reissued by Scholarly Book Services in 2000, and Deryl P. Sellmeyer's *Jo Shelby's Iron Brigade* (Gretna, La.: Pelican, 2007). O'Flaherty was a journalist with a flair for the dramatic as well as a thorough researcher; unless otherwise indicated, the personal details in my account of Shelby come from his book. Sellmeyer's study of Shelby and his Iron Brigade during the Civil War is particularly useful in providing a detailed, reliable account of Shelby as a military leader and in outlining the lives of some of his men who joined the expedition to Mexico.

Two other works deal specifically with my primary focus, Shelby in Mexico.

Edwin Davis's *Fallen Guidon: The Saga of Confederate General Jo Shelby's March to Mexico* (Santa Fe, N.M.: Stagecoach Press, 1962), reissued by Texas A&M University Press in 1995, is effective for its descriptions of the terrain in Texas and Mexico, and where it describes the experiences of the author's grandfather, who was one of Shelby's men. Andrew Rolle's *The Lost Cause: The Confederate Exodus to Mexico* (University of Oklahoma Press, 1962; reissued 1992) is a fascinating portrayal of the overall Confederate experience in Mexico. Additionally, a number of other studies that I have found helpful are identified in the notes below.

ONE: FROM PRIVILEGED YOUTH TO BORDER RUFFIAN

3 **In the early 1850s** Evan Shelby's eccentric marriage pronouncement is found in *Proceedings of the Council of Maryland,* 133, and more accessibly in Pynchon's 1997 novel *Mason & Dixon,* 582, in which Shelby is a recurring character.

3 **Evan's energetic sons** For the complicated Shelby family genealogy, see O'Flaherty, *General Jo Shelby,* 404–5. Colonel James Shelby of Lexington, Mo., has compiled revised and updated research on his family, which he generously made available to me. Isaac Shelby, a Revolutionary War hero and the first governor of Kentucky, in 1792, was the first cousin of David Shelby, Jo Shelby's grandfather; the many town and county place names of Shelby in Kentucky and Tennessee derive from Jo Shelby's great-uncle.

4 **In the opening decades of the nineteenth century** Concerning the education of the Gratz children, see Ashton, *Rebecca Gratz,* 124: "Their children learned a mix of Judaism and Christianity, leaning heavily toward Christianity."

5 **But the most striking of his youthful influences** Information on Frank Blair is from Wurthman, "Frank Blair: Lincoln's Congressional Spokesman," 267; and Parrish, *Frank Blair: Lincoln's Conservative.*

6 **Young Jo was not only indifferent to formal study** "Lift me gently" is from O'Flaherty, *General Jo Shelby,* 21.

7 **Born in 1781, Rebecca Gratz was still a beautiful woman** For the Irving-Scott story and for Rebecca's association with her brother's family, see Ashton, *Rebecca Gratz,* 13, 301; and *Letters of Rebecca Gratz,* 327–28.

10 **Shelby enjoyed his bachelor years in Waverly** Waverly details are from O'Flaherty, *General Jo Shelby,* 26–29; the "finest looking man" quote is on p. 28.

12 **Such weapons shipments were confiscated** Johnson, "Genesis of the New England Emigrant Aid Company," 118–20.

13 **Several months later, in early October** The John Brown association with Shelby's Waverly is described in DeCaro, *"Fire from the Midst of You,"* 223, 226–27.

13 **Jackson was born in Kentucky in 1806** Information on Jackson, Atchison, and other details concerning the border wars are from Monaghan, *Civil War on the Western Border, 1854–1865,* 119ff. It is one of the most readable and generally reliable histories of this period.

15 **Shelby was not always so polite** O'Flaherty, *General Jo Shelby,* 39.

15 **Shelby's neighbors in Waverly and the region** Ibid., 46.

16 **A tragic consequence of this farcical affair** Shelby's comment about John Brown's victims is from Connelley, *Quantrill and the Border Wars,* 288. Connelley interviewed Shelby several times in the 1890s.

17 **The unrest would continue for another two years** Casualty figures are from Watts, "How Bloody Was Bleeding Kansas?" 116–29. Watts enumerates 56 documented political killings in Kansas from 1854 to 1861 and says that "157 violent deaths" occurred during that period. Watts also writes: "During this same time frame, 583 killings took place in the California gold fields in 1855, while over 1,200 murders occurred in San Francisco over a 3-year period alone—all mostly ignored by a national press more interested in hyping 'Bleeding Kansas' as a political issue in the run-up to the 1860 presidential election." See also Schmeller, "Propagandists for a Free-State Kansas," 7–14.

18 **He found his subject in the holy Southern cause** Beasley, "Splendid Paladin," xx.

TWO: ON THE MARCH WITH THE IRON BRIGADE

21 **On April 12, 1861, the Civil War** The Blair telegram to Shelby is from O'Flaherty, *General Jo Shelby,* 51.

21 **Several hundred men strong** Ibid., 52.

22 **It is fair to say that the Blair family** The *New York Herald* quote is from Wurthman, "Frank Blair: Lincoln's Congressional Spokesman," 266; the

New York Sun quote is from Parrish, *Frank Blair: Lincoln's Conservative,* ix.

23 **Shelby arrived in St. Louis on May 10, 1861**   Details on Camp Jackson come from Parrish, *Frank Blair: Lincoln's Conservative,* 100; Brownlee, *Gray Ghosts of the Confederacy,* 12; and Castel, *General Sterling Price and the Civil War in the West,* 13. Castel's biography of Price is exceptionally good.

25 **The North was scrambling**   Lafayette is cited in McPherson, *Battle Cry of Freedom,* 210.

26 **In fact, Shelby had never intended**   The Morgan arms purchase anecdote is from Edwards, *Shelby and His Men,* 42.

27 **Personal tragedy for Jo Shelby ... "Beloved Cary"**   Edwards, *Shelby and His Men,* 35; and *Letters of Rebecca Gratz,* 426.

29 **The forces these generals commanded**   Bailey, "Role of the Trans-Mississippi Region," 5. This is the most useful brief account of the subject that I have found. It is accessible online.

29 **Shelby's greatest fame**   Details are drawn from O'Flaherty, *General Jo Shelby,* 189–207; and Sellmeyer, *Jo Shelby's Iron Brigade,* 125–42. Sellmeyer's estimate of six hundred Federals rendered unable to fight is more authoritative than the figure of 1,500 in O'Flaherty, which comes from John Edwards's exaggerated after-battle report filed under Shelby's name.

30 **Such raids extracted a price**   Edwards, *Shelby and His Men,* 76.

30 **Shelby's example on these marches**   Ibid., 452.

30 **When he was finally wounded**   O'Flaherty, *General Jo Shelby,* 186; Billy Hunter's wound is described in *The Kansas City Star,* 1897 (n.d.), WHMC, Columbia, Mo.

31 **Shelby's genius as a commander**   O'Flaherty, *General Jo Shelby,* 141–45; and Sellmeyer, *Jo Shelby's Iron Brigade,* 51–55.

31 **Throughout the war there would be lighter moments**   Edwards, *Shelby and His Men,* 33. A variant on this story is found in John Prinze, "An Eyewitness Account: The Capture of the *Sunshine,*" *The St. Louis Republic,* March 8, 1894. According to Prinze, Shelby did fire on the *Sunshine,* causing it to dock at Waverly.

32 **There could even be humor**   Ford, "Recruiting in North Missouri," 335.

32 **The romantic patina of these tales**   Edwards, *Shelby and His Men,*

448–49. The Virginia-born Edwards's "Puritan against Cavalier" comparison is elaborated by the great historian Francis Parkman in his *Montcalm and Wolfe*, 43–44. Comparing the New England colonies to Virginia in the eighteenth century, he writes, "The one was Puritan with Roundhead traditions, and the other, so far as concerned its governing class, Anglican with Cavalier traditions." The Virginians "were few in number; they raced, gambled, drank, and swore; they did everything that in Puritan eyes was most reprehensible," and they provided "a body of statesmen and orators" without equal: "A vigorous aristocracy favors the growth of personal eminence, even in those who are not of it, but only near it."

33 **Edwards was hardly alone . . . "Strange and true"**   Edwards, S*helby and His Men*, 128.

33 **But Shelby himself could be courtly**   Joseph Shelby to Col. White, July 31, 1861.

33 **And his grandiloquence . . . "One great aim"**   Shelby's Proclamation.

35 **A few weeks later, during the Battle of Prairie Grove**   O'Flaherty, *General Jo Shelby*, 361, says Shelby later "gave an interview to the press in which he credited Frank with having helped to save him from capture by the Yankees."

35 **Shelby's association with the guerrillas**   Bowen, "Quantrill, James, Younger, et al.," 48, n. 12.

35 **Operating independently, for the most part**   Ibid., 42.

36 **Shelby's receptiveness to the guerrillas**   Gilmore, *Civil War on the Missouri-Kansas Border*, 13.

36 **Like most Missourians, Bingham**   The Bingham and Frank James quotes are from the Boonslick Area Information Network, http://www.mo-river.net/Arts/georgecalebbingham.htm/.

37 **Among the families dispossessed**   "War Experiences, by Mrs. Bettie Shelby," 103–5.

37 **Caleb Bingham took experiences like Betty Shelby's**   The Bingham description is found online at the Missouri Partisan Ranger Virtual Museum and Archives, http://www.rulen.com/partisan/gcb11.htm/.

38 **When Shelby learned what was happening**   Parrish, *Frank Blair: Lincoln's Conservative*, 172; see also O'Flaherty, *General Jo Shelby*, 188.

38 **Shortly after Shelby's family was rescued**   O'Flaherty, *General Jo Shelby*, 128; Edwards, *Shelby and His Men*, 109–12; and Cothrum, "Jo Shelby: Reluctant Guerrilla," 121.

39 **Occasional encounters with raiding parties**   Cothrum, "Jo Shelby: Reluctant Guerrilla," 111.

40 **Official Confederate policy encouraged brutality**   The Seddon quote and the Fort Pillow murders are from McPherson, *Battle Cry of Freedom*, 793, 748. Regarding Fort Pillow and Forrest's culpability, McPherson says the charges against Forrest are now "generally accepted" as true.

40 **The new commander of the Trans-Mississippi Department**   Urwin, "We Cannot Treat Negroes," 141.

40 **Shelby's brigade was part**   The Union commander's summary is from O'Flaherty, *General Jo Shelby*, 211, citing *Official Records of the Union and Confederate Armies*, ser. 1, vol. 34, pt. 1, 663.

41 **The significance of the Confederate**   See Hanson, "Joseph Orville Shelby," 14.

41 **Marks' Mills was a triumph**   Soldiers' quotes on atrocities are from Urwin, "We Cannot Treat Negroes," 142–43.

41 **One Shelby biographer, Dallas Cothrum**   Cothrum, "Jo Shelby: Reluctant Guerrilla," 201.

42 **The origin of the specific charge against Shelby**   Rea, *Sterling Price*, 110.

42 **The larger charge by Cothrum**   On efforts to hold the men back, see Edwards, *Shelby and His Men*, 279.

43 **General Edmund Kirby Smith, not surprisingly**   Castel, *General Sterling*, 197; and Edwards, *Shelby and His Men*, 266–67, 312–13.

43 **Shelby sent out a stern warning**   Edwards, *Shelby and His Men*, 312.

44 **Price's greatest coup came early**   The description of Price is from Castel, *General Sterling Price*, 69, citing Dabney H. Maury, "Recollections of the Elkhorn Campaign," *Southern Historical Society Papers* 2 (1876): 181–83.

44 **Shelby's impression of Price was less favorable**   Details on Price are from Castel, *General Sterling Price*, 69. The 1968 novel by Charles Portis from which the movie *True Grit* was made in 1969 also mentions Shelby in the context of his later role as U.S. marshal for western Missouri and his help in getting Rooster Cogburn his job.

45 **Shelby had begged Price**   Shelby to Lt. Col. J. F. Belton, July 27, 1864.

46 **There was no subtlety**   Sellmeyer, *Jo Shelby's Iron Brigade*, 261, citing *Civil War Reminiscences of General M. Jeff Thompson*, 137–39.

THREE: REBELLION AGAINST SURRENDER

47 **As the war progressed, the Blair family continued**   The Lincoln anec-
dote is from Burlingame and Ettlinger, *Inside Lincoln's White House,* 239.
The story of Blair's visit to Richmond was originally told in Hay and
Nicolay, *Abraham Lincoln: A History.*

50 **When Shelby heard from Blair**   Sellmeyer, *Jo Shelby's Iron Brigade,* 265.

51 **Accompanied by the wife . . . "the bottom was badly"**   "War Experiences, by Mrs. Bettie Shelby," 103–5. Loula Grace Erdman's novel for
young people, *Save Weeping for the Night,* is based on Betty Shelby's experiences during the war as imagined by the author, and includes an account of her trip to Texas. The Whitsett quote is from a memoir in the
possession of his descendant Hayden Whitsett, provided to me by Deryl
Sellmeyer.

53 **In 1853, Brown's political attacks on Reynolds**   The duel is described
in Gerteis, *Civil War St. Louis,* 69–71.

53 **By the time he and Kirby Smith were planning**   Castel, *General Sterling
Price,* 166, 202.

53 **In December 1864, while Price and Shelby**   Ibid., 259, 258. A full account of the Price-Reynolds dispute is found in Edwards, *Shelby and His
Men,* 461–84 and 517–19.

54 **Edwards, too, had little use for Price**   Castel, *General Sterling Price,*
253; Edwards, *Shelby and His Men,* 477–78, 482.

54 **Price asked to be court-martialed**   Castel, *General Sterling Price,*
260–61.

54 **Kirby Smith stalled on Reynolds's request**   Ibid., 263.

55 **Kirby Smith, for his part, had been less than eager**   Ibid., 265.

56 **It took two weeks for the news of the surrender**   Shelby's reaction to
Lincoln's death was described at his funeral by one of his officers, Jake
Stonestreet; Kate Stone's reaction is found in Stone, *Brokenburn,* 340.

57 **Shelby's measured response**   Edwards, *Shelby and His Men,* 517.

57 **Price asked Shelby to approach Kirby Smith's chief of staff**   Kerby,
Kirby Smith's Confederacy, 414; see also Castel, *General Sterling Price,*
268–70. Castel, it should be noted, admits that John Edwards is "practi-
cally the only source providing details on what took place in the Trans-
Mississippi during the spring of 1865," but adds that his account in this

affair "appears to be generally accurate and, allowing for his prejudices and exaggerations, can be used with fair confidence," 269, n. 34.

58 **Kirby Smith did, however, prudently stay put in Shreveport**   Edwards, *Shelby and His Men,* 522; Castel, *General Sterling Price,* 270.

58 **Kirby Smith readily agreed with Reynolds's request**   There is no record of Kirby Smith and Shelby discussing plans to travel together or separately to Mexico at this time. It seems likely that Shelby, as well connected as he was, knew of them, as he did of many other similar plans. For the time being, though, Shelby's own focus was not on flight to Mexico but continuing the war against the Union.

58 **According to Kirby Smith biographer**   Parks, *General Edmund Kirby Smith, CSA,* 463.

59 **A second meeting of the generals**   Edwards, *Shelby and His Men,* 524.

59 **Shelby then met with Kirby Smith alone**   Edwards, *Shelby's Expedition to Mexico,* 5–6. For Parks's objections to Edwards, see his *General Edmund Kirby Smith, CSA,* 467–68.

60 **In the end, both Kirby Smith and Shelby were undone by Buckner**   Castel, *General Sterling Price,* 271.

60 **Shelby was the leader**   Edwards, *Shelby's Expedition to Mexico,* 8.

FOUR: SHELBY PACIFIES TEXAS

Incidents and background material in this chapter are from Edwards, *Shelby's Expedition to Mexico,* 13–57, unless otherwise noted.

65 **Jo Shelby finally had to admit**   Westlake's remarks are from "Confederate Trooper Thomas Westlake's Journal," 134.

FIVE: "SHALL IT BE MAXIMILIAN OR JUÁREZ?"

Incidents and background material in this chapter are from Edwards, *Shelby's Expedition to Mexico,* 27–40, unless otherwise noted.

75 **Shelby's response the following day**   Details on Union troop movements are found in Richter, *Army in Texas during Reconstruction,* 13, 17.

77 **The former commander of the Trans-Mississippi Department**   Kirby Smith's crossing into Mexico is from Parks, *General Edmund Kirby Smith, CSA,* 482.

77 **Shelby had both more and less freedom**   Edwards is not always precise

with dates for Shelby's journey; assuming Shelby made 20 to 25 miles a day during the 130-mile trek from San Antonio, he would have arrived at Eagle Pass on June 29 or June 30.

82 **The next morning, July 1, 1865** The Slayback poem is from Davis, *Fallen Guidon,* 17. As Deryl Sellmeyer points out in *Jo Shelby's Iron Brigade,* 353, Shelby identified the date of the flag burial in a note to the newly elected President McKinley as July 3, Edwards as July 4, and a soldier, Sam Box, as July 1: See Box, "End of the War," 121–23. If General Magruder is correct in identifying the attack at the Sabinas as occurring on July 4, then Box's date of July 1 must be the accurate date for the flag burial.

83 **Shelby sent a man back** Piedras Negras information is from Hanna and Hanna, *Napoléon III and Mexico,* 166; the Westlake quote is from "Confederate Trooper Thomas Westlake's Journal," 134.

SIX: "BEWARE OF THE SABINAS!"

Incidents and background material in this chapter are from Edwards, *Shelby's Expedition to Mexico,* 41–50.

SEVEN: SHELBY REACHES MONTERREY

Incidents and background material in this chapter are from Edwards, *Shelby's Expedition to Mexico,* 58–72, unless otherwise noted.

99 **A *New York Times* article in 1863** Hanna and Hanna, *Napoléon III and Mexico,* xiv, 61.

100 **And the Monroe Doctrine** Ibid., 64–65, 90.

100 **For all of Napoléon's talk** Ibid., 80.

101 **Napoléon initially kept his part of the bargain** Dabbs, *French Army in Mexico 1861–1867,* 31.

102 **Early in 1864, before Maximilian's departure** Gold cargo speculation is from Hanna and Hanna, *Napoléon III and Mexico,* 141, citing a January 7, 1864, letter from Confederate Secretary of State Judah Benjamin to Preston.

102 **Unfortunately for the ambitions** Quotes and army distribution figures are from Hanna and Hanna, *Napoléon III and Mexico,* 90, 117, 145.

103 **In January 1865, Preston Blair's scheme** Sheridan's actions are from ibid., 230–40.

103 **Seward was appalled by Grant's idea** Seward's actions are described in Schofield, *Forty-Six Years in the Army*, 383–85, and examined in Hanna and Hanna, *Napoléon III and Mexico*, 243–47.

104 **Grant's own motivation remains obscure** The "no life to lead" speculation is William S. McFeeley's, in his *Grant: A Biography*, 221.

104 **Still others had already arrived** The Terrell story is from Terrell, *From Texas to Mexico and the Court of Maximilian in 1865*, 8–18.

106 **Good luck played a role** John Edwards identifies the killer of General Parsons as "Figueroa," but Andrew Rolle in his reliable *Lost Cause* identifies him as Cortina; the Dobie quote on Cortina as "the most daring" bandit is from Rolle, 83.

107 **When the French arrived** The Lozada story is from Dabbs, *French Army in Mexico 1861–1867*, 267.

107 **The atrocities of Gutierrez** Ibid., 105.

108 **Bazaine issued a tongue-in-cheek warning** Ibid., 233.

108 **Ernst Pitner, the young Austrian lieutenant** Pitner, *Ernst Pitner*, 58, 88–89, 96.

110 **The most compelling of these tales** O'Connor, *Cactus Throne*, 79–82.

111 **Though indisputably brave** Bazaine's remarks were made in an April 1864 letter to the French minister of war and are cited in Dabbs, *French Army in Mexico 1861–1867*, 230.

112 **A more pleasing aspect** Kirby Smith's disappointment is from Parks, *General Edmund Kirby Smith, CSA*, 482.

115 **His success appeared imminent** Gwin's fears are cited in Andrew Rolle, *Lost Cause*, 65.

115 **Unfortunately for Gwin** Maximilian's reservations are quoted in Hanna and Hanna, *Napoléon III and Mexico*, 179.

EIGHT: "YOU WILL TURN ASIDE"

Incidents and background material from this chapter are from Edwards, *Shelby's Expedition to Mexico*, 78–121, unless otherwise noted.

117 **And he was saddened by Ben Elliott's determination** The "iron colonel" characterization is from Sellmeyer, *Jo Shelby's Iron Brigade*, 310. Elliott's admiring colleague was General M. Jeff Thompson, who referred in his book, *The Civil War Reminiscences of General M. Jeff Thompson*, to the "iron Elliott," 257, and elsewhere said his "nerves were steel,"

251. That they would not see each other for twelve years is from Sell-meyer, *Jo Shelby's Iron Brigade*, 290.

117 **On their third night out of Monterrey** On Taylor and the Battle of Buena Vista, see Perrett, *A Country Made by War*, 155–56.

119 **It did not detract from Prince John's appeal** Casdorph, *Prince John Magruder*, 2. See also NationMaster.com, s.v. "John B. Magruder," http://www.nationmaster.com/encyclopedia/John-B.-Magruder.

125 **As Shelby's biographer Daniel O'Flaherty perceptively notes** O'Flaherty, *General Jo Shelby*, 279.

129 **Douay was responsible for pacifying** Dabbs, *French Army in Mexico 1861–1867*, 222. Edwards writes that Magruder and Bazaine had known each other in the Crimea, and that Magruder was instrumental in having the order sent for Shelby to proceed to Mexico City, in *Shelby's Expedition to Mexico*, 115.

131 **Thrailkill was a twenty-two-year-old house painter** Thrailkill's letter is cited in Farley and Farley, *Missouri Rebels Remembered*, 93–94.

NINE: MAXIMILIAN SAYS "NO"

Incidents and background material in this chapter are from Edwards, *Shelby's Expedition to Mexico*, 132–43, unless otherwise noted.

136 **The most eminent of Shelby's fellow Confederates** The Freeman description of Maury is from Dabbs, *French Army in Mexico 1861–1867*, 221; biographical information is from Wayland, *Pathfinder of the Seas*, 121.

137 **While in England, Maury had followed** Hanna and Hanna, *Napoléon III and Mexico*, 119–204.

138 **But Shelby's optimism** Davis, *Fallen Guidon*, 149.

142 **The final mustering of the Iron Brigade at sunset** Ibid., 170.

143 **About fifty men did end up serving** The Zouave officer's account is by Noir, *Campaign of Mexico*, cited in O'Connor, *Cactus Throne*, 63.

144 **The wheels of Maximilian's bureaucracy** The Salm-Salm description is from Agnes Salm-Salm, *Ten Years of My Life*, 140.

144 **Born in Virginia in 1820, Allen earned** Cassidy and Simpson, *Henry Watkins Allen of Louisiana*, 20.

145 **In an account written by a female admirer** Ibid., 38.

145 **Unlike some of his Confederate brethren** Ibid., 137–38.

145 **Allen was able to point out**   Cassidy and Simpson, *Henry Watkins Allen of Louisiana*, 139–40.

147 **On the evening her ship left**   Stevenson, *Maximilian in Mexico*, 102.

147 **Before her ship had docked**   Ibid., 60–61. Sara Yorke's observations about the French plans to exploit Mexico sound much like Joseph Conrad's at the beginning of *The Heart of Darkness:* "The conquest of the earth, which mostly means the taking it away from those who have a different complexion or slightly flatter noses than ourselves, is not a pretty thing when you look into it too much. What redeems it is the idea only. An idea at the back of it; not a sentimental pretence but an idea; and an unselfish belief in the idea—something you can set up, and bow down before, and offer a sacrifice to."

147 **By the time the Confederates**   Stevenson, *Maximilian in Mexico*, 79.

148 **But Shelby's benefactor, Marshal Bazaine**   Ibid., 87, 123. Sara omitted the sad truth about Bazaine's wife's death, which Bazaine's officers kept from him for a time. Her affair with a young lover while her husband was out of the country was exposed and she killed herself.

148 **A year later**   "A very pretty girl" comes from Haslip, *Crown of Mexico*, 318.

148 **Sara wrote that her mother**   Stevenson, *Maximilian in Mexico*, 117.

149 **Among these contentious Confederates**   Magruder's influence is cited in Terrell, *From Texas to Mexico*, 45.

149 **Magruder was appointed chief**   Rolle, *Lost Cause*, 137.

149 **The problem was that Maury's**   Reynolds's "amanuensis" complaint is from ibid., 150.

151 **The newspaper was Henry Allen's weekly**   Cassidy and Simpson, *Henry Watkins Allen of Louisiana*, 143.

151 **The *Times* had only a relative handful**   Hanna, "Confederate Newspaper in Mexico," 70. Hanna's excellent article is supplemented by Rolle's "A Voice in Exile: Henry Watkins Allen and the *Mexican Times*," chap. 16 in his *Lost Cause*, 155–73.

152 **The remaining pages of the *Times***   The Tara quote is from Cassidy and Simpson, *Henry Watkins Allen of Louisiana*, 142.

152 **In private letters and in the pages of the *Times***   Ibid., 151.

152 **Allen and Edwards frequently met**   Ibid., 145.

153 **Edwards grew increasingly fascinated**   Maximilian's remarks are from O'Connor, *Cactus Throne*, 33.

153 **Maximilian's admiring biographer** Corti, *Maximilian and Charlotte of Mexico*, 1:42–44.

154 **But Edwards, at heart . . . "there was not"** Maximilian's handbook and its problems are discussed in Guedalla, *Two Marshals*, 119.

155 **Carlota gave a weekly ball** O'Connor, *Cactus Throne*, 149–50.

155 **Sara Yorke attended one such ball** Stevenson, *Maximilian in Mexico*, 224–25.

155 **Carlota did try, like her husband** Niles, *Passengers to Mexico*, 144.

156 **Carlota's ineffectual attempt** Stevenson, *Maximilian in Mexico*, 131.

156 **John Edwards saw a different side** The tribute appeared in *The Kansas City Times*, May 29, 1870, and was reprinted in *John N. Edwards*, 65.

156 **Poor Carlota indeed** The Allen quote is from Cassidy and Simpson, *Henry Watkins Allen of Louisiana*, 151.

TEN: "A FORTUNE AWAITS"

Incidents and background in this chapter are from Edwards, *Shelby's Expedition to Mexico*, 152–64, 170–76, unless otherwise noted.

158 **Privately, Shelby was still bitter** Shelby's letter is from *Message of the President of the United States of January 29, 1867, Relating to the Present Conditions of Mexico*, 39th Cong., 1st sess., H. Doc. 76, 502; it is cited in Rolle, *Lost Cause*, 99.

159 **Nevertheless, Shelby had reason to feel good** On Betty's arrival and Santa Anna, see O'Flaherty, *General Jo Shelby*, 290. Santa Anna had been the owner of vast areas of land between Xalapa and Veracruz. Will Fowler, author of *Santa Anna of Mexico*, has advised me via personal communication that he does not think Santa Anna owned property in Córdoba.

159 **Córdoba itself elicited different reactions** Pitner, *Ernst Pitner*, 45–46.

161 **The social center for the colonists** Details are from Rolle, "Carlota, Queen of the Confederate Colonies," chap. 9 in *Lost Cause*, 92–99. Rolle notes elsewhere that there were probably no more than "several thousand American exiles in all of Mexico," 181, while Albert Hanna writes that fewer than one thousand Confederates immigrated to Mexico during the 1865–67 period in "Confederate Newspaper in Mexico," 8, n. 23.

161 **Shelby's closest neighbor, Isham Harris** Details on Harris are from Rolle, *Lost Cause*, 79–81.

162 **"This culprit Harris"**   Brownlow's description of Harris is from Watters, "Isham Green Harris," 125–26.

163 **Shelby was also doubtless encouraged**   Brownlee's execution is described in Sellmeyer, *Jo Shelby's Iron Brigade*, 298.

164 **But Anderson warned Maximilian**   Anderson, *American in Maximilian's Mexico 1865–1866*, 50–51.

165 **Bazaine headed up a branch**   O'Connor, *Cactus Throne*, 76, citing Guedalla, *Two Marshals*.

166 **But Bazaine's triumph was short-lived**   The massacre at Tacámbaro is from O'Connor, *Cactus Throne*, 156; the train incident is from Pitner, *Ernst Pitner*, 91.

167 **The Black Decree was an even harsher**   O'Connor, *Cactus Throne*, 194–95.

167 **An immediate consequence of the Black Decree**   Ibid., 197.

168 **The *préstamo*, or protection money**   The Slayback quote is found online at the following website, which is based on information provided by Slayback's descendants: "Col. Alonzo W. Slayback," http://www.usgennet.org/usa/mo/county/stlouis/slayback.htm.

169 **A more surprising departure**   Maury's complaints are from Corti, *Maximilian and Charlotte of Mexico*, 2:539–40.

169 **Shelby knew that it was Carlota**   Hanna and Hanna, *Napoléon III and Mexico*, 233–34.

170 **In New Orleans, General Phillip Sheridan learned**   Sheridan to Grant, November 26, 1865; April 16, 1866, Philip Henry Sheridan Papers.

171 **Although he exaggerated the numbers**   The Allen quotes, including emphasis, are from Cassidy and Simpson, *Henry Watkins Allen of Louisiana*, 153; and O'Flaherty, *General Jo Shelby*, 297.

ELEVEN: THE COLLAPSE OF THE CONFEDERATE COLONIES

172 **Readers of the major newspapers**   *The New York Herald*, April 19, 1866.

172 **The reporter also spent time with Sterling Price**   Ibid. Rolle, *Lost Cause*, 100–107, discusses Price in useful detail.

173 **Henry Allen continued to boost Price and Shelby**   The Allen quotes and his death are from Cassidy and Simpson, *Henry Watkins Allen of Louisiana*, 35, 154, 158.

174 **John Edwards took on the editing** Edwards to his sister Fanny, September 18, 1866.

174 **Edwards was no businessman** Edwards to "darling Sisters," April 6, 1866.

174 **Edwards was prescient** Details on Omealco are from "American Captives in Mexico," *The New York Times*, June 20, 1866, cited in Rolle, *Lost Cause*, 179–80.

176 **Among those who lost their homesteads** Details on Price are from O'Flaherty, *General Jo Shelby*, 301; and Castel, *General Sterling Price and the Civil War in the West*, 276–77.

176 **But not to Jo Shelby** O'Flaherty, *General Jo Shelby*, 302.

177 **After Carlota's departure** Edwards to Tom Edwards, September 18, 1866.

177 **As for himself** Edwards to family, n.d., ca. September 1866.

182 **Most of all, Maximilian . . . "has been the greatest"** Carlota's arguments to her husband are from Corti, *Maximilian and Charlotte of Mexico*, 2:638–41.

184 **Around November 20, 1866,** Bazaine's use of Magruder as a messenger to Sherman is from Hanna and Hanna, *Napoléon III and Mexico*, 286–87.

184 **After all of Grant and Sheridan's . . . "to hold off"** Hanna and Hanna, *Napoléon III and Mexico*, 288; and Sheridan to Grant, November 20, 1866, Philip Henry Sheridan Papers.

185 **Magruder, too, was going home** O'Flaherty, *General Jo Shelby*, 309.

185 **It was not easy** Sheridan to Grant, November 4, 1866, Philip Henry Sheridan Papers.

186 **As Shelby struggled . . . "Several pieces of cannon"** The Bazaine and Kendall quotes are from O'Connor, *Cactus Throne*, 289.

186 **On February 5, 1867, Marshal Achille-François Bazaine** The Laurent quote is from ibid., 289. For Salm-Salm, see his memoir, *My Diary in Mexico*, 18. This book is available through Google books.

187 **Most of the remaining colonists** Figures on the French evacuation are from O'Connor, *Cactus Throne*, 291.

188 **He arrived to learn that Maximilian** Edwards, *Shelby's Expedition to Mexico*, 175–76.

189 **A week later, Shelby put Betty** The Edwards interview is from O'Flaherty, *General Jo Shelby*, 312.

190 **In yet another curious historical coincidence**   Fowler, *Santa Anna of Mexico*, 333–34.

191 **The defeat this time**   The Jefferson Davis release is described in Blight, *Race and Reunion*, 67.

191 **Some support for this speculation**   Schroeder, *Fall of Maximilian's Empire as Seen from a United States Gun-Boat*, 40–41. Schroeder would later be decorated for bravery during the Spanish-American War and end his naval career as a rear admiral. His book is available through Google books.

TWELVE: SHELBY SAVES FRANK JAMES FROM HANGING

195 **In August 1877, ten years after**   O'Flaherty, *General Jo Shelby*, 352.

196 **Shelby's later accomplishments**   Ibid., 334.

196 **In the years to come**   Ibid., 350.

197 **Shelby remained a Democrat**   Ibid., 351.

197 **It was the only time the two ever met**   Lincoln's description is from Morris, *Sheridan*, 1.

197 **"I was very anxious" . . . "Shelby," replied Sheridan**   O'Flaherty, *General Jo Shelby*, 355–56.

198 **Privately, Shelby was less sanguine**   Ibid., 354.

198 **John Edwards was the archetypal Bourbon Democrat**   Ibid., 358–59.

200 **The continuing fascination**   Beasley, "Splendid Paladin," xxix.

201 **To be sure, Jesse James**   O'Flaherty, *General Jo Shelby*, 363.

201 **In April 1882, shortly before Jesse's death**   Ibid., 367.

201 **When Jesse was shot**   The estimated worth today of $10,000 in 1870 is $1,138,450.70, using the unskilled wage category provided by Measuring Worth. See http://www.measuringworth.com.

202 **Frank James's surrender**   O'Flaherty, *General Jo Shelby*, 365–66.

202 **As had been the case**   Petrone, *Judgment at Gallatin*, 102.

203 **The trial was held in the small town of Gallatin**   Ibid. According to Petrone, there is no full transcript of the James trial; his book, which uses a number of different newspaper stories and other materials, provides the basis for the discussion here of Shelby's part in the trial.

204 **The defense counsel was John Philips**   Petrone, *Judgment at Gallatin*, 125, 187.

204 **The prosecution's case against Frank**   Ibid., 104.

205 **"The afternoon session opened" . . . "God bless you"**   Ibid., 127–28.

206 The next day Shelby returned ... "he spoke truth"   Ibid., 129–30.

207 Later that afternoon, Wallace and Shelby met   Ibid.,135.

207 Unmollified, Wallace later complained   Ibid., 161, 177–78. Petrone is certain that Frank was guilty, and he is persuasive. However, T. J. Stiles, in his exhaustive biography, *Jesse James*, 365, accepts Clarence Hite's assertion before his death that it was Jesse who shot both of the men who died, more or less by accident in a "terrifying fusillade" of bullets fired mostly into the roof of the train car.

THIRTEEN: U.S. MARSHAL

209 It is true that some of those men survived   Details on Shelby's men are from Sellmeyer, *Jo Shelby's Iron Brigade*, 306.

210 But many of Shelby's associates   The Hindman and Reynolds deaths are from Rolle, *Lost Cause*, 196–98.

210 The men most associated with Shelby's Mexican adventure   Hier, "Fatal Temper of Alonzo W. Slayback," 36–38.

211 Though he sided with Shelby   The fullest account of the Slayback killing is King, *Pulitzer's Prize Editor*, 101–14. See also the Slayback website "Col. Alonzo W. Slayback," http://www.usgennet.org/usa/mo /county/stlouis/slayback.htm/.

213 Edwards's own demise seven years later   The Foster duel is from *John N. Edwards*, 20–23.

215 Many of these tributes   O'Flaherty, *General Jo Shelby*, 380.

215 In 1892, Shelby's name   Ibid., 383.

215 Shelby was more vulnerable   *New York Tribune*, February 18, 1893.

216 For example: His victories, Shelby had said   O'Flaherty, *General Jo Shelby*, 384.

217 Another attack on Shelby's fitness   *St. Louis Journal*, n.d., WHMC, Columbia, Mo.

218 The once hard-bitten soldier   O'Flaherty, *General Jo Shelby*, 386–87.

219 Marshal Shelby actively participated   Ibid., 393.

220 The most obvious of these issues   *The Kansas City Star*, n.d.

221 "I was in Kansas at the head of an armed force"   Connolley, *Quantrill and the Border Wars*, 288.

221 Much of Shelby's popularity   For Shelby's last words to his wife, see O'Flaherty, *General Jo Shelby*, 394.

222 **Two thousand people attended Shelby's funeral**   Sellmeyer, *Jo Shelby's Iron Brigade*, 309. See also O'Flaherty, *General Jo Shelby*, 394–401. Newspaper accounts cited here regarding Shelby's death and funeral are from undated clippings in the *Joseph O. Shelby Scrapbook*, WHMC, Columbia, Mo.

223 **One of the more touching responses**   Dick Collins to "Friend Pritchard," February 14, 1897, WHMC, Columbia, Mo.

BIBLIOGRAPHY

Anderson, William Marshall. *An American in Maximilian's Mexico 1865–1866.* San Marino, Calif.: Huntington Library, 1959.

Ashton, Dianne. *Rebecca Gratz: Women and Judaism in Antebellum America.* Detroit: Wayne State University Press, 1997.

Bailey, Anne J. "The Role of the Trans-Mississippi Region." Historical Text Archive. http://www.historicaltextarchive.com/sections.php?op=viewarticle &artid=663.

Beasley, Conger, Jr. "The Splendid Paladin: The Life and Times of John N. Edwards." Introduction to *Shelby's Expedition to Mexico: An Unwritten Leaf of the War,* xiii–xxxvii. Fayetteville: University of Arkansas Press, 2002.

Blasio, Jose Luis, *Maximilian: Memoirs of His Private Secretary.* New Haven: Yale University Press, 1934.

Blight, David W. *Race and Reunion: The Civil War in American Memory.* Cambridge: Belknap Press of Harvard University Press, 2001.

Bowen, Don R. "Quantrill, James, Younger, et al.: Leadership in a Guerrilla Movement, Missouri, 1861–1865." *Military Affairs* 41, no. 1 (1977): 42–48.

Box, Sam. "End of the War—Exiles in Mexico," *Confederate Veteran* 6 (1903): 121–23.

Brownlee, Richard S. *Gray Ghosts of the Confederacy: Guerrilla Warfare in the West, 1961–1865.* Baton Rouge: Louisiana State University Press, 1958.

Casdorph, Paul D. *Prince John Magruder: His Life and Campaigns.* New York: John Wiley and Sons, Inc., 1996.

Cassidy, Vincent H., and Amos E. Simpson. *Henry Watkins Allen of Louisiana.* Baton Rouge: Louisiana State University Press, 1964.

Castel, Albert M. *General Sterling Price and the Civil War in the West.* Baton Rouge: Louisiana State University Press, 1968.

Collins, Dick. Dick Collins to "Friend Pritchard," February 14, 1897. Western Historical Manuscripts Collection (WHMC), Columbia, Mo.

Connelley, William Elsey. *Quantrill and the Border Wars*. Cedar Rapids, Iowa: Torch, 1910.

Corti, Egon Caesar. *Maximilian and Charlotte of Mexico*. New York: Knopf, 1928.

Cothrum, Dallas Lee. "Jo Shelby: Reluctant Guerrilla." PhD. diss., Texas Christian University, Abilene, 1999.

Dabbs, Jack Autrey. *The French Army in Mexico 1861–1867: A Study in Military Government*. The Hague, Netherlands: Mouton and Co., 1963.

Davis, Edwin Adams. *Fallen Guidon: The Saga of Confederate General Jo Shelby's March to Mexico*. College Station: Texas A&M University Press, 1995. Originally published in New Mexico by Stagecoach Press in 1962. Page references are to 1995 edition.

DeCaro, Louis A., Jr., *"Fire from the Midst of You": A Religious Life of John Brown*. New York: New York University Press, 2002.

Edwards, John Newman. *John N. Edwards: Biography, Memoirs, Reminiscences and Recollections*. Kansas City. Jennie Edwards, 1889.

———. John Newman Edwards to "darling Sisters," April 6, 1866, WHMC, Columbia, Mo.

———. John Newman Edwards to family, n.d., ca. September 1866, WHMC, Columbia, Mo.

———. John Newman Edwards to his sister Fanny, September 18, 1866. WHMC, Columbia, Mo.

———. John Newman Edwards to Tom Edwards, September 18, 1866, WHMC, Columbia, Mo.

———. *Shelby and His Men; or The War in the West*. Waverly, Mo.: General Joseph Shelby Memorial Fund, 1993.

———. *Shelby's Expedition to Mexico: An Unwritten Leaf of the War*. In *John N. Edwards: Biography, Memoirs, Reminiscences and Recollections*. Kansas City: Jennie Edwards, 1889.

Erdman, Loula Grace. *Save Weeping for the Night*. New York: Dodd, Mead, 1975.

Farley, James W., and John Farley. *Missouri Rebels Remembered: Si Gordon and John Thrailkill*. Independence, Mo: Two Trails Publishing, 2005.

Ford, S. H. "Recruiting in North Missouri." *Confederate Veteran* 19 (1911): 335.

Fowler, Will. *Santa Anna of Mexico*. Lincoln: University of Nebraska Press, 2007.

Gerteis, Louis S. *Civil War St. Louis*. Lawrence: University Press of Kansas, 2001.

Gilmore, Donald L. *The Civil War on the Missouri-Kansas Border*. Gretna, La.: Pelican Publishing Company, 2006.

Gratz, Rebecca. *Letters of Rebecca Gratz*. Philadelphia: Jewish Publication Society of America, 1929.

Guedalla, Philip. *The Two Marshals*. London: Hodder and Stoughton, 1943.

Hanna, Alfred J. "A Confederate Newspaper in Mexico," *Journal of Southern History* 12, no. 1 (February 1946), 67–83.

Hanna, Alfred Jackson, and Kathryn Abbey Hanna, *Napoléon III and Mexico: American Triumph over Monarchy*. Chapel Hill: University of North Carolina Press, 1971.

Hanson, Joseph. "Joseph Orville Shelby." *Cavalry Journal* 42 (1933).

Haslip, Joan. *The Crown of Mexico*. New York: Holt, Rinehart, and Winston, 1971.

Hay, John. *Inside Lincoln's White House: The Complete Civil War Diary of John Hay*. Edited by Michael Burlingame and John R. Turner Ettlinger. Carbondale: Southern Illinois University Press, 1997.

Hay, John, and John Nicolay. *Abraham Lincoln: A History*. Project Gutenberg, http://www.gutenberg.org/.

Hier, Marshal D. "The Fatal Temper of Alonzo W. Slayback." *St. Louis Bar Journal*, Winter 1994, 36–38.

Johnson, Samuel A. "The Genesis of the New England Emigrant Aid Company." *New England Quarterly* 3 (1930): 95–122.

Kerby, Robert L. *Kirby Smith's Confederacy: The Trans-Mississippi South, 1863–1865*. New York: Columbia University Press, 1992.

King, Homer W. *Pulitzer's Prize Editor: A Biography Of John A. Cockerill 1845–1896*. Durham, N.C.: Duke University Press, 1965.

McFeeley, William S. *Grant: A Biography*. New York: Norton, 1981.

McPherson, James Alan. *Battle Cry of Freedom*. New York: Oxford University Press, 1988.

Message of the President of the United States of January 29, 1867, Relating to the Present Conditions of Mexico. 39th Cong., 1st sess., H. Doc. 76.

Monaghan, Jay. *Civil War on the Western Border, 1854–1865*. Boston: Little, Brown, 1955.

Morris, Roy, Jr. *Sheridan: The Life and Wars of General Phil Sheridan*. New York: Crown, 1992.

Niles, Blair. *Passengers to Mexico: The Last Invasion of the Americas*. New York: Farrar and Rinehart, Inc., 1943.

Noir, Louis. *Campaign of Mexico*. Paris: A. Faure, 1867.

O'Connor, Richard. *The Cactus Throne*. New York: Putnam, 1971.

O'Flaherty, Daniel. *General Jo Shelby: Undefeated Rebel*. Chapel Hill: University of North Carolina Press, 1954.

O'Flaherty, Daniel. *General Jo Shelby: Undefeated Rebel*. Scholarly book Services, 2000. Includes an excellent introduction by Daniel E. Sutherland.

Parkman, Francis. *Montcalm and Wolfe*. New York: Collier Books, 1962.

Parks, Joseph H. *General Edmund Kirby Smith, CSA*. Baton Rouge: Louisiana State University Press, 1954.

Parrish, William E. *Frank Blair: Lincoln's Conservative*. Columbia: University of Missouri Press, 1998.

Perret, Geoffrey. *A Country Made by War*. New York: Random House, 1989.

Petrone, Gerard S. *Judgment at Gallatin: The Trial of Frank James*. Lubbock: Texas Tech University Press, 1998.

Pitner, Ernst. *Ernst Pitner, Maximilian's Lieutenant: A Personal History of the Mexican Campaign, 1864–7*. Albuquerque: University of New Mexico Press, 1993.

Proceedings of the Council of Maryland. Vol. 32, *1761–1769*. Baltimore: Maryland Historical Society, 1913.

Pynchon, Thomas. *Mason & Dixon*. New York: Henry Holt, 1997.

Rea, Ralph R. *Sterling Price: The Lee of the West*. Little Rock, Ark.: Pioneer Press, 1959.

Richter, William. *The Army in Texas during Reconstruction*. College Station: Texas A&M University Press, 1987.

Rolle, Andrew. *The Lost Cause: The Confederate Exodus to Mexico*. Norman: University of Oklahoma Press, 1962. Reprint, 1992. Page references are to 1992 edition.

Salm-Salm, Agnes Elisabeth Winona Leclerq Joy. *Ten Years of My Life*. New York: R. Worthington, 1877.

Salm-Salm, Felix. *My Diary in Mexico in 1867: Including the Last Days of the Emperor Maximilian*. London: R. Bently, 1868.

Schmeller, Erik S. "Propagandists for a Free-State Kansas: *New York Times*' Correspondents and Bleeding Kansas, 1856." *Heritage of the Great Plains* 23 (Summer 1990): 7–14.

Schofield, John McAllister. *Forty-Six Years in the Army*. New York: Century Company, 1897.

Schroeder, Seaton. *The Fall of Maximilian's Empire as Seen from a United States Gun-Boat*. New York: Putnam, 1887.

Sellmeyer, Deryl P. *Jo Shelby's Iron Brigade*. Gretna, La.: Pelican, 2007.

Shelby, Bettie. "War Experiences, by Mrs. Bettie Shelby." In *Reminiscences of the Women of Missouri During the Sixties: Gathered, Compiled and Published by Missouri Division, United Daughters of the Confederacy*, 103–5. Dayton, OH: Morningside House, 1988.

Shelby, Joseph. *Joseph O. Shelby Scrapbook*. WHMC, Columbia, Mo.

———. Joseph Shelby to Col. White, July 31, 1891. Shelby Papers. WHMC, St. Louis, Mo.

———. Joseph Shelby to Lt. Col. J. F. Belton, July 27, 1864. *Official Records of the Union and Confederate Armies*, ser. 1, vol. 41, pt. 2, 1027–28.

———. Shelby's Proclamation. Shelby Papers. WHMC, St. Louis, Mo.

Sheridan, Philip. Philip Henry Sheridan Papers. Library of Congress, Washington, D.C., 2005.

Stevenson, Sara Yorke. *Maximilian in Mexico*. New York: Century, 1899.

Stiles, T. J. *Jesse James: Last Rebel of the Civil War*. New York: A. A. Knopf, 2002.

Stone, Kate. *Brokenburn: The Journal of Kate Stone, 1861–1868*. Edited by John Q. Anderson. Baton Rouge: Louisiana State University Press, 1955. Reprint, 1972. Page references are to 1972 edition.

Terrell, Alexander Watkins. *From Texas to Mexico and the Court of Maximilian in 1865*. Dallas: Texas Book Club, 1933.

Thompson, M. Jeff. *The Civil War Reminiscences of General M. Jeff Thompson*. Dayton, OH: Morningside House, 1988.

Urwin, Gregory J. "We Cannot Treat Negroes . . . as Prisoners of War." In *Black Flag Over Dixie: Racial Atrocities and Reprisals in the Civil War*. Carbondale: Southern Illinois University Press, 2004.

Watters, George W. "Isham Green Harris, Civil War Governor and Senator from Tennessee, 1818–1897." PhD. diss., Florida State University, Tallahassee, 1977.

Watts, Dale E. "How Bloody Was Bleeding Kansas? Political Killings in Kansas Territory, 1854–1861." *Kansas History: A Journal of the Central Plains* 18, no. 2 (Summer 1995): 116–29.

Wayland, John W. *The Pathfinder of the Seas: The Life of Matthew Fontaine Maury.* Richmond, Va: Garrett amd Massie, 1930.

Westlake, Thomas. "Confederate Trooper Thomas Westlake's Journal," 1865. WHMC, Columbia, Mo.

Wurthman, Leonard B., Jr. "Frank Blair: Lincoln's Congressional Spokesman." *Missouri Historical Review* 64, no. 3 (1970): 263–288.

INDEX

ANTHONY ARTHUR was a professor emeritus of literature at California State University, Northridge, and the author of five books, including three on twentieth-century American culture, politics, and history. Two of them were History Book Club and Military Book Club selections. The third, *Literary Feuds,* was a Book-of-the-Month Club selection in 2002. He was the author of *Radical Innocent,* a biography of Upton Sinclair, and also the co-author of *Clashes of Will: Great Confrontations That Have Shaped Modern America.* Anthony Arthur died in 2009, shortly after finishing this book.

ABOUT THE TYPE

This book was set in Caslon, a typeface first designed in 1722 by William Caslon. Its widespread use by most English printers in the early eighteenth century soon supplanted the Dutch typefaces that had formerly prevailed. The roman is considered a "workhorse" typeface due to its pleasant, open appearance, while the italic is exceedingly decorative.